The Peripatetic Perambulations of a

Fiddlefoot

By Bryce Babcock

Order this book online at www.trafford.com
or email orders@trafford.com

Most Trafford titles are also available at major online book retailers.

Printed in the United States of America.

ISBN: 978-1-4669-7999-4 (sc)
ISBN: 978-1-4669-7998-7 (e)

Trafford rev. 02/21/2013

 www.trafford.com

North America & international
toll-free: 1 888 232 4444 (USA & Canada)
phone: 250 383 6864 ♦ fax: 812 355 4082

CONTENTS

DEDICATION

This book is about my life. It is dedicated to all the people who have been a part of that life. In particular, to those who have shared in it the most and been the closest to me. That would be my parents, O.T. and Beulah, my first wife Carol, and our children, Taavi, Talitha, Kemet & Kevin, and, of course, my Zenith who has shared the last 24 years with me. My faults and shortcomings belong to me alone. The good times and the happy times belong to me and all of those who are mentioned in these pages.

I'm also dedicating this to my grandchildren: Travis, Rose, Kara, Ben, Steve and Elizabeth. I've not known you as well as I would have liked, but I hope that this book will help you to know me a little better.

I can't mention everyone by name, but a special word of appreciation goes to closest friends, Charles Mossop and Clif and Dick Boehm. You have small parts in this book, but large parts in my life and my heart.

Bryce
December 2012

FOREWORD

For several years my wife has been nagging me to write my autobiography. I've resisted but she has finally worn me down. I realize that by committing myself to this effort I'm going against the best advice I ever saw about writing an autobiography. That advice came from motion picture producer Samuel Goldwyn who is supposed to have said, "No one should write their autobiography until after they're dead." That makes a lot of sense to me. But it won't be the first time in my life that I've ignored good advice. *

The reason I've done so in this instance is that the end result will be that the effort will produce [if all goes well] a book—and I love books. [I also love quotations, as will be readily apparent as you read on.] A lady named Jane Hamilton captured my feeling about books with the statement, "It is books that are the key to the whole wide world; if you can't do anything else, read all that you can." Another quote that I like is from the Dutch humanist Erasmus who anticipated my outlook perfectly when he wrote, "I buy books. If anything is left, I buy food and clothes."

Probably the reason those statements appeal to me is that reading books is one thing in life that I seem to have a talent for. I'm not mechanically inclined, dislike hard physical work, have no talent for numbers or languages, and have difficulty carrying a tune when singing. But I have always loved to read. Books have been this man's best friend, unlike Groucho Marx who rated books only in 2nd place when he said, "Outside of a dog, a book is man's best friend. Inside of a dog it's too dark to read." Well, I rate books even ahead of dogs. And I say that without even putting the last part of Groucho's comment to the test.

The next problem I faced in making the decision to write an autobiography was what to call it. I suppose I could have waited until I finished it before giving it a title, but I have a very linear mind and I didn't feel comfortable without beginning at the beginning.

The most enjoyable autobiography I ever read was that of humorist James Thurber. He gave his book the title, "My Life and Hard Times." A great title. I wish I'd thought of it before Thurber, but for me to use it now would be flat out plagiarism, and even I wouldn't stoop <u>that</u> low. Nor has my life really been characterized by "hard times." Only a few relatively minor difficulties now and then.

In thinking more about my life I realized that it's taken a lot of twists and turns [and may take more before I'm through.] So, I thought of calling it "My Life and Convoluted Times." But, that seemed still a bit too close to plagiarism. So, back to the drawing board. At one point I decided to just regard my life as a "Journey" which it certainly has been and as I think will become obvious to anyone so bold or bored as to read about it. That title survived for some 70 pages or so, but the feeling that I wanted something a bit more personal never left.

Then, waking up early one winter morning and unable to get back to sleep, a sudden inspiration seized me. I'd been dredging the dim recesses of memory about some of my wanderings through life when a word suddenly jumped into my semi-conscious mind: "fiddlefoot." I even remembered where it came from. I'd gone through a period in my youth where my discovery of the American West led me into reading and rereading dozens of "western" novels, most particularly those of Ernest Haycox and Luke Short. It was the latter who introduced me to the word "fiddlefooted" in reference to the nameless drifters and aimless riders who traveled the back trails and roads of the American West.

It struck a chord, and with my penchant for long or interesting words, the title of my nascent tome was born, springing like Athena from the forehead of Zeus: "The Peripatetic Perambulations of a FIDDLEFOOT."

So here we go. Ernest Hemingway wrote of Thurber's book, "We knew he had it in him if he could only get it out." So, I'm going to make a start on my autobiography and see if there's really "anything in there" and, if so, can I "get it out"? Stay tuned.

A word or two of warning to anyone who has read this far: I once read an autobiography that began, "As a boy I was very young." I plan to go into a bit more detail. I'm not known—whether in writing or speaking—for brevity. So this opus is probably going to be LONG.

Which reminds me of one of my favorite comic strips, "Calvin and Hobbes." [For any unfortunate human creature who is not familiar with Bill Watterson's—sadly, no longer in production—creation, it revolves around Calvin, a precocious [to say the least] six-year-old and his imaginary friend and *alter ego*, Hobbes, who is just a stuffed tiger to everyone but Calvin. In one of my favorite episodes, Hobbes finds Calvin sitting at a table assiduously writing on a sheet of paper, and asks what he is doing. "I'm writing my autobiography," replies Calvin. Hobbes observes, "But you're only 6 years old!" "I know," says Calvin, "but I've only got one sheet of paper." So, heed my warning: I'm now over 82 years old and I have a multi-GB computer, so what follows is not likely to suffer from brevity. 'Nuff said.

*In the Preface to his autobiography, "_My Life and Hard Times_," James Thurber quotes Benvenuto Cellini as saying a man "should be at least forty years old before he undertakes the task of writing an autobiography" and that he should have "accomplished something of excellence." Thurber then notes that he's not yet, at the time of his writing, 40 years old and has accomplished "nothing of excellence except a talent for throwing stones at empty ginger ale bottles." I don't even claim <u>that</u> kind of excellence. I have, however, reached 82 years of age in 2012 which is more than 40, the last time I figured it on my wristwatch calculator, so that's my excuse. Not long ago a man asked me where I was from. I said, "Cottonwood, Arizona." He asked, "Have you lived there all your life?" I said, "Not yet." So here goes.

—Bryce Babcock,
October, 2012, and beyond . . .

Bryce 1 year   **Bryce 81 years**

PART I

Youngster Years

CHAPTER 1

Loca et Parentes

I was born on April 6, 1930, at Mercy Hospital in Janesville, WI. My parents lived in the nearby village of Milton, about 8 miles from Janesville, the site of the nearest hospital. My parents were O. T. and Beulah Vincent Babcock. My father's name was Oscar (after his grandfather) True (his mother's maiden name) but, for reasons that I can quite understand, as an adult he was always called O.T. (except by his mother, who always called him Oscar.)

My parents were both unfortunate in the choice of names their parents burdened them with. My mother never escaped her given name [except briefly in school where some of her classmates called her "Skeeter" due to her small stature, and with her sister, Doris, who tried to fasten on her the nickname "Boo"]. Given Doris' alternative my mother wisely stuck with Beulah. [My aunt Doris had a "thing" about nicknames. She preferred to be called "Do"—pronounced 'Dough'—or "Dodie" and she had a sister-in-law named Florence who she always called "Fluff". She even insisted on giving her younger son, Gary Gene, the nickname of "Buster" [that's right, Buster Baker!] until he was old enough to insist that he wanted to be called Gene. I believe Doris mistakenly thought nicknames like these were "cute," but I should add that I always liked her in spite of that handicap.

My parents burdened me with the name Bryce Vincent Babcock. I'm frequently asked if I was named after Bryce Canyon National Park. I usually reply by saying, "No, it was the other way around." Actually, the explanation my parents always gave was that they were just looking for an "unusual" name and finally settled on Bryce. Further probing elicited the information that the specific inspiration was provided by the Irish-born British historian and statesman, James Bryce. [That may explain my lifelong interest in history!]

A brief digression: As a young boy, surrounded by friends with nicknames such as Jim, Bob or Bill, I hated the name Bryce. Well, initially I only <u>disliked</u> it. I longed

3

for a nickname but Bryce didn't lend itself to being shortened. [Bry?? Naaw!] I never thought of it until just now, but "Ice" might have worked when I was young. Then, again, a nickname such as "Ice" might have condemned me to perpetual bachelorhood when I grew older. I thought of going by my middle name. Vince would be OK. But what if Vincent got shortened to Vinnie instead? That would be too girlish. Initials were out, too. BVB sounded too much like BVD which, as a type of underwear, was also unacceptable to me. I was stuck.

Hating my name came later, after I once made the mistake of mentioning to several of those "friends" that I envied them their nicknames. They sympathized and immediately decided they could solve the problem by giving me one! For reasons that I cannot account for except as pure unadulterated maliciousness they decided on "Percy." It was gleefully adopted by those who must have secretly borne me a deep-seated grudge and lingered for several years among those long weaned from the milk of human kindness. Eventually, as my circle of acquaintances widened, the sobriquet "Percy" fortunately faded away. As a result of that whole traumatic experience, I decided that the name Bryce wasn't so bad after all.

The ten-year U.S. census was due that year of 1930 and my father happened to be the census-taker for the village of Milton. The rules of the census game were that anyone born before April 1st of that year could be included. Later, my mother would jokingly recount how disappointed in me she and my father were, that I was six days late! [I think she was joking.] So I was born in 1930, but didn't statistically become a real person to the U.S. government until 1940. Somehow, though, in spite of that I'm still 82 [as this is written] and not 72. The world is a strange place, indeed.

My father was the Registrar at Milton College, a small liberal-arts college in Milton, Wisconsin, where he at one time had also taught classes in Political Science and Business Law. The college had started as a denominational college of a small religious sect known as Seventh Day Baptists (SDBs). The denomination began in England as an offshoot of the Baptist church there. It was brought to America in the mid-1600s and, as far as I've been able to ascertain, the only major difference between SDBs and "regular" [northern] Baptists, was in the day of worship. The Seventh Day people taking seriously the injunction to "remember the seventh day and keep it holy," felt it necessary to separate from the denomination of those they often referred to as "First Day People" who's day of worship was Sunday the first day of the week.

The SDB denomination has always been very small and although it still exists I've found that, among people I meet, few have ever heard of it. Milton College had initially attracted mainly SDB students, but by the time I was arrived on the scene had become more eclectic. There were never a large number of students [only about 350 on campus at its' peak and far fewer during the World War II years] and the school throughout its history struggled financially and finally, for financial reasons, closed in 1982.

My father was born and raised in Nebraska in the tiny town of North Loup which had been founded by his grandfather and namesake, Oscar Babcock, an SDB minister

and two term member of the Wisconsin State Legislature. Oscar's eldest son was my grandfather, Edwin J. [E.J.], who married Jessie True. They had one daughter, the eldest child, Katharine followed by my dad, then Edwin, Archie and Arthur. Archie, died as a young man. This photo of the family [minus Archie] was taken when they were all younger than when I knew them: [L to R] Edwin, Katharine, Art, Grandma Jessie, and my dad, Oscar.

After finishing high school my dad had attended the University of Nebraska for two years receiving a "certificate to practice law." He practiced law in his father's law office in North Loup for two years, then came to Milton and enrolled at Milton College, graduating in 1925. Immediately upon graduation he was hired by the College as a combination Registrar and professor. He taught courses in Political Science and Business Law for several years and then served full time as Registrar for the rest of his life.

My mother grew up [so to speak—she was almost 5' tall] on a farm a few miles north of Milton. She was a member of the first class of the new High School from which she graduated in 1924. She then enrolled at Milton College which she attended from 1925 to 1927 when she dropped out of school and married my dad. After I was born in 1930 she remained a full-time wife and mother until I was 10, when she resumed her studies at the college and graduated in 1942.

Even before graduation she began working in the Registrar's Office. After graduation she worked there full time and after a few years was officially designated as Assistant Registrar. She continued in that position after my dad died until she retired in 1971, ending a 30 year career. This photo was probably taken in the early 1040s.

As a youngster, I used to spend a lot of time in the office and no one seemed to mind. Those times were in the summer when there were few college students around, and my school summer recess was in full swing.

I remember that there were two "treasures" that I particularly liked that were kept in the fire-proof walk-in vault in the office. There was no money in the vault, only records and files of various kinds, so during the day it was usually left standing wide open. One "treasure" was a large lever-operated "stamp" gadget that by inserting a piece of paper and pressing down on the lever would create an embossed Milton College Alumni seal. I loved to play with it, affixing the seal to a variety of discarded pieces of paper I salvaged from wastebaskets. [I think it made me feel that I was working as another "assistant Registrar".]

The other "treasure" was a late 1800's American flag neatly folded and kept in a shallow cardboard box. I learned that it was a gift to the college from a Brother Dutton, a former student of the old Milton Academy that preceded the College, and who had succeeded the Belgian missionary, Father Damien, who for many years had charge of the leper colony on Molokai, one of the Hawaiian Islands. Father Damien had contracted the disease himself and died of it in 1889. Brother Dutton had sent as a gift to his *alma mater*, one of the flags that had flown over the Leper Colony. I remember that I liked to open the box and look at the folded flag, but was afraid to touch it for fear of contracting leprosy, though my parents assured me that it was perfectly safe. The flag is presently on display in the old college Main Hall which is being maintained

as a museum by an alumni group, the Milton College Preservation Society to which I belong.

As I said, my parents were married in 1927. I haven't been able to find a wedding photo of them, but this is what they looked like at the time. Horn-rimmed glasses, spit curl and all! [No laughter, please!]

My mother had a favorite story that she loved to tell about their wedding, which took place at her parent's home on their farm about five miles north of Milton. The main floor of the house consisted of a kitchen and an enclosed porch in the back, a bedroom and dining room side by side in the center and toward the front two rooms also side by side, a living room and a "parlor" which were separated by sliding double doors. The bride and groom, along with the minister, stood in the living room while guests were seated in the parlor, the double doors open. Mom and dad—well, they were just O.T. and Beulah then—were facing the guests and the minister stood in front of them with his back to the guests. Just the opposite of the format favored for most weddings today.

Just inside the parlor and out of sight of the wedding party stood Eunice Thomas, a cousin of my mother, who was to play a brief violin solo during the prayer by the minister. As my mother told it, the minister's prayer went on and on . . . and on . . . and on . . . . and Eunice kept leaning out and peering around the corner of the doorway to see if the prayer had ended which was her cue to end her violin piece. Mom said that she could hardly restrain herself from bursting out laughing each time she saw Eunice poke her head around the corner, until the minister's prayer finally droned to a long-awaited and welcome close.

Just two years after my parents married in 1927, the U.S. was hit by the Great Depression and as a result salaries at the college were miniscule. With my father's small salary and my mother not working things were a struggle financially during those years, of which I have only a few vague memories. As a result of my parent's very limited income, their housing was a series of small, second-floor apartments in other people's homes. We lived in two different upstairs apartments during the first two years of my life.

Then when I was 3 years old we moved to an apartment on the second floor of one of the buildings on the college campus. The building, originally built as the home for the college President, had become the domain of the college music department which only needed the ground floor, so the 2ⁿᵈ floor was remodeled into an apartment.

Because my dad worked for the college he was allowed to rent the apartment for $10 a month! Known as the Music Studio, or more often as just "the Studio" at that time, it was to be my home for 10 years, and the site of many of my happiest days as a child. I have many fond memories of the 10 years that I lived there. The building still stands. After the College closed it was purchased by a private family and they occupy it for only part of the year. Happily, it has not been torn down.

Here's what it looked like when we lived there. We lived on the second floor. The center window on that floor was to a hallway. The two windows on the left in the

picture were to our living room. Behind it was my parent's bedroom. The two 2ⁿᵈ story windows on the right were to my room. Behind it was a room, with a "half-bathroom" [meaning just a toilet and sink but no bathtub] that was sub-let by my parents, usually to a college student. Behind these rooms were our bathroom, a closet, kitchen and dining room all part of a somewhat narrower addition on the back of the building.

The downstairs rooms were used by the college music department. I loved living in the "studio" except when music students [including both those studying instrumental music or voice] would be practicing their seemingly endless and repetitious exercises up and down the musical scale, on the floor below! The rooms were <u>not</u> soundproofed!

CHAPTER 2

Home, Sweet Home

Living there between my 3rd and 13th years, the Studio was closely associated with most of my childhood memories. It was a wonderful place to grow up. I had the whole college campus for a yard or playground—complete with a gymnasium, a football field, tennis courts and a cinder running track! There were trees to climb, a hill for sledding and skiing in the winter as the Studio stood on top of a hill. There was lots of space to roam and play which I could share with my friends and I was a constant presence for the college football and basketball practices and games, as well as track and field and tennis matches and practices.

The Studio itself had a long curved banister to slide down from the second floor to the first, plus a cupola with windows all around that I had access to and which provided a private sanctuary plus great views over Milton and for miles around as the Studio occupied one of the highest points in town. There was also a dark, dusty basement that was accessible to me as my father had to tend the coal furnace there in the winter. One room in the basement, which could be closed off so as to keep it relatively free of the omnipresent coal dust, served as our family laundry room.

I became a kind of unofficial "mascot" around the college and to the athletic teams in particular as I was always underfoot and got to know a lot of the students including most of the athletes. It was a fun environment in which to grow up.

One event involving the Studio that wasn't fun was the time it caught fire, although it had a happy ending, as I'll explain. It happened during the summer when I was 5 years old. The Studio was of brick and had a metal [tin] roof. In order to keep the roof watertight during rains and times of snow melt, it was necessary to coat the roof with tar every few years, thus sealing seams and nail holes.

On this occasion several college students were employed to "tar the roof." We had an old two-burner kerosene stove in the basement that at one time had been our kitchen cook stove. It was seldom used in 1935, but for this task the fellows working on the roof employed it to heat the tar. They used large five-gallon metal pails, partially filled one with tar and heated it until it was of a consistency where it could be spread over the roof with brooms. Then they would carry it up ladders pour it on the roof and spread it around while another pail of tar was being heated on the stove. It was heavy, hot and difficult work!

On this particular day a pail of tar was over-filled and left on the stove too long and it boiled over. Instead of turning off the burner [maybe the hot tar prevented that] one of the student workers tried to jerk the bucket off the stove and it tipped over and the tar caught fire. Fortunately the workman got out of the way and wasn't hurt, but the burning tar ignited the wooden basement stairs beside the stove and some partitions and immediately began to burn up through the floors above.

For some reason the fire spread straight upwards through stairwells, closets and the bathrooms on both floors above. Someone thought to call the fire department and they got there quickly and started fighting the fire and managed to keep it from spreading—except upward. Dad was at work when the accident occurred, and my mother and I were outside in the yard watching the workmen and so were in no danger.

For me it was exciting and not really that scary. I remember one of the firemen on the roof of the two-story building with an axe trying to chop through the metal roof! The volunteer firemen did a great job to keep the fire from spreading and keeping the damage to a minimum. We were able to return to our apartment and assess the damage the next day. The only major damage was to our bathroom, a closet and the bathroom and closet directly under ours on the ground floor.

I soon feared, however, that the fire had resulted in a casualty! Living in an upstairs apartment I wasn't allowed to have a dog or cat for a pet. [Actually, we'd learned that I was very allergic to cats, there being several around my grandparent's farm, so that would have been out of the question anyway.] As a substitute I'd talked my parents into letting me keep as a pet a turtle, which I'd "captured" in Burdick's Woods across the street. He or she [I never knew which] lived in a large metal can about two feet deep and maybe a foot across which occupied a corner on the floor of the kitchen. I believe the can had been purchased as a container full of pre-popped popcorn. It had been converted, however, to a home for my pet turtle with a couple of inches of water and a few rocks and some sand to provide a bit of "dry land" for it.

My mom broke the sad news to me the next day. One of the firemen had apparently noticed the can and had emptied it to use in carrying water to aid in putting out the fire. My turtle was nowhere to be seen and was assumed to have been the lone casualty of the conflagration. A couple days later my mom opened the glass paneled door to the dish cupboard to get something and there on a shelf between some plates and cups was Muddy, my turtle!

The tender-hearted fireman had noticed the resident of the can and had carefully removed said occupant, placed it safely on a shelf, and then closed the cupboard's doors, before proceeding to use the turtle residence to carry water. Thus, thanks to the volunteer firemen, were two major tragedies averted, one to the Studio and one to my faithful pet. I've had both respect and admiration for firemen ever since!

I can't remember what finally happened to old Muddy (well he—or she—WAS a mud turtle). I think I finally felt sympathy for it living in what amounted to a prison and turned it loose in the woods where I'd found it. Dad and Mom went to the 1936 Chicago World's Fair the following year, leaving me with my grandparents while they were gone, and brought me back a tiny little turtle with its upper shell painted white and the Fair's logo stenciled on it. I don't remember what its fate was, either, but I think I turned it loose, too, and allowed it to waddle off to that great swamp in the sky after only a brief sojourn with the Babcock family.

My neighborhood when we lived in the Studio on campus was well populated with boys around my own age. We were on High Street and the Studio was at the top of a fairly long hill. Directly across the street lived a boy my own age, Winston, who we called Windy for short, much to the consternation of his parents. [It took me many years to realize that the reason they disliked the nickname Windy was that to them the term implied that the owner of the name was someone afflicted with flatulence. To us it was just a shortened form of Winston and had no such connotation.]

Next door to Windy lived Bob B. He was about three years older and was, at that time, the eldest of four children. Up the street lived two brothers, Jim and Bob L. Jim was Bob B.'s age and Bob L. was a year younger. In the other direction, at the bottom

of the hill lived Bill who was in the same grade as Windy and I and although a few months younger was taller and the best athlete of the three of us. All through elementary school we were inseparable, a more or less non-violent version of The Three Musketeers.

We laid out a small baseball diamond on a flat terrace area on the college campus near the Studio and would spend many hours in the summer playing baseball. Here's a photo showing the Studio with a few of us playing baseball on our little "diamond." I'm the one pitching in this photo. [Bob B., Bill, Windy and I from left to right.]

Often, six of us would form teams of three each. Jim, as the oldest, always assumed leadership in everything. [Actually, Bob B. was the same age, but was a very easy-going, happy-go-lucky type and content to follow rather than lead.]

Whenever we decided to have a game Jim would immediately announce, "OK, Bob 'n me 'n Bill 'll stand." The Bob named being his brother, which meant the three best players were on one side, so the outcome of the games were pretty much a foregone conclusion. Windy and I would occasionally comment about this but without effect. Bob B. really didn't care.

My parents, for some reason quite obscure to me, thought that I should learn to play some kind of musical instrument. The college piano instructor, a nice but elderly spinster named Alberta Crandall, had her classroom on the first floor just under my bedroom. At my parent's insistence, I was enrolled as a private student of hers during one summer while there were no college classes going on. It turned out that I had no talent whatsoever for playing the piano, and the lessons were pure agony for me.

It undoubtedly aggravated the situation that my friends would frequently cluster around on the big front porch, peering in through the windows, clutching their baseball gloves, bats and balls, waiting for me to join them. At last the allotted lesson time would expire, Miss Alberta would dismiss me, the door to my prison would swing open and I would be paroled to the custody of my friends, much to both my relief and, I suspect, to Miss Alberta's!

A few years before we moved from the Studio Jim and Bob L.'s family moved out of town and a new family moved in next door to Bill's home at the bottom of the hill. The H.'s had two daughters, Virginia, a year ahead of me in school, Lois who was in my grade and a son, Bob, who was a year younger than I was. Bob H. was small in stature like me and soon was christened by the "High Street" crowd as "Shrink." That helped take some of the sting out of "Percy" and as I got into High School and began to make new friends, Percy gradually fell into disuse, and soon disappeared altogether. One of my life's great burdens was lifted!

The village of Milton was actually one half of twin towns. The other half was known as Milton Junction and the two towns physically ran together. Milton was the original community and "the Junction" [as we always referred to it] grew up years later when the railroad bypassed Milton by about a mile. The reason the Junction developed as a separate community was that Milton was a "dry" village and the people that settled in the Junction wanted establishments where beer and liquor could be sold.

Each town had its own Elementary school, but a single High School served both communities. With separate elementary schools, we kids from the two towns didn't really have that much contact with each other until we got to be of high school age, and in our elementary years there was a lot of rivalry. So, occasionally each community would put together a team and one would challenge the other to a game. We played both baseball in the summer and football in the fall.

We weren't sissies. We played baseball or "hardball" not softball, and we played "tackle" not "touch" football even though we had only the rudiments of equipment—a few bats, balls and baseball gloves and mitts. For football a few boys had kid's shoulder pads or a helmet but most had no equipment.

At first, I played shortstop on the baseball teams as I was the shortest one and that seemed appropriate. Then someone discovered that shortstops were supposed to be tall, lanky types and I had to play 2nd base! I never liked the change and felt put upon by the decision, but my protestations fell on deaf ears. Later, in high school I always had to play 2nd base. To me, playing second base was like playing "second fiddle." Sometimes life is so unfair!!

As for football, we mostly played a game with no teams or positions. We called it "Tackle-the-Man-With-the-Ball" and the only equipment required was a football. Someone would throw the ball in the air and whoever got hold of it would try to run with it and everyone else would chase the "man with the ball" and try to tackle him. When the person with the ball was in the process of being tackled he would throw or "fumble" the ball and whoever managed to capture it first was now "the man with the ball" and everyone else would try to tackle him! It wasn't really that dangerous as mostly the game consisted of grabbing people, falling in a heap and then getting up and doing it all over again . . . and again.

I seem to have had an interest in sports from a very early age. Here's a photo of me ready for a game of football at the age of three or four just after moving to the studio. [Pretty neat *chapeau*, eh?]

In winter it was mostly individual sports: sledding, skiing, and ice skating. The High Street hill was good for sledding with snow packed hard after the snowplows went through, and fortunately traffic wasn't too heavy in those days. The Milton fire department would flood the tennis courts in the town park in the winter. They would soon freeze and made fine ice skating rinks. They were always too crowded to play hockey, but occasionally we'd hike out of town for a hockey game on a farmer's pond that was frozen over. Of course, we usually had to take a snow shovel and clear the snow from the ice first. We used the hill on campus for skiing. As we grew older we would slog our way out of town to where there were some steeper slopes.

There was an abandoned gravel pit a mile or so south of town and it was a favorite location for some of our winter sports. I remember one day we discovered a large sheet of tin that had been used as a billboard sign and when it was removed it had just been dumped and left in the old, unused gravel pit. We thought it would make a great toboggan as it was long and narrow and quite flexible. We dragged it to the edge of the steep drop-off and a bunch of us [there must have been 6 or 8 of us altogether] sat on the sheet of metal with those on the front pulling the front edge up and back like the curved front of a toboggan. We never thought that it might not be the best idea to have all the bigger, heavier kids up front and lighter kids behind. [Blame it on the innocence of youth.] Then we pushed off.

The "hill" was an almost sheer 20 or 25 foot embankment and the front of the contraption plunged straight down while the back rode up over the top. Kids went plummeting headlong, landing in a tangled heap while the back end of the "toboggan" curled over on top of us. Then the snow bank came down on top of everything. We were completely buried, but managed to tunnel ourselves out and nobody was hurt but we got quite a scare from the experience of being "buried alive" in the snow underneath a large sheet of metal. We never experimented with the tin "toboggan" again, but for several years it lay there at the bottom of the slope like a mute and evil reminder of another not very bright idea gone wrong!

Another bad idea that we came up with, involved skiing. Our equipment was not very sophisticated. [These were "depression years," remember, and no one had much money for purchases.] Our wooden skis just had leather straps that we stuck our feet into, so controlling our course was difficult. We had found a nice hill adjacent to the gravel pit that had scattered pine trees growing on it. We thought we could ski down the hill avoiding the small trees as we could make simple turns. We knew, however, that "real" skiers used ski poles to help make turns but none of us had the money to buy "real" ski poles.

No problemo. We could make our own. Just take a couple of old broom sticks, saw them to the desired length, drive a large nail into one end of the broomstick and then file off the head of the nail. *Voila!* Ski poles—and on the cheap!

Several of us manufactured sets of ski poles. They didn't work to perfection, but they made us feel more sophisticated and "professional." Then one day Windy had the misfortune to hit a stump that was buried in the snow. **Disaster!** Windy went flying heels over head, lost hold of his ski poles and fell with the nail end of one pole catching him right in the mouth. The nail punched through his cheek and the broomstick followed with about a foot of its length poking out through the tear in his cheek while the other end was projecting from his mouth!

We who were with him were afraid to try to extricate the pole [and Windy wouldn't let us touch it anyway], so we proceeded to walk him back into town—nearly a mile—to the doctor's office, Windy bawling his head off all the way as you might expect. Doctor Davis sawed off the pole and removed it, then sewed up the hole in his cheek. Windy carried the nearly two-inch long scar on his cheek from that day on. I last saw him at our 50th High School graduation reunion in 1998 and the scar was still there. Either good sense or faint hearts prevailed after the accident and we gradually discontinued using the "homemade" ski poles, discarding them into the dustbin of history.

It was a good thing or I might have had a similar accident. Not long after that I was skiing in the same area (*sans* the home made ski poles, thankfully) when it was my turn to hit a mostly buried stump with one ski. I, too, went flying heels over head [as my Grandma Babcock used to say] but wasn't hurt. The only damage was that one of my wooden skis—the one that hit the stump—was split down the middle for half its length. Better the ski than me, I concluded, and I quit skiing on that hill altogether.

As a young boy I was well coordinated and enjoyed all sports. My favorite at this time was baseball. My major handicap in all sports was being short and rather skinny. That wasn't really a major handicap, however, until I got into organized team sports in high school and began playing basketball as well as football and baseball. I'll get to that a bit later in this saga.

We didn't spend all of our time playing sports. One summer when I was 7 or 8 years old we decided to become businessmen—or businessboys. We decided it would be nice to have a few extra nickels and dimes to buy ice-cream cones or phosphates. [Phosphates, for the edification of more modern generations, were "soft drinks," sold in most drug-stores or soda fountains in those days. They consisted of several squirts of flavored syrup from the soda fountain dispensers into a "coca cola" glass and then filling it with carbonated water. They were an alternative to a "coke", 7-Up or Nehi Root Beer, and you could get a variety of flavors like lemon, lime, cherry, orange or pineapple. They were good, but cost a nickel, and this was still during the Great Depression which meant that a nickel was almost a fortune to kids our age.]

So Bill, Windy and I with two or three others decided to earn the money we needed by going into business—the selling business to be exact. What to sell that did not require a cash investment? After much discussion we had a brainstorm. [Who says that committees can't make decisions?]

Out on the edge of town, about a half-mile from where we lived, was an old neglected apple orchard, known as Plumb's Nursery. The apples were no longer being harvested, but that summer the gnarly old trees that remained were loaded with wormy little green apples. We could make "apple cider" and sell it to passers-by! We began

gathering apples and carrying them by bicycle to a spot by our baseball "diamond" in front of the Studio where we would establish our place of business.

We even hand-painted a large sign which you can see in the photo. [That's me on the far left and my cousin Reg, who was visiting at the time, on the right.]

I borrowed my mother's meat-grinder, an old-fashioned device that clamped to a table top and was equipped with a hand-turned crank. [It was the implement that families used to convert leftover beef or other meats into "hamburger" or "ground beef", in those days of yore.] We had a small table for a "counter," and behind it a small tent. We put another table behind the tent, out of sight of customers, and it was here that we set up the meat-grinder.

On this table we would cut up our green apples [trying occasionally to avoid the wormiest parts] and feed the pieces into the grinder taking turns turning the crank. The resulting juice we caught in a metal dishpan held underneath. The pulp was fed into old cloth sugar sacks which we could squeeze to get more juice. *Voila!* "Apple cider"! [Well, actually apple juice, but what the heck—close enough!] We sold this delicious beverage for 10 cents a glass to pedestrians or motorists who happened by, saw our sign and stopped to see what it was all about.

We did this for several days and actually made enough money for several phosphates for each of us. We decided to go out of business after a customer, upon tasting his delicious "cider", asked Windy how we made the product? Windy, proudly showed him our secret [until then] manufacturing process which we'd cleverly placed so that it was hidden from nosey passers-by. One look at our manufactory and the man promptly poured his "cider" on the ground and walked away without a word. Thankfully, he'd already paid, but we were discouraged by his action and decided that we'd been in business long enough and closed up shop thinking that we'd rather close than risk facing a lawsuit.

CHAPTER 3

A Fullness of Falling

I need to back up a bit to describe some other experiences of mine as a young boy. For some reason I did a lot of falling as a youngster and I've carried a number of scars to show for it. As a baby I'd fallen out of my highchair and got a cut over my right eye. One time I slid down the banister in the Studio, fell off at the bottom [performing what must have been a somersault worthy of a trained acrobat] and landed on my chin, somehow, and carried another scar there. I had several other scars, one on my knee from falling on a piece of broken glass hidden by snow on my way home from school one winter, plus another on my head the cause of which is long lost in the mists of time.

But I've never forgotten the one I got in Kindergarten. Every day we had a "nap time" of 15 minutes or so during which time we'd get small woven or braided "throw rugs" which were kept in a closet, spread them on the hardwood floor and lie down on them for "a nap." I always thought it was a silly exercise as I don't think anyone ever napped even for a single "wink", let alone 40 of them. I think it was really intended just to calm us down for a few minutes and let the teacher catch her breath. It never seemed to accomplish those results, either, as we were all raring to go when it was over. [All of that doesn't really figure in my story. Just thought I'd mention it.]

Kindergarten was in the mornings only and one day when the bell rang signaling that the school day for us was over and the "real" day (well, half day) of play about to begin, I made a dash for the door and freedom. As I rounded the end of the upright piano heading for the door I lost my footing. I've never known whether I just slipped or if someone else in a similar bid for freedom bumped me from behind. (I remember well that I was in the lead and my objective was to be the first one out the door!) Anyway, the result was that I lost my balance and crashed headfirst into a radiator against the wall beside the door.

Few that read this will remember those old corrugated cast-iron steam radiators that were a common means of heating homes and other buildings in those days. They

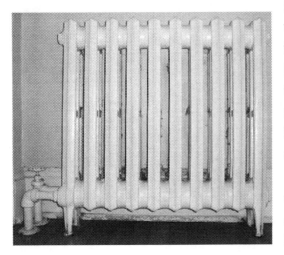

stood probably three or four feet high and were maybe about the same length and less than a foot deep. They had a series of vertical hollow "fins" that hot steam could circulate through and a valve at one end that could be used to adjust the amount of steam allowed into the radiator. The picture will provide a clearer idea of what I'm trying to describe.

At any rate I crashed into it head first at a dead run. I sat up, a bit dazed, but laughing about it while putting my hand to my sore head. The teacher and a bunch of morbidly curious classmates gathered around. Then I took my hand away from my head and saw it was covered with blood! My laughter stopped abruptly and turned to howls of fright as copious tears joined the blood running down my face.

The blow had split my scalp open, a wound about an inch and a half long. The teacher got a cloth to hold against the cut and sent someone to get an older girl out of another class. That was DeEtta Lippencott whose parents were good friends of my parents. The teacher (I think her name was Miss Davis) asked DeEtta to walk with me over to the Doctor's office about three or four blocks away, which she did.

Someone, the teacher I believe, called my parents who came down to the office just as Doctor Davis [no relation to my teacher] was shaving an area of my scalp preparatory to taking some stitches. As I recall, it only took three stitches to close the cut and I went home having learned an important lesson in life: a cast iron radiator is harder than even <u>my</u> head.

Actually, my most famous fall happened before I was old enough to remember it. I only know the story as my mother would relate it whenever she had an audience of one or more that she thought might not have heard it before or would be too polite to complain if they were enduring a repetition. Here's how it happened:

My dad's mother lived in North Loup, NE, where he had been born. It was probably 650 or 700 miles from Milton, depending on which of several routes we took. At three to four year intervals we drove out to visit my grandmother, Jessie Babcock [grandfather, E.J., had died before I was born]. Grandma would come out to Milton by bus to visit us most other summers. Visits usually lasted a week or so. I must have been about two years old at the time of the visit in question. At any rate I was too young to have any personal memory of the illustrious event. I only remember hearing about it from the adults who were there at the time.

Grandma Babcock was less than five feet in height and my grandfather had a rather unique house built for her when they were married. All the built-in counters, cupboards, etc. were lower than normal for her convenience. Even the stair steps were lower and also the height of the windows above the floor. Here's a faded photo of the house as it looked in the 1930s. [When visiting I usually slept out on the 2nd-story porch, as Nebraska summers were notoriously hot and rooms stuffy!] Sadly, the house has since then succumbed to the wrecking ball, and sledge-hammer, a fate it did not deserve! It was one-of-a-kind and ought to have been preserved!

After grandpa died, grandma had the second floor converted into an apartment. She lived there and rented out the downstairs. The window sills in her apartment on the second floor were only a foot or so off the floor, and the windows were fitted with screens that were hinged on one side so they could swing outwards. (Don't ask me why they were this way. I've always wondered myself.) The screens had a hook on the side opposite the hinges so they could be secured and not accidentally swing open. Summers in North Loup were always hot and windows were usually open most of the time, with just a screen to keep insects at bay.

Grandma's kitchen table normally was placed in front of one kitchen window which, as a result was seldom opened and for some reason the screen had not been hooked to keep it from swinging open if pushed. On this particular day, my mother and grandmother decided the apartment needed a thorough cleaning, and the kitchen table had been moved from its usual space in front of the window which had been opened wide to let in some fresh air on a typical hot Nebraska summer day. No one noticed that the screen, although closed, was not hooked.

I had been playing happily, though apparently somewhat bored, on the floor. As mother liked to tell the story she happened to look up just as I pulled myself up to the open window and leaned out against the [unhooked] screen. Out it swung and overboard I went in what must have been a medal-worthy swan dive. Below the window on the ground floor level was a small roofless porch. There were wooden railings along each side and against one stood an old-fashioned washing machine with the wringer assembly exposed on top over the tub. I landed smack [I think that's an appropriately descriptive word] on my hands and knees, on the wooden floor in between the washing machine and the opposite railing, a space of perhaps 3 feet.

My mom ran out, desperate to reach the mangled remains of her only offspring. She had to go down the inside stairway, out the front door and then run around the house. When she got there a young neighbor boy about eight or nine years old was holding me in his arms. Mom said that before she could speak the boy looked at her and blurted out, "I'd 'ave caught 'im if I'd seen 'im comin'." No damage was done. Mom said I had some small red spots on my knees and palms. It's always been a source of pride for me to be able to counter the brags of others by replying, after hearing them describe their own trials and tribulations as children, "That's nothing. I fell out of a second story window when I was two and wasn't hurt at all."

CHAPTER 4

Grandparents Galore

My grandma Jessie was the only grandparent I had on my dad's side of the family. She was my favorite as she would spend lots of time playing with me when she visited us in Milton or when we visited her in North Loup. She also would read and sing songs to me. One of my favorite books was a story called "Ab the Cave Boy." It was set in prehistoric times when humans lived in caves and the main character was a boy growing up in those times of cave bears and other dangerous creatures. Dad had built me a sand box beside the Studio where we lived, and grandma and I would create a cave village in the sand and I would be Ab and she would be Ab's mother.

Grandma Babcock loved to sing and when she would be staying with us she would sing to me every night when I was ready for bed. Before she married my grandfather she had attended a small college in Nebraska called Doan College. She had a book of Yale College songs that they'd used at Doan. [Since both schools had one-syllable names they could easily substitute "Here's to good old Doan" to replace "Here's to good old Yale."]. So she would sing and encourage me to sing along with her.

The interesting thing about this was that almost all the songs were what would be considered "drinking songs" and grandma and her family were all strict abstainers from alcohol! [Her husband, my grandfather, had led the campaign to keep North Loup "dry" and not allow the sale of any alcoholic beverages in the town. [The last I heard, North Loup was still "dry."] The songs all had catchy tunes, though, and were easy to sing and I really enjoyed them. [She did, too!] I didn't think anything strange about it at the time but later on I've always thought it a bit odd that grandma so enjoyed those old college drinking songs! I still have the old song book and get it out now and then and sing some of the songs that I liked the best.

Here is a picture of Grandma Babcock as I remember her. [She's standing on the front porch of the Studio, c.1940]. Her gray hair, which she always braided and wore in a kind of bun on top of her head, hung well below her waist when she let it down before combing it out every morning.

From Grandma Babcock I learned that my father as a small boy had developed a "language" all of his own. She had learned to decipher it and she alone in the family could understand him. I only remember one sentence of his personal language that she passed on to me: "Bra-pra-oh-na-ki-ki-dah-kah." My spelling is phonetic, but it translated as "Grandpa's over across the creek in the corn field." According to grandma my dad as he grew older had suddenly quit speaking like that and began speaking in English as though he'd always done so.

This unique talent was not something that was passed on to succeeding generations except in very minor ways. I had a few words [according to my parents] that might have been a left-over residual or an undeveloped beginning of such a talent that I never could bring to germination. Where we lived, every farm in those days had a windmill to pump water from a well and I do remember that at an early age I called a windmill an i-lo [with a long i and o, as in eye-low]. Most farms also had a tall round silo or two beside the barn for storing corn silage, a major winter food for the milk cows. And my word for a barn sounded like bairn.

Milton and the surrounding area was visited one year when I was about 4, by a rather destructive cyclone which knocked down a number of trees, barns and structures such as silos and windmills. When out for a drive afterwards to view the damage I noticed a windmill still standing beside the ruins of a destroyed barn and excitedly pointed it out to my parents saying, "There's an i-lo without a bairn!" That, I realize, is a pretty feeble example of a personal language. I was undoubtedly just confusing windmills with silos, which also usually stood beside barns, just not sounding the initial letter "s". But for some time afterwards I always called windmills 'ilos'.

I thought at one point many years later that the gene that enabled one to invent a personal language had skipped a generation and was about to resurface in my daughter, Talitha. But in the end the private language gene was even weaker in her than it had been in me. She only managed to garble a few names of creatures calling a chipmunk a "munk-munk" and a caterpillar a "culler-puhller." For a time we thought she was going to develop a personal sign language as well, but that hope died after a single example. When waving "goodbye" she would always turn her palm inward toward herself so it appeared that instead of signaling farewell she seemed to be beckoning the people to return rather than leave. [They never did.]

Grandma Babcock was the only grandparent I ever knew on my dad's side of the family. On my mother's side it was a different story. Her parents, Floyd and Mignon [actually Mignonette Whitford] Vincent, lived on a farm about 5 miles north of Milton, so I saw them frequently.

This photo was taken on Grandpa and Grandma's 50th wedding anniversary. That's my mother in back on the left and her sister, Doris on the right. The two girls were their only children, except for a baby boy who died shortly after birth.

Grandpa and Grandma would look after me whenever my parents had to go out of town for overnight or longer. I enjoyed staying with them, and, as far as I could tell they enjoyed having me.

Grandpa Vincent's farm was 140 acres at this time [later he sold the "back 40" acres]. He kept four horses and milked about 20 or 25 cows. Grandpa grew alfalfa, oats, corn, melons and other crops and grandma always had a big vegetable garden and kept a rather sizeable flock of chickens. I'd have probably enjoyed staying on the farm even more except that I had allergies and early on found that I couldn't spend much time around the hay in the barns [grandpa had both a cow barn and a horse barn] without being reduced to fits of sneezing and itchy, watery eyes.

Fortunately, I didn't have that kind of reaction to the corn silage that was also fed to the cows and I enjoyed climbing up into the silo and using a special broad-tined pitchfork to throw down silage thus helping Grandpa complete his chores a bit more quickly. Other jobs I could handle and enjoyed was walking out to whichever one of several pastures the cows were grazing in, and driving them to the cow barn to be milked. I also enjoyed helping Grandma feed the chickens and collect the eggs.

Grandpa took great pride in the melons he grew on the farm, especially muskmelons. [They're what we now usually call cantaloupe]. Fortunately, I wasn't allergic to those! I loved to help grandpa pick the melons when they were ripe. Probably one reason was that every so often he would pick up a melon and remark that perhaps we should sample that one to see if it was worth picking! He'd pull out his big jackknife, open it and cut a slice for each of us. If it was especially tasty we'd usually have another slice or two before throwing the rest away.

This photo shows Grandpa with his first car an old Model "A" Ford, with my mom, before she married my dad. Later he upgraded cars several times, but would never own anything but a Ford! He'd load the melons into his car and then he'd drive to neighboring towns and sell the melons to grocery stores. He had a regular route and clientele that he'd built up over the years. In

those days grocery stores were privately owned and the big chain stores were still years in the future. When I was young I often got to go with him on these trips.

In later years, when he had retired from farming, sold the farm and moved to town, Grandpa would rent an acre or two from one of his former farm neighbors so that he could still grow melons and sell them.

The photo here shows Grandpa Vincent holding a prize watermelon. The trunk of the car is packed with muskmelons. The photo was taken after he'd retired and moved into town.

Grandpa had played semi-pro baseball as a young man and had an old-fashioned baseball glove with no webbing between the thumb and first finger. When staying at the farm, I'd spend hours bouncing a tennis ball off the side of the house and catching the rebound. It must have driven Grandma to distraction with the constant thump-thump-thump of my bouncing the ball off the house, but she never complained or asked me to stop. [And, wonder of wonders, I never broke a window!]

Grandpa had a serious accident when I was 5 or 6 years old. He was working in a field with a team of two horses and a binder. This machine would scoop up stalks of wheat or barley lying on the ground after the grain had been mowed and harvested. It would gather the stalks into a bundle called a "shock" or sheaf, bind the sheaf with a coarse twine (called, not surprisingly, "binder twine"). As the binder rolled forward, a large knife blade about 8 or 10 inches long would drop down to cut the twine and then spring back to its normal position. The binder then deposited the sheaves upright on the ground to dry for straw.

One day when grandpa was working with the binder in one of the grain fields, something jammed in the machine. Grandpa stopped the team, climbed off the binder and reached inside to free the jam. As he did so, one of the horses, probably bothered by a biting horse-fly, moved just a single step. It was enough to bring the knife down and it went right through the back of his right hand pinning it in a way that he could not reach to free it with his other hand.

Grandma, in the house a quarter of a mile away, noticed that the noise of the binder had ceased and did not start up again and suspected that something was wrong. She went out to investigate and heard Grandpa calling her name. She found Grandpa pinned by the binder knife which had gone clear through his hand and then stopped. He directed her to get the team to move forward just enough to cause the knife to retract which she did. She wrapped the wounded hand in her apron and they walked back to where Gramp kept his old Model A Ford car. Grandma did not drive so grandpa drove with one hand the 5 miles or so to the doctor's office in town to have the wound treated.

While Grandpa was recovering, my mother would act as chauffeur driving him into town for appointments with the doctor. I begged to go along and was finally allowed to do so. One look at the badly swollen wounded hand as the Doctor dressed and bandaged it, and I almost lost my breakfast. I never asked to go along again!

Grandpa recovered from the ordeal and did not lose movement of his fingers, although he was never able to clench that hand into a fist, but that was a handicap that didn't prevent him from continuing to work the farm. He did, however, employ a "hired man" to help during the busiest times. A single man, Howard Drake, worked with Grandpa for several years, occupying an upstairs bedroom in the farm house.

Among the 140 acres on the farm there were three areas of woods. The closest to the house was just called "First Woods." The others had names, too, but I've forgotten what they were. Grandpa Vincent, like almost all farmers in those days, was an occasional hunter. Always on his own land, he would take his shotgun and shoot a pheasant or wild duck or goose once in a while. I don't remember him ever hunting anything else.

He didn't make a big deal out of occasional hunts with a shotgun, but he loved to tell how one day while "shucking" [husking] corn with team and wagon, he sighted a pheasant some 15 feet away along the fence line. He took the ear of dried corn he was holding and broke it in half against the side of the wagon. Picking up the butt-end he threw it at the pheasant hitting it on the side of the head stunning it. He picked up the bird, wrung its neck, tossed it in the wagon and he and grandma enjoyed roast pheasant for supper that evening. Grandma vouched for him, so I'm sure it was all true. Grandpa, of course, loved to tell that story. I can't say that I blamed him.

In addition to his 12-guage shotgun he had a .22 rifle. One time, when I was maybe 10 or 12, he let me take the rifle and accompany him hunting in the First Woods. I happened to spot a squirrel up in an oak tree, and took a shot at it with the rifle. To the amazement of grandpa, though not to me, I hit it. We took it back to the house and grandma skinned and cooked it for supper that night. I felt quite proud of my marksmanship, but had disquieting feelings about killing a harmless squirrel. As a result I refused to eat any of the squirrel meat and never went hunting again. Grandpa never invited me to go hunting again, either.

I had a similar experience in fishing, which grandpa also would engage in once in a while. One afternoon he took me fishing on nearby Rock River. Grandma's sister, my Aunt Edna Thomas, owned a cottage on the river a few miles from Grandpa's farm. We went there and fished off a pier that jutted out over the water from the riverbank. We spent several hours fishing and I was lucky enough to catch two catfish [we called them bullheads] while grandpa never had a single bite! He never asked me to go fishing with him again. I'm not sure that <u>he</u> ever went fishing again, either. [The bullheads were so ugly and slimy looking, I also refused to eat <u>that</u> food!]

When I stayed overnight with Grandma and Grandpa on the farm occasionally, we'd listen to our favorite comedy programs, like Jack Benny, Fibber McGee and Charlie McCarthy on the radio [this was long before TV], or play cards. They had a favorite card game called "Smear" [I've since heard it, or a very similar game, called "High, Low, Joker, Jack, Game."] It was fun to play and was about the only card game I ever enjoyed playing. I was fairly good at it, partly because Grandpa loved to make outrageously high bids and often couldn't make his bid, which would set his score back.

In those days and in that part of the country the noon meal was always referred to as "dinner" and the evening meal was "supper." Grandpa had an interesting habit. After working all morning he would come to the house to eat dinner, and every day after the meal he would go into the living room, put a small pillow on the floor for his head, lie down on the floor and almost instantly fall asleep. He would nap for half an hour, then wake up and head out to whatever job was waiting to be done that afternoon.

These short naps were a daily week-day ritual, not in evidence on weekends. I always wished that I had that ability. If ever I happen to fall asleep during the middle of the day, I wake up so groggy that I'm pretty useless for several hours afterward. But for Grandpa, it was a way of revitalizing himself, and enabled him to return, rested and refreshed to whatever tasks were required of him in the afternoon.

Grandma Vincent's parents and Grandpa's mother were still living when I was a young boy. Grandma's parents, Algernon and Vernette Woolworth Whitford were in their mid-80s and lived in Milton. We would visit them fairly often but I have few memories of them. Grandpa Whitford died when I was 7 and Grandma Whitford when I was 10. Grandpa had a large white "walrus" moustache that I greatly admired! The photo on the previous page shows Great-Grandpa [mustache and all] and Great-Grandma as I remember them.

Algernon had homesteaded in Nebraska for a few years before returning to Wisconsin and marrying Great-Grandma. He worked at a number of different jobs including working on a land surveying crew and even had a township in neighboring Custer County, NE, named 'Algernon' for him by the survey crew. I'm sure he had a lot of interesting stories to tell if I'd only thought to ask him about his life. Sadly, I never did.

Grandpa Vincent's father died about 3 months after I was born, so I never knew him. His name was Joseph Vincent. I remember Grandpa's mother, Artilda [Tillie]. She lived in northern Wisconsin, so we didn't see her except when she would come to the farm to visit her son and granddaughters. Grandpa was the eldest of 4 brothers and all the others lived near their mother. When she visited, during my early boyhood years, it confused me to have two grandmothers in the same house and with the same last name. So when talking to my parents, in order to keep the grandmothers straight, I always referred to Tillie as "A-Gramma" with a "long" a, and to mom's mother as "Just-gramma." A-gramma lived until I was 18, but as I saw her so seldom I have few memories of her.

The thing I remember most about A-Gramma was that she always scolded Grandpa for wearing a cap or hat when he was working. She "knew" that wearing a cap or hat was what caused men to grow bald! [Grandpa never grew bald.]

The photo here shows what she looked like when I was a baby. Others in the photo are Grandpa Vincent, my mom and me at 6 ½ months old! [I remember the occasion vividly! NOT!]

The only thing I disliked about spending time with Grandpa and Grandma Vincent on the farm was that they did not have a bathroom! Actually, there was no running water in the house. Outside the back-porch was a windmill with both an electric and a hand pump, which provided water for drinking and cooking. There was always a pail of water with a metal dipper on the little enclosed back-porch just off the kitchen which provided drinking water. Grandma cooked on a wood-burning stove that had a tank or reservoir built in beside the fire box. This provided a source of warm, if not always hot, water.

Baths were performed in a round galvanized washtub which would be placed on the kitchen floor near the stove. The bathee [is that a word?] would crouch in the tub with a few inches of warm water in it and give himself/herself a "sponge bath" [only using a dish cloth instead of a sponge]. At least that's how grandpa took a bath, and so did I. [I was never granted the privilege of being present when grandma took her bath. I just assume that the mechanics of the operation were roughly similar.] I always found it interesting to see Grandpa taking a bath. When working outdoors he always wore a blue cotton shirt with the sleeves rolled up to his elbows. So his forearms, face and neck were very darkly suntanned, while the rest of his body was white as a snake's belly. Since we were all SDBs, bath nights on the farm or in town were on Friday nights.

But back to the lack of indoor plumbing: The facility for human waste disposal was a small "two-holer" outhouse, a short distance downhill from the main house. It was cold in winter, unlighted, and worst of all one would occasionally see **spiders**! I was terrified of spiders, so I hated having to use the outhouse, especially after dark. The substitute of choice for toilet paper consisted of the [not very absorbent] pages we would tear from old Sears Roebuck or Montgomery Ward catalogs. At least having pictures to look at helped take one's mind off of any lurking spiders!

CHAPTER 5

A Surfeit of Surgeries

Aside from allergies I really had no major health problems as a boy, but those were the days when the medical profession's attitude was that certain human body parts were created, apparently, by mistake and that people would be better off in general to be rid of these "organs of error." Since I was bothered by allergies you may be able to guess what the first application of this medical belief system involved for me.

If you guessed tonsils and adenoids you passed your first test. I was, I think, only about 6 or 7 when it was decided by Dr. Vogle that the allergies would be less of a problem if my body was relieved of the presence of those useless organs. I remember a few things about the ordeal. First of all the operation was not serious enough to warrant going to a hospital. It was performed in a doctor's office in Janesville, where I was laid on a table on a blanket. Then I was rolled over and over in the blanket with my arms at my sides until I was totally immobilized from the shoulders down.

The anesthetic of choice in those days was ether. Being anesthetized by ether was a major trauma for me [and probably for anyone else who's been subjected to it]. They put a folded cloth over my nose and mouth and dripped liquid ether onto it and told me to breathe deeply. That was unnecessary as the sensation was that I was being smothered and as a result I was gasping for air. Being given ether was the most traumatic experience I ever remember. I think the sensation must have been similar to that of "waterboarding" that's been in the news recently. I haven't the slightest doubt that it would now be considered a form of torture and if employed today would be a violation of the Geneva Conventions!

When I came "to" later I had a horribly sore throat and a throbbing headache to go along with vomiting up blood. There was only one aspect of the whole experience that I remember with any pleasure. That was when I learned that because of the operation in my throat, one food that was recommended for the first few days was ice cream! So there was a ray of sunlight after the darkness of the experience. But, no, my allergies did not vanish in the aftermath of the torture inflicted on this small helpless child. [Not surprising, as torture never elicits useful results!]

My second experience with ether was my own fault and was probably a well-deserved punishment. I DID learn a valuable lesson, however, so I guess that as Shakespeare said, "all's well that ends well." It came about thusly:

I was the world's most picky eater as a young boy [I've improved little over the years I'm sorry to say] and that may have been the cause of periodic stomach upsets. At some point along the way I discovered that when I experienced stomach pains or cramps, that it was, on occasion, enough of an excuse to keep me home from school. I don't claim to be a "fast learner," but I'm not the slowest learner either. Stomach pains, I learned, could be a ticket to miss a day or half day of school!

It was convenient, I had discovered, to exaggerate a mild "stomach ache" to the point of being able to miss school. It was not difficult to carry it one step further and fake totally non-existent pain. I did it only rarely, but it worked to perfection. You're undoubtedly familiar with the old adage that "curiosity killed the cat." You may not be familiar with a corollary that "faking illness can cost you your appendix." Well, now you know.

As it happened, I tried my devious little trick once too often. I was 10 years old at the time and in 6th grade and was faced one day with a test in arithmetic or something equally daunting. [Brief aside: I'm sure that one reason I've always had a deep dislike for arithmetic or mathematics in any form, is that the usual punishment for misbehavior in school in those days was to be kept after school and made to do long-division problems. If you got any wrong, you had to do more!] Anyway, on this occasion, I conjured up a sudden stomach ache!

My dad had had enough. [Or maybe he suspected my little game!] "We'd better take you to the doctor," he said. And he did. I was trapped! I couldn't admit that I was faking. I had to continue the charade. Doctor Vogel announced that it was probably my appendix that was causing these periodic painful seizures, and the best thing to do was to remove it. Like the tonsils and adenoids, according to Dr. Vogel's thinking, the appendix was a useless body part that I might as well be rid of if it was causing me problems. And there was always the dreadful possibility that some time in the future it might rupture and become life-threatening. Well, I couldn't admit that there was no problem without admitting to being a base, despicable and contemptible poltroon. "Hoist by my own petard," as the saying goes!

So I had my appendix out. This time it was in the hospital in Janesville and this time there was again the ether, every bit as traumatic as the first time, but I learned an invaluable lesson about truth and falsehood.

Oh, yeah, the doctor told my parents after the surgery that my appendix looked OK, no inflammation or indication of a problem, but it was probably best to have had it out as it served no purpose and "might cause problems sometime in the future."

Actually, there may have been a problem that the doctor missed, since—what do you know?—With the useless appendix gone, my stomach cramps never resurfaced! Odd, perhaps, but true!

In addition to learning an important lesson, there was, as there had been with the tonsils, an indirect benefit from this experience. During my recuperation from the surgery I was bored and prevailed upon my dad to read to me, an activity I dearly loved. I don't remember what kind of reasoning I used to persuade him to undertake this task. I think perhaps he felt sorry for me, not realizing that I had brought this all on myself and was only receiving my "just deserts" as a consequence of my dissembling.

He agreed, on the condition that I allow him to choose what he was going to read to me. I was always anxious for my dad's attention, so I didn't hesitate to accept his condition. He picked Victor Hugo's *Les Miserable*, saying that it might be a little "heavy" for a 10 year old, but assuring me that if I paid attention he thought I'd enjoy it as it was a very famous and highly regarded novel.

My dad read to me for an hour or so every day for some 10 days to 2 weeks. He could read with expression and would explain things to me if I wasn't quite sure what Monsieur Hugo was getting at. I found that I really got into the story and was thoroughly enjoying it. But, then, wonder of wonders, I recovered from the surgery and my bed-ridden status came to an end.

One day when dad finished reading, he put the bookmark in the book, closed it and handed it to me. He said that I was well now and he wasn't going to read any more to me and suggested that I could continue reading the book myself [he knew that I liked to read] if I was interested in what was happening to Jean Valjean and M. Hugo's other protagonists.

I whined a bit (probably) but he was firm—and I was curious. It WAS a very interesting tale. So it wasn't long before I picked up the book and began reading from where dad had left off. [Would Jean Valjean be sent back to the galleys for stealing the old Priest's silver candlesticks? I HAD to find out!] Dad even told me that there was a rather long section about the Battle of Waterloo which had little to do with the plot and that I could skip that part if I found the going too difficult.

Well, I got so interested and so involved that I finished reading the entire two-volume book [**including** the section dealing with the Battle of Waterloo!] I could hardly put it down. I've read the entire book at least four times since then. And I have three different film versions on VCR tapes or DVDs, each of which I've watched several times. [And now another film rendition of Les Miserable has just been released.] It is, in my opinion, the finest novel ever written. Nor can I resist the admission that if I hadn't faked a stomach ache on that occasion, I might never have discovered a literary treasure of incomparable value. MORAL: Crime doesn't pay . . . but a little fib isn't always the end of the world . . . not if you're willing to pay the price of a non-essential body part.

CHAPTER 6

Various Vacations

Some of my happiest memories as a young boy were of summer vacations with my parents. Every few years we would drive to North Loup, Nebraska, where my father was born and where his mother, my grandma, lived. We would usually make stops in Omaha where dad's sister, Katherine, lived and in Lincoln, NE, where his brother Edwin and family lived. I enjoyed visiting with my cousins, Patty and Jacque, in Lincoln even though they were both older than I was. One summer, I remember the three of us had great fun "printing," by hand, what we called a "newspaper." Their house had an old-fashioned laundry chute which could be accessed on the first and second floors as well as the basement. We would send our "news bulletins" back and forth from floor to floor via the laundry chute.

Their mother, Mary, was not my favorite aunt. I always felt that she didn't approve of me. I think I know why, and, as you might guess, it was not too difficult for me to understand why that may have been true. I mentioned earlier that I was probably the world's most finicky eater. One time when I was only 2 or 3 years old, we were visiting and Aunt Mary had fixed [as usual] a fairly elaborate dinner. [She DID enjoy impressing people with her culinary skills.] As you might guess I absolutely refused to eat anything that she served. Finally my parents were embarrassed enough to take me down from the dining room table and leave the others to enjoy their dinner.

At one point Aunt Mary got up and went into the kitchen only to voice a loud shriek! My mother came to see what was wrong. The kitchen stove was one of those old-fashioned gas stoves on legs with an open space below the burners and oven. In that open space on the floor was a dish where they fed their pet cat. There I was sitting on the floor under the stove eating the food from the cat's dish! [I was too young to have any personal memory of the incident, but in later years I remember my mother related the incident on many occasions to anyone who would listen.]

There were several other cousins in North Loup and sometimes Patty and Jacque would come with us and we would have a grand time. My closest friends among my North Loup cousins were Joe and Belva, children of two of my dad's first cousins. Each had older siblings as well. I think the most fun was when the North Loup cousins introduced Patty, Jacque and I, to an irrigation ditch not too far out of town. The water in the ditch was carried across a little valley by a long open metal flume. The water ran quite fast in the flume and we could sit down at the upper end and the water would carry us along to the lower end at a good rate of speed. Great fun, although it proved rather hard on bathing suits as we skidded along on the metal that formed the bottom of the flume.

We couldn't afford a trip to Nebraska every year. Summers when we could not afford a trip to Nebraska, Grandma Babcock, would come to Wisconsin and stay with us for a week or so. I always looked forward to her visits, as she would read to me almost every night when I went to bed, and also sing to me. I've already mentioned how much I enjoyed her reading to me and singing the old college songs from the Yale College Songbook which I still have, it's broken binding held together with adhesive tape, glue and rubber bands!

Nearly every summer when we did not go to Nebraska, my parents would take me to State Parks and other places of scenic or historic interest in southern and central Wisconsin. My favorite was Devil's Lake State Park near Baraboo. My parents were not your typical "outdoorsy" people. But I remember two summers my dad rented a small home-made camp trailer and we camped the first year at Devil's Lake and the next year at Peninsula State Park on the Door County peninsula north of Green Bay.

The camp trailer was a bit of a pain as it suffered from "flat tire syndrome". The first year we used it, it had three flats. In those days flat tires were a major problem for car owners. When you experienced a flat tire, you jacked up the vehicle with a hand "jack" [an essential piece of equipment for all cars in those days], took off the wheel using a "lug wrench", then removed the tire from the wheel using other "made for the purpose" tools, removed from the tire and patched the inflatable "inner tube" using a special kit, replaced it within the tire, pumped it up with a manually operated hand pump and then replaced the wheel.

That rather complex process made flat tires a major pain in the nether region. To make matters worse, the builder of the trailer had constructed it with plywood "skirts" over the wheel wells which made it extremely difficult to access the wheels. After the first year my Dad convinced the owner/builder to remove the wheel well skirts. It didn't prevent the flats we experienced [two or three more that year], but did make the whole repair operation a little easier.

Devil's Lake State Park was my favorite place as a boy. There was great wading or swimming in the lake at the shallow north end adjacent to the campground. Also near the campground were a number of Indian "effigy mounds" in the shapes of various birds and animals. Best of all were several miles of hiking trails along the sides of the bluffs that formed both the east and west sides of the lake. Along these trails were a number of rock formations with interesting names like Devil's Doorway, Tomahawk Rock, Elephant Rock and Cleopatra's Needle to name just a few.

Here's a photo of the rock formation called Devil's Doorway, taken in the winter. The lake is on the left under a white sheet of ice.

The summer when we spent a week up in Door County, the peninsula that separates Green Bay from Lake Michigan, was fun, too. Other summers we would take day trips to interesting places nearer home such as Wisconsin Dells, Tower Hill State Park, Cave of the Mounds and Little Norway.

I enjoyed visiting these places so much that later when in high school I interested my best friends at that time, Clif and Dick Boehm, in going camping at Devils Lake and visiting some of the other places.

I can't resist telling about one eventful day-outing with my parents and Grandpa and Grandma Vincent. It was basically a picnic outing to a small park near Madison, called Blue Mounds. Mom and Grandma had packed a large picnic lunch which we laid out on a picnic table. You know the kind of table: all one unit with the table part between two benches that were attached on either side. This table happened to be located on a slight slope. After eating, I'd gotten up to explore, and mom and grandma had finished eating and had gotten up from the table also. This left my dad seated on the uphill side of the table and Grandpa on the downhill side. Then dad got up.

Now you can picture the scene. Grandpa is the only one still sitting at the table and he's on the downhill side. Got the picture? As soon as my dad got up from his seat, grandpa's weight over-balanced the table. Down went the lower side of the table with Grandpa still sitting on the bench which was now on the ground. Everything on the table slid off onto the ground on grandpa's side. I remember a big bowl of potato salad going bottom up on the ground beside a very startled grandpa.

Now my grandfather had a very strong dislike for only one kind of food and that was green olives! All the rest of us loved green olives and, hey, a picnic wouldn't be a picnic without them. Wouldn't you know that a large bottle of green olives—with the cover removed—overturned right in Grandpa Vincent's lap! The four of us who witnessed this sudden and unexpected catastrophe, thought the whole scene was hilarious and doubled up laughing. Needless to say, Grandpa did not share our spontaneous mirth but as the good sport that he was, he picked himself up off the ground and stoically endured the rest of the day while trying not to let other people we encountered notice the brine-soaked crotch of his trousers.

Probably the highlight of all my boyhood vacations came about in the summer of 1940 when I was 10. [That was the summer prior to my appendectomy!] My dad decided or was asked by the College [I can't remember which] to take a 6 week long summer school course at the University of Colorado in Boulder. We rented a small cabin near the UC campus. My parents knew a lady who lived in Boulder who had a son about my age. Billy and I had great fun. He earned a little spare change by selling magazines on street corners, and he arranged for me to do this as well. Colliers, Redbook, Saturday Evening Post, at 25 cents each, for anyone who might be old enough to remember. It was fun and never seemed like work . . . and had the benefit of providing a bit of spending money for Billy and me.

The UC campus had a small creek running through it and Billy showed me how to catch crayfish. These were what in the southeastern states are called crawdads and are like small lobsters with a pair of claws or pincers at the ends of their front appendages. The technique for catching them was simple. All it took was a baited piece of string 2 or 3 feet long. Billy would filch pieces of bacon from his mother's refrigerator, and we would each tie a piece of bacon to the end of a piece of string and lower it into the water along the edge of the little creek. It didn't take long before we would see a crayfish emerge from under a rock and grab onto the bacon with its pincer or claw. All we had to do was pull up on the string and up would come the bacon, crayfish and all. We could catch dozens within a half hour or so. Then we'd let them all go back in the stream, move to a different place on the bank and do it all over again.

The city of Boulder lies just at the foot of the Front Range of the Rocky Mountains and on weekends my folks and I would go for drives into the Mountains. To me it was a wonderland, and I was thrilled at all the scenic and interesting places we traveled to and visited. Ghost towns from the early gold mining days like Central City, seeing the famous "Face on the Bar Room Floor" that a thirsty miner painted to pay for a few drinks, driving up Boulder and other narrow canyons, "Buffalo Bill" Cody's grave on Lookout Mountain, stopping at the entrance of the over 6 mile long Moffat railroad tunnel under the Continental Divide, making a big loop around Rocky Mountain National Park to Grand Lake the source of the Colorado River and back over the Trail Ridge Road to Estes Park.

It was my first experience of real mountains and I remember marveling at mining towns laid out on the sides of steep slopes. I was especially impressed by a "switchback" street in the little town of Ward where we drove past the front door of a house, made a hairpin turn and drove by the back of the house at the level of the 2nd story windows.

We always did a lot of sightseeing when my folks and I traveled and I feel I was fortunate to have the chance to visit and see so many places of interest. Traveling with my parents always whetted my appetite for learning and I've always felt that I owed them a great debt for this opportunity. When our 4 children were young, Carol and I tried to make sure that we gave them similar opportunities.

"Read a lot and travel all you can," is my advice to everyone, child or adult, male or female! Or as St. Augustine so aptly put it, "The world is a book and those who do not travel have read only one page." Combine that with this statement by Ian Myrdal, "Traveling is like falling in love; the world is made new!" These brief quotations do a pretty thorough job of summing up a major guiding principle of my life. **"Read a lot and travel all you can," is my personal motto for living!** Reading and traveling are, I believe, the two activities that have given me the greatest satisfaction in life.

CHAPTER 7

Relatively Speaking

I've written about the various grandparents and other relatives that were part of my early life, and have mentioned some, but not all of the others. So, I've decided on slipping in a special section here highlighted with some pictures and introducing readers to some of my aunts, uncles and cousins.

My mother had only one sibling, a younger sister, my Aunt Doris. I've mentioned her earlier in this story, but I wanted to add a photo. Here she is on the right with my mom on the left. Doris was really a very nice lady. Her husband, Harold Baker, was an executive with the YMCA organization. I first remember when they lived in Quincy, IL, and remember visiting them there and going to nearby Hannibal, MO, where we got to see the enormous labyrinthine cave Mark Twain described in "Tom Sawyer", the cave from which Tom and his friend Becky Thatcher had their narrow escape from Injun Joe!

Sometime after that, the Bakers moved to Michigan, living in several different places. Later in his career "Uncle Bake" as I called him, was in charge of the entire State YMCA program for the

state of Michigan. Their two sons, Reg and Gene, were both younger than I, and as we didn't see them that often I really never got to know them that well. The photo on the previous page shows Doris with her two sons, my 1st cousins, Gene [left] and Reg [right]. After Harold's retirement he and Doris had become avid "Aerostreamers" spending their summers in an Aerostream Trailer Park in Florida and later after "Uncle Bake" retired, living there in the trailer park the year around.

I've written about Grandma Babcock, my Dad's mother, and that his father, my grandfather, Edwin, died before I was born. In contrast to Mom, my dad had a sister and three brothers. There is a photo of my Dad, his mother and siblings [minus Archie] in Chapter 1, page 5. My Dad's sister, Katharine, suffered a bout of smallpox and lost her hearing when she was two years old. She was totally deaf but lived a full and productive life, although she never married. She learned to communicate through sign language, and when her parents learned of a school in Massachusetts, Clark School for the Deaf, that taught lip reading ["the oral method" of communication for the deaf], they decided to send her there. Kate wanted to learn that skill and traveled alone by train, a very brave teen-age deaf girl, from Nebraska to Massachusetts!

Kate became proficient in both methods of communication and I remember her telling me once that her parents always encouraged her to associate with "hearing people" and not only with the deaf. Since she was unable to hear her own speech, her pronunciation of words was often a bit distorted and difficult to understand. When I was young I was fearful of being alone with her as I was afraid that I wouldn't understand her and didn't want to embarrass her. Later, I discovered that I could understand her quite well and communicating was never a problem. She, in turn, could understand virtually everything that others said to her, as long as she could see their lips. She was a remarkable lady!

For a number of years after finishing school Kate lived with her brother Edwin's family in Lincoln. She learned the art of retouching and color tinting black and white photographs [this was before the "age of Kodachrome"] and moved to Omaha, where she shared an apartment with another deaf lady for many years, and continued her employment as a retoucher for a photo studio.

This color photo of me in my cowboy outfit was a black and white photo that Katharine color tinted. [When I was a boy my parents never had much money, but they always splurged and got me something extra-nice for Christmas. I think this cowboy outfit was my all-time favorite Christmas present. [Maybe that's how I became a Fiddlefoot!]

Grandfather Edwin J. Babcock, served three terms in the Nebraska State Legislature and one of his proudest accomplishments was a successful effort to change the method of teaching at the Nebraska State School for the Deaf from the old "manual method" of sign-language, to emphasis on the "oral [lip-reading] method." In July, 1954, Katharine and her mother began sharing an apartment in Omaha. Grandma passed away there in July 1966, just 2 months short of her 101st birthday! Katharine died less than four months later.

Dad was the oldest of the four boys, and was named for his grandfather. Next came his brother Edwin named for their father. "Deke," as he was known in the family, served as a Lieutenant in the army during World War I, and worked after that for the Nebraska State Highway Department. During World War II, he worked as an engineer on the ALCAN Highway, built largely through Canada as a link between the "lower 48" states and the territory of Alaska. Deke and his wife, Mary, lived most of their lives in Lincoln, NE. They had two daughters, Patty and Jacque, a few years older than I.

The next son, Archie, also lost his hearing in his youth, the cause of which I never learned. He attended the Nebraska State School for the Deaf in Omaha, graduating in 1922, and then attended Wayne State Normal College for two years, specializing in manual training and drafting. [Several items of his wood work are still in the family.] Archie was very athletic and was a star football player despite his handicap. He also attended the University of Nebraska for a short time until he took a job as a draftsman in the State Engineer's Office in Lincoln, NE. Two years later, in 1928, he died of meningitis after a short illness, so I never had the privilege of knowing him.

My dad's youngest brother was Arthur Sidney, or as Grandma always called him, Art-Sid. Art suffered from epilepsy throughout his life, which his mother believed was due to a head injury suffered when playing football for North Loup High School. Art saw a doctor regularly and took medication and kept the epilepsy under control. Still, Art was not positive that the disease was caused by the injury and that it might possibly be passed on to any children he might sire. So Art made the selfless decision that he should not marry or have children due to the possibility, however slight, that he could pass on the disease to another generation.

For most of his adult life Art worked for the Nebraska State Highway Department, a job that took him "on the road" to different parts of the state, often for days or weeks at a time. Unfortunately, Art was a heavy smoker and in later years suffered from advanced pulmonary emphysema. After one particularly difficult pulmonary attack he had to be hospitalized and after being released was transferred to a nursing home facility. A month after his 68th birthday, he had another severe attack, complicated by pneumonia and after being transferred to the hospital again, died there, January 11, 1972.

END PART I

PART II

School Daze

CHAPTER 8

Elementary, My Dear . . .

I'm going to fast-forward, to some extent at least, through my grade school and high school years. As I look back on those years, they weren't GREAT, but they weren't BAD, either. Perhaps I'm being unfair to myself when I suggest that my elementary school years in particular, were not <u>memorable</u>. After all, they all happened quite a few years ago and my <u>memory</u> has weakened with time!

I was always a good student, but also tended to be a rather lazy and somewhat under-achieving student as well. All through grade school another boy, Ray D., and I were usually the top two students in our class. [I think Ray worked harder at it than I did and I like to think that's why he was at the "head of the class" as often as I was!] Ray wasn't much for sports, while I thought of little else, so I always felt I was at a disadvantage in competing with him for top academic honors! It's also true that I wasn't really interested in competing for that "honor." I don't think it would be wrong to say that I was a somewhat lazy student who did very well at things I liked or enjoyed, and was content to just get by in other things. I was best in subjects like history, geography, reading and social studies.

Geography was one of my favorite subjects. I was 9 years old when Hitler's Germany invaded Poland to set off World War II. The newspapers would frequently print maps on the front page showing what the troop movements were in various theaters of war. I soon developed the habit of drawing my own maps of the various war zones. I think it was as a direct result of this that I developed a love and fascination for maps which has never left me. I have lots of individual maps, both current and historical, plastered on walls of my home, as well as stacks of maps around the house and **many** atlases—again, both current and historical.

I hated arithmetic and never felt motivated to do well in that subject. In English I did very well in the reading part of it, but couldn't have cared less about learning the rules of grammar. There's a bit of an anomaly there. My use of vocabulary and grammar as well as spelling have always been above average, but I never did learn the <u>rules</u> of grammar and still find it almost impossible to tell what is the difference between an adjective and an adverb, how to define a conjunction or a preposition, or to identify the correct "part of speech" in which a given word belongs. Because I was small for my age my parents did not start me in school at the earliest possible time, but waited another year. As a result I was three to six months older than most of my classmates. I can't say that I enjoyed going to school from kindergarten through high school, but neither did I have a strong dislike for school. Going to school was something that was expected and taken for granted. I was never a "troublemaker" in school, but could be a tad "mischievous" at times, I recall.

Where I went to school we did not have "school uniforms." [Thank goodness for small favors!] In a way, I had my own uniform and that was the way I dressed all through the lower grades. After "graduating" from short pants, I'd hoped to be able to move on with my friends to being a "long pants" person which was the definitive sign of being "grown up." My parents, however, had other ideas, and for several years I found myself to be in a "tweener" class—a class that I shared with no one else among my class-mates. This photo will illustrate what I mean. I think I was about seven years old when it was taken.

Probably because we had little money, and clothes were costly, consideration *numero uno* for my parents was for clothes to last! Their solution to that was to dress me in what were then called 'knickers', actually a kind of modified jodhpur. Trousers that were flared at the thighs and gathered at the knees and were worn with long stockings that folded over the pants cuff just below the knees. My Mom then sewed leather patches on each knee so that I wouldn't wear out that area of the trousers so quickly. Fortunately, my parents DID permit me to wear lace-up boots that were known in that day and age as "high tops." This photo shows how I dressed over the course of several years. It wasn't so bad, I guess, as I don't ever remember being teased by classmates about my garb. [Actually, I think some of the other boys were a bit jealous of the boots!]

I remember little about grade school years. Our school was a rather massive two story brick building with inside stairways and outside metal fire escapes. Four large classrooms on the first floor held grades one, two and three, plus Kindergarten and a teacher's lounge. On the second floor were classrooms for grades four through eight, if I remember correctly. The below ground-level basement had restrooms [boys on one side, girls on the other], the coal heating plant, a room for the janitor along with a workshop and a kind of "utility" room for band practice, etc. This photo of the building was taken during one of two great Milton floods of 1936 and 1938, if my  memory is correct. The school was near the edge of the village park and in the spring of each of those years, the entire park and much of the "downtown" area was under water. I'm not sure which year this photo was taken.

I can best describe my elementary school years by observing that they just sort of happened. For the most part I got along with the teachers, although I liked some more than others. I'll try to elaborate a bit about the few memories I have of them. I mentioned my kindergarten teacher when I described the altercation between my head and the radiator. She was fairly young and was new at our school, if I recall correctly. I don't even remember her first name for certain, although I'm pretty sure that her last name was Davis. Kindergarten was kind of fun, as there was no studying or homework required. My view of Kindergarten is that it's not "school." It exists to get kids out of their homes . . . and out of their parents' hair for a few hours each day.

First and second grades were both taught by older ladies, first grade by Leta Lanphere and second by Rachel Coon. Kindly ladies, with <u>many</u> years of teaching experience, and "no nonsense" disciplinarians, as I remember them. They were "veterans" at Milton Elementary School, having taught their respective grades for a number of years and seemed as if they would go on teaching them forever.

Third grade was a bit of a change. Miss Moore was new to our school, younger and less strict. We were all, I believe, a bit in awe of her as we learned that she was ambidextrous! She could write on the blackboard with either hand and could even write simultaneously with both hands! How could anyone not admire and respect a person with such skills? I remember that year as being more 'fun' than most of the others, although I have no particular memories of it, other than Miss Moore demonstrating her ambidexterity on the blackboard.

We entered fourth grade somewhat with fear and trembling, as we had heard stories about how "tough" and strict that teacher was—at least compared with Miss

Moore. This was a lady, I'd guess of about 40 years, Miss Marie Enlow. At least, I think she was a Miss, but I'm not sure. I don't really have any specific memories of that year, except for the recollection that she wasn't quite the tyrannical despot that rumors had made her out to be. Rather, 'strict but fair' is how I would describe her.

Fifth grade was one of the more interesting years, and we had a teacher who was new both to our school and to the state, Miss Rosalie Pole. This rather masculine lady, probably in her late 20s, came from Brownsville, Texas, and was intent on convincing all of us that she came from God's chosen country populated by a race of almost mythical beings. She regaled us with tales of her proficiency with a "six-shooter" and how she could fearlessly face and shoot the head off of an angry rattlesnake, a feat she led us to believe she had accomplished more than once.

We were quite in awe of her until one fall day during the daily recess period we discovered a 6-inch-long baby grass snake in the school yard. Several of us thought that Miss Pole might be pleased to see this rather puny specimen of a harmless Wisconsin snake. My friend, Windy, picked it up and several of us trooped behind him and approached our fearless Texan teacher who was sitting at her desk in our class room. Windy, holding our snake baby by its tail, thrust it in front of her face saying, "Miss Pole, look what we found."

Miss Pole's response was a sharp scream, as she jumped out of her chair and quickly put the desk between herself and her now equally startled and amazed students. She quickly, and in no uncertain tone, ordered us to return the [also startled] little reptile to where we found it. We did so, and somewhat to our surprise, Miss Pole went on with the day's lessons, as though nothing out of the ordinary had happened. For the rest of the school year she never mentioned the incident nor did she any longer try to impress us with what, from that point on, we dismissingly referred to as her "Texas stories" which we now concluded were largely fictitious!

Miss Pole was a good sport, however. She had never seen snow before and after the first snowfall that winter she would often come out with us for recess, and we showed her how to make and throw snowballs. It wasn't long before she would even join in friendly snowball "fights" with us. The fact that we were able to throw snowballs at our teacher—even hitting her occasionally—without being scolded or punished was a great thrill for us, and also helped restore our rather tattered respect for the "terrible Texan."

Sixth grade, we had a youngish lady Miss [or Mrs., I'm not sure] Callahan. She was a pleasant person, fair and good natured, and that helped make for a generally pleasant and uneventful year in school. Outside of school was another story, as that was the year of my unfortunate faked stomach ache and ensuing appendectomy, which I've described in Part I.

Miss Elfrida Hermann, our seventh grade teacher was another strict teacher with a rather tough, no nonsense reputation. We were somewhat intimidated by that blot on her professional escutcheon, until one eventful day when an unexpected incident served to 'break the ice' and we decided that she was more or less human after all. Miss Herman liked to read to us, and she would pick a book that she thought might be interesting as well as educational, and every Friday she would read to us for 20 minutes or so just before class let out in the afternoon. I don't recall how many books she read to us that year. It was, in fact, a rather enjoyable and relaxing way to end a school week, but we still had nervous reservations about her.

All was well, however, until the time Miss Herman got so wrapped up in her story that she neglected her concomitant role of "literary censor." It was only later that we discovered that she had carefully made a practice of omitting any, and all, profanity or curse words that happened to "salt" the text that she was reading to us. This was 1943, mind you. World War II was raging and was the center of everyone's attention, and the book she had chosen a few weeks before was the recently published, *They Were Expendable.*" It's the story of the U.S. Navy's Motor Torpedo Boat squadron and crews operating in the Philippine Islands at the time of the Japanese invasion. Now, in a war story like this, I discovered when I bought my own copy a few years later, there was no lack of "salt." But Miss Herman was determined to spare what she imagined were our innocent ears, and she had adroitly skipped over all the curse words . . . . until, "the day."

Indeed, Miss Herman had performed magnificently in her role as 'language censor' until near the end of the book. Then, [the scene is still vivid in my mind] a tense and enthralled roomful of students on the edges of our seats, listened with rapt attention as Miss Herman's voice, capturing perfectly the tenseness of the situation, describes how a Japanese plane is mistaken for an expected U.S. aircraft by the crew of Lieutenant Kelly's PT 41 boat. The supposedly friendly plane drops a bomb that barely misses the 41 boat and Miss Hermann's voice rises to a climactic pitch as she read's Kelly's shout of, "Those crazy bastards! Don't they know we're on *their* side?" [Look it up, if you doubt me—page 172 in my copy!]

There was a stunned silence in our classroom, punctuated only by a few astonished gasps from several girls, and a half-smothered chorus of snickers from some of us boys. For an instant, Miss Herman's face turned white, then bright red, but there was hardly a noticeable break in her reading, as—to her credit—she continued on as if nothing out of the ordinary had happened. Afterward, neither we nor she ever made mention of the incident. But I think we students, for the rest of the school year felt a new respect for a teacher who, if only for a brief second or two, showed herself to be an excitable and mistake-prone human, just like the rest of us. From that moment on, Miss Herman was one of us!

Our eighth Grade teacher was Mrs. Nancy Kidder. She was an institution at Milton Grade School, a very well-liked middle-aged lady and an excellent teacher. What more can I say? Years later she was to play a small role in my years at Milton College as, by that time, she had moved on to the position of Matron at Goodrich Hall, the women's dormitory on the campus. I have one, lingering, unpleasant memory of 8th grade. The punishment for any misbehavior, real or imagined, was to be kept after school, and given a set of long-division problems to work before we could leave the classroom. To this day I'm convinced that this form of punishment was at the root of my lifelong dislike of anything to do with arithmetic or mathematics. Simply put, to me arithmetic was a form of punishment.

From, I believe, about fifth grade on up we had a special music teacher who came in once or twice a week for a 50 minute period. [Each school day was divided into 50 minute "periods" each devoted to a different subject like, English, Arithmetic, History, etc.] Our music teacher—he taught singing—was a pleasant young man and very talented singer who shared my last name although Ken Babcock was only very distantly related to me. He made singing fun and I enjoyed it. I still have a copy of one of the songbooks that we used in his classes. It's called "Discovery" from a series known as "The World of Music" and has songs from many different countries and parts of the world. I really enjoyed our singing classes.

There was also a school band, but it was an "extracurricular activity" and met after school in the basement, once or twice a week. For many years my parents were filled with an unrequited desire for me to learn to play a musical instrument. I've mentioned the rather hopeless and short-lived attempt to have me take piano lessons while we lived at the studio. At one time I must have said something to the effect that I thought perhaps playing a trumpet might be more fun than that "girly" instrument the piano. My parents checked into the possibility but there were two problems. First, they were told that learning the cornet would be a better idea [it was very similar to a trumpet, but easier to play]. Second, they couldn't really afford to buy me a musical instrument, but my Dad's unmarried younger brother, my Uncle Art, came to their rescue and bought a cornet for me.

My then best friends, Bill and Windy, also took up instruments at the same time, so I didn't have to worry about them standing outside the window with baseball bats and gloves while I took lessons. We all tried out for the after-school band class conducted by a lady named Roxa Pritchett. Both Bill and Windy became fairly adept at playing, Bill the cornet, and Windy the trombone. As with the earlier piano experience I turned out to be rather hopeless at the cornet as well, didn't really enjoy trying to play it, and soon dropped out of the band altogether.

To show what one-track minds my parents had, it was necessary for me to endure one more "musical chairs" fiasco before they finally abandoned their orchestral plans for me. [Both of my parents were singers, singing in choirs or other groups, but neither played an instrument.] I've mentioned that while we lived in the studio at the college there was a spare room that my parents rented out to college students. The last one before we moved out was a music student named Bernhardt Westlund. He was, to my way of thinking, a musical genius. After he graduated he was hired by the college to be the head of the music department and directed both the college orchestra and *a cappella* choir as well as non-college community music groups. As a student Bernie had little money so *en lieu* of paying rent to my parents, he would often refinish antique pieces of furniture, with which my parents loved to fill our home. Bernie was super-good at that kind of work, as well as being a masterful musician, and some of those pieces of furniture are still in my possession or with my children.

Anyway, to make a short story shorter, they asked Bernie if he could teach me how to play a snare drum. Even a nearly tone-deaf twelve-year-old should be able to play a drum. Right? Wrong! Bernie was quite aware of my musical deficiencies, but still agreed to undertake the task. He was astute enough, however, to advise them not to purchase a drum, but to start with investing in just a pair of drumsticks. Bernie said he could show me how to drum on a table top, and if I showed promise, THEN they could buy me a real drum. I won't keep you guessing how it all turned out. Another dashing of parental hopes! In my feeble defense, I can only say that rattling two sticks on a table top, was counterproductive to producing in me either talent or interest in becoming a drummer.

Over a period of years, I grew to like Bernie, even though I never quite forgave him for a remark he once made to my parents. I LOVED to sing, and still do for that matter. Unfortunately, I've always had problems carrying a tune and staying on key. One day after listening to my off-key singing in an adjacent room, Bernie commented to my parents that "I don't think Bryce could carry a tune in a bushel-basket." It was some years later that my mother told me of the incident, adding that it was said sadly and not maliciously. By that time I realized the truth of the matter so never took offence. Nor have I ever stopped singing, and feel that my continued efforts were rewarded. I'm still not a GREAT singer, but singing WITH someone, I can match my voice to theirs reasonably well.

What did I do for entertainment, other than playing sports games with friends during these "formative" years? Television was still years in the future and computers and cell phones didn't exist. We did have radio, however, and I enjoyed listening to some of the really outstanding radio comedians. Jack Benny, Fred Allen, George Burns and Gracie Allen, Fibber McGee and Molly, Bob Hope, Bud Abbot and Lou Costello, and Red Skelton were among my favorites. Mostly they had half-hour long shows once a week, so there were enjoyable laughs almost every night of the week.

Another radio feature was the late afternoon "serials." Buck Rogers, Captain Midnight, Henry Aldrich, The Lone Ranger, The Green Hornet, and Jack Armstrong ["the All-American Boy"], to name a few. Most were 15 minute episodes that carried a continuous storyline that would go on for several weeks. These serial adventure or comedy programs were an almost constant way of filling in the period between the end of the school day and the evening meal.

And, one can't leave out the fascination of "comic books." Some were actually "comics", but most were adventure stories usually featuring some superhuman crime fighter. Superman, Batman, Captain Marvel, the Flash, Tarzan, and Wonder Woman were among the most popular. With a price of just 10 cents apiece, most every kid of grade school age had a large collection of comic books, and it was a common practice to trade them, so they got passed around from hand to hand. This stage of life faded quickly for most of us, I think, when we "graduated" into High School.

CHAPTER 9

The Lowdown On High School

The summer before I entered High School, my parents bought a house, and we moved out of the Studio. The house was on the corner of Davis St. and Plumb St., facing onto the two-block-long Davis Street. My mother lived in the house until she retired from work at the college, when she sold it. It had been the home of John Daland, the Dean of the college, who wrote the tribute to my dad [see page 59]. It was a two story house, with an attic. Dean Daland's son had left a lot of books in the attic, and I was thrilled to think that now they were mine.

One treasure was a complete hardback set of Edgar Rice Burroughs' Tarzan books. As it turned out, after a few years, Dean Daland's grandson heard about them and wanted them, so I reluctantly passed them on to him. I still have some of the other books from the attic treasure, and have since purchased paperback editions of all the Tarzan books, plus many of E.R.B.'s other great stories. The new home was a little

closer to the High School that I would be starting in the fall, but I would still have a walk to school of about a half a mile.

Our new home was a two story house and larger than we needed with an unused bedroom upstairs. After a few years, my parents had the upstairs remodeled into an apartment, with an outside stairway. A spacious screened porch was also enclosed and would become my bedroom. The work was done by Wilton "Wil" Hurley, who would later be my chemistry professor in college and marry my cousin, Mary Babcock. The corner lot was large enough to allow for a garden, and for a garage. The photo on the previous page, taken about 1951 shows my parents and I standing in the yard. You can see the lower end of the stairs going up to the apartment, which was quickly rented to a Professor at the college named Zea Zinn.

Here is a photo of Milton Union High School [MUHS] as it looked when I attended between 1944 and 1948. It served students from both Milton and Milton Junction and was located where the two villages physically joined each other. In 1967 the two villages finally amalgamated into a single small city called Milton. This building is no more. It was torn down and a new High School, Milton High School, was built in a new location.

The four years I spent in High School were fairly uneventful. I got decent grades for the most part. The pattern established in elementary school generally continued. If I enjoyed the subject I did very well, but if I disliked the subject [or the teacher!] I did rather poorly. With "in between" subjects, I did well enough to get by, but was not a "straight A" student by any means. Fortunately there were only two subjects in the four years in which I had major problems.

The first was algebra. I've mentioned how much I always disliked mathematics. Algebra came in my sophomore year [10th grade], and was the only class that was taught by our High School Principal, Charles "Charlie" Dorr. My father knew him well after serving for a number of years on the School Board. To this day I know absolutely nothing about algebra. It was then, and is today, a totally foreign language to me. Mr. Dorr "passed" me with a grade of D. I really should have flat out failed, and I'm sure I received the undeserved D, mainly on account of Dad having been on the School Board!

The other class in which I "earned" only the dreaded "D" was a course in German which I took in my third or junior year. A new teacher had been hired that year to teach English. [I say "new" as in new to MUHS. In life, she was rather ancient.] Her name was Ella Kneller, and she had been born and raised in Germany. She persuaded the Principal and School Board to let her teach a German Language course in addition to her English courses which were mandatory courses for freshman and sophomore students. Fortunately, as a junior that year, I didn't have to endure her as an English teacher.

My parents, however, were strongly of the opinion that I should take a foreign language class. Until that time the only foreign language class taught at MUHS was a class in Latin. I'd told my parents that I wasn't interested in learning Latin, and they didn't push me into a course in a so-called "dead" language. But, when they learned that there was an opportunity for me to learn a language in current use, they practically insisted that I take it. So I did . . . and soon regretted the decision.

I hated the course, mainly, I think, because I developed a strong dislike for Miss Kneller. Why THAT was, I'm not entirely sure, but it was true without a shred of doubt. I learned absolutely nothing about algebra, but I actually did learn a little about the German language. I learned to recite the alphabet in German [*aah, bay, tsay, day*, etc.] and learned to count [*ein, tswei, drei, fier*, etc.] up to a hundred! I also learned the basic pronunciation rules well enough that I can still read words in German and pronounce them more or less correctly, even though the meaning of 90% of them is still a mystery. Perhaps that is the reason that Ms. Kneller passed me with another D grade.

Good teachers had a positive effect on me as a student. After the fiasco of algebra, in fear and trembling I took geometry the next year. I was lucky enough to have an excellent teacher, a youngish man named Edward Rood, and enjoyed and passed that class with no trouble. My friend Ray, D. and I [rivals in grade school] had become best friends in our Junior year and had fun during "free" periods, inventing a "Geometry Language" by giving geometrical terms like secant, cosine, tangent and sine, specific meanings of English words. Unfortunately this worthy effort has been lost to posterity. I wish I'd preserved it.

Ray and I, who had given ourselves nicknames of Buckets [me] and Bones [Ray] also engaged in a long, detailed collaborative effort during our Junior years, of transposing Shakespeare's play *Julius* Caesar [which we were studying in English class] into a bastardized combination of "Dogpatch", the language used in the "Lil Abner" comic strips, and pseudo-German dialect reminiscent of Ms. Kneller's German class which we had both taken the year before. It followed Shakespeare's play in terms of plot and characters, with total exactitude, just different names and language.

The title page read: *"The Tragical Tragedy of Good Kink Nogoodnik, II, by Buckets Papooshnick and Bones Slushpump. "A Drama of Lower Slobbovia." Time: About the year 44 BB [Before Bagles]. Dedication "To Ella Kneller, mit many pleasant [?] memories uf High School."* We never finished it, but I still have a hand printed copy of our masterpiece through Act IV, Scene III, which is as far as we got. Writing it was great fun for us, however, and gave us many laughs.

As in grade school, I did well in the reading parts of English courses which were required all four years with 3rd and 4th year English taught by a nice older lady, Edith Stockman. I remember reading "Ivanhoe" and enjoying it. Some of the other books we read, such as "The Return of the Native" I found far less enjoyable, but got through with no trouble.

Some of the classes were actually fun. At times, anyway. We had another new to MUHS teacher for biology, Miss Avis Hosbach, and although I hated having to dissect a variety of strange creatures, she was easy-going and good natured. Social Science classes from Robert Shorey and U.S. and world history from Curtis Hotlen were among the classes I enjoyed the most. My last two years, I joined the school's *a capella* choir that was directed by the same Ken Babcock that taught us singing when we were in grade school. As I mentioned earlier, I always had trouble carrying a tune or melody when trying to sing alone. Surrounded by other voices, however, I found that I could match my voice to theirs and manage to get by reasonably well. Even without the aid of a bushel-basket!

I almost forgot to mention another class in which I did rather poorly. That was a class in typing, which I took because I needed an extra class my Junior [3rd] year. Our instructor, Miss Ruby Agnew, was an older lady who probably should have retired some years earlier. Miss Agnew was notable for having a "wooden leg". [Well, I don't know if it was actually made of wood, but an "artificial" leg at least.]

The thing I remember most about her classes was that she would frequently give us tests to evaluate our typing speed. These were usually intended to be either 5 or 10 minute timed tests. Not infrequently, however, Miss Agnew would doze off at her desk shortly after we began the timed test. We would merrily type away far beyond the intended limit. Suddenly Miss Agnew would awake from her unintended slumber. She would <u>never</u> acknowledge that she'd dozed off, but would just announce that the "timed" test had only been a "practice" exercise, and go on with the class. I never was able to top the minimum passing requirement of correctly typing 20 words per minute, but that modest achievement was enough to pass the course with another "D".

I had a pretty limited "social life" in High School. For over a year I dated a pretty dark haired girl, Janet H., who was a year behind me in school. It was not a very eventful or exciting courtship. I was terribly shy around girls, and felt too embarrassed and inept to attend school dances. I did take Janet to the Junior Class Prom, but one venture onto the dance floor convinced me that I didn't belong there, and I think Janet recognized my lack of skill and my obvious embarrassment and we stayed for only a short time.

The major dating activity for shy, socially inept teens like me was to go to "movies". There were no motion picture theaters in Milton but Fort Atkinson, 12 miles away, had two, and Janesville just 8 miles from Milton had four movie theaters! Admission for kids under 18 years of age was only a quarter [$.25] at first, although inflation's ugly head bumped it up to $.50 later, and a "show" would include a cartoon, newsreel, the ubiquitous previews, and feature film [even a "double feature" sometimes]. So it was an affordable and pleasant way to take a girl on a date.

Janet lived on a farm a few miles out of town, but my parents would let me use their car, so transportation didn't pose a major problem. By then I was 16 and had my driver's license. When there was no movie that interested us, I'd drive out to Janet's home and we'd go for a drive, then find a secluded spot on a back road, park, and engage in a session of kissing, cuddling, or "necking" as it was referred to in those days. Then I'd drive her home. Very exciting! But I have pleasant memories of my first "romance." The photo on the previous page was copied from my HS yearbook. It doesn't do justice to Janet, who was a very pretty girl, but it's the only photograph of her that I have!

It all came to an end sometime towards the end of my final year in High School. A near neighbor of Janet, named Bob B., had graduated 2 years earlier and immediately enlisted in the U.S. Navy. Having served his enlistment he was discharged and returned home midway through that year of 1948. It didn't take him long to ask Janet on a date. She said, no, that she had a boyfriend, but Bob was persistent. Janet finally told me, and asked if it would be OK with me if she went out with Bob. She didn't want to "break up" with me, she said, but she no longer wanted to "go steady."

It didn't take me long to say "no". As I think I've already made clear, my self-confidence was near zero, especially when it concerned girls. On top of that, Bob was older, had been 2 years in the Navy, and *everyone* knew how promiscuous sailors were with "a girl in every port!" I saw my chances of competing as being exactly nil . . . or worse. So I said either we continued going steady, or not at all. I was disappointed but not surprised by Janet's reply. A few years later Janet and Bob were married and, as far as I know, it was a successful and, I hope, happy union.

My parents were very accommodating about letting me use the family car evenings. My trips were all fairly short during my High School years, and there always seemed to be enough gas in the tank for my travels. I was a careful driver and was never ticketed. I remember only one "accident" and that had no particular bearing on my driving.

It was in my senior year after my breakup with Janet, that I found myself "on my own" one evening, a bit bored, and decided to go to see a movie by myself. In our old 1938 "battleship grey" Plymouth sedan, I headed toward Ft. Atkinson alone in the car about dusk. About 3 or 4 miles from home something made me look down at the floorboard. The openings around the brake and clutch pedals of cars in those days created narrow gaps around the pedal shafts. When I looked down I was shocked to see flames through the openings. I immediately pulled off onto the shoulder of the road, stopped, turned off the ignition and jumped out of the car.

So far I'd acted correctly, but that was about to end. No flames were visible so I opened the hood to see what was happening inside and the sudden inrush of oxygen caused the flames to flare up several feet in the air as old oil and grease on the engine ignited. I slammed the hood down quickly, but the conflagration had taken hold by that time, and I was rather scared!

Not knowing what else to do I ran over to a farmhouse just down the road. It happened to be the home of a girl in my high school class. I told her that my car was on fire and asked if I could use her phone. She showed me where it was. I had no idea what to do, so I did what most any kid faced with a new and unexpected, possibly dangerous, situation would do. I phoned home!

Trying to sound calm and collected, I told my dad where I was and that the car was on fire and could he bring me a fire extinguisher! Duh! He said to stay away from the car and not to worry. I went back to the car to wait but didn't get too close! It never occurred to me that we were a "one car family," or to wonder how they would get to where I was. It was not long before I heard a siren, and to my total surprise and embarrassment, here came the Milton fire truck from town. Following close behind a neighbor's car conveyed my parents. By this time I think they were more frightened that I was.

My first reaction was to scold them! I'd asked for a fire extinguisher, not the whole dang fire department, siren blaring, and a string of 6 or 8 cars containing morbidly curious townspeople. [There was always a contingent of nit-wits who would go chasing after fire trucks in those days. I guess, maybe, there still are.] In fact a fire extinguisher was all that was needed to put out the, by that time, dying conflagration.

The car had to be towed into town to be repaired and my parents had to walk to work [only about 3 blocks] for the next week or so. A "short" in the electrical wiring had ignited some oil or grease, we were told later. The whole incident was quickly forgotten, I think, by everyone but "yours truly."

In High School, besides the regular interschool athletics and curriculum of "for credit" classes, there were what were considered "extra-curricular activities". There were choir concerts, and intramural sports like volleyball which I enjoyed. My junior year I performed in a comedy "Barbershop Quartette" routine with 3 other fellows, and also had a part in our Junior Class play, a comedy called "Spring Green," directed by our English teacher, Mrs. Stockman. I played an elderly, absent-minded doctor who was an earthworm specialist!!

I was also in a short one-act play called "The Dear Departed" which involved funeral preparations for an elderly man who turns out to be "dead drunk" rather than deceased. I enjoyed acting on stage as will become more apparent as this story unfolds. I would have tried out for the Senior Class play except that I learned it would be directed by Ms. Kneller, so I wanted nothing to do with it!

Sports, however, were my main interest [aside from Janet!] during my High School years. I've probably done more stupid things in my life than I want to admit to, but the absolute stupidest was going out for the H.S. football team all four years. Consider. I was, as a freshman, almost 5 feet tall, and weighed less than 100 pounds when soaking wet. By my senior year I was almost 5' 2" and may have weighed nearly 110 lbs. I was, however, determined to pursue a High School "career" in sports. I was on both the football and basketball teams all four years, and also played baseball one year.

MUHS had very good football teams during my years in school. My freshman year we won the Rock Valley League championship going undefeated. We placed 2nd the following year, again undefeated, but with two ties. My junior year we won 5 and lost 2 and my senior year we were again Conference champions, with 5 wins although we lost a non-conference game. I keep saying "we", but I have to admit that I had very little, if anything, to do with the outcomes.

I dutifully went out for practices, and my senior year, actually got on the field for the final few seconds of two or three games. Due to my size, or rather lack of it, Coach Anderson had me play quarterback. I could hand off the ball from the T-formation, but I could not throw passes at all well as my hands were too small to effectively grip the ball and I was too short to see over the heads of defensive linemen. In those days

everyone played both on offence and on defense, so I played as a single 'safety' in the defensive backfield. I can quite honestly say that I took a good beating. No major injuries but I tore ligaments in my knee one year and still have a crooked nose as a result of getting kicked in the face [accidently] when I tried to tackle our star halfback during a practice scrimmage!

Basketball was the sport I really enjoyed, although my lack of height was a major handicap. I was very good at shooting baskets in practice, but when I did get into a few games my senior year I was so nervous that my shooting eye suddenly went "blind." The skinny kid in this photo, copied from the Blackhawk, our school "Annual" for 1948, the year I graduated, as you no doubt guessed, is me.

Because I knew how to keep score for games, Coach Anderson gave me the job of being the official score-keeper for the Varsity games during my first 3 years on the squad. I enjoyed that, and have always enjoyed "keeping score" for baseball, football and basketball games, "live" or over the radio or later TV.

I should have mentioned this in Part I, but my dad taught me how to keep score to Chicago Cubs baseball games which we listened to on the radio, from the time I was somewhere around five years old! I enjoyed it immensely, made myself score-sheets, a quantity of which Dad ran off for me on a mimeograph machine at the college. As an outgrowth to that, I also taught myself to keep score to basketball and football games.

I did have one moment of "glory" on the basketball floor. Those not good enough to play on the Varsity team would play preliminary games before the main event. My junior year, I was a starting player on the "Junior Varsity" team and in one home game we trailed by a point in the closing seconds. As we brought the ball up the floor someone threw it to me near center court. I turned and heaved the ball toward the basket just ahead of the game-ending buzzer and by some miracle the ball banged off the backboard and dropped through the basket to win the game. My one "moment of glory!"

I was a school hero, for perhaps 24 hours! I mentioned earlier that Ray D. and I had adopted nicknames. I'd chosen "Buckets" which was the nickname of a Green Bay Packers player "Buckets" Goldenberg. The next day a couple varsity players greeted me with, "Now we know why they call you "Buckets." The miracle was never repeated.

Coach Anderson was primarily a football coach and a good one. In a small high school he had to coach all inter-school sports. During my first two years in HS this was just football and basketball, but in my junior year the school decided to field a baseball team as well. Coach Anderson never really enjoyed coaching sports other than football, and it showed in the results. I was a reserve on the baseball team my junior year, playing 2nd base, but did not go out for the team my last year in school, as I'll explain.

The big reward for High School athletes was to earn a "letter." This was a rather ostentatious cloth letter of the alphabet that identified a particular school. Ours was a "U" for Union. Each student who played in a certain number of "quarters" or innings of a varsity-level game would receive a "Letter." The custom was that then you could have the Letter sewn on a sweater fashioned in the "school color". [Our school color was red, and the team's knick-name was "Redmen."] If you didn't play in enough games but went out for the sport all four years, a Letter would also be awarded. I finally received a Letter for going out for football [and almost getting killed!] for four years.

I should have received a Letter for basketball as well. Actually I'd played in enough quarters of games my senior year and I'd also been on the team all four years. In addition to playing, however, team members were expected to obey a set of "training rules." Many of the basketball players had started smoking which was a training rules infraction, and Coach Anderson decided to punish them by not awarding the Letters they had earned.

In actual fact I was one of only two members of the team that had not "broken training", but Coach decided to punish the entire squad! So no Letters were awarded, and I felt I'd been unfairly punished. I was so angry and disappointed with Coach Anderson that I refused to go out for the baseball team that, my senior, year. So I was denied two Letters that I felt I should have received. In hindsight, it seems totally unimportant to me now, but it really rankled at the time.

As I noted earlier, my parents had purchased a home after all those years of renting and we had moved into it just before I started High School. My new home was several blocks from the Studio, and I'd pretty much grown away from my early boy-hood friends.

Walking to High School from our new home at the corner of Davis St. and Plumb St., I soon made new friends. My two best friends were fraternal twin brothers, Clif and Dick Boehm. They were two years ahead of me in school, but lived down the hill from me and we soon were walking the half-mile or so to High School together.

We became pretty much inseparable friends during my first two years in High School. Clif [he always spelled his name with a single "f"] and Dick and I would play at baseball nearly every day during the summers, taking turns with one of us hitting grounders and fly balls to the other two. We were all avid Chicago Cubs baseball fans. That's Clif on the left, me in the center and Dick on the right.

In the winter, when weather permitted, we'd shoot baskets at a hoop over their garage door. The friendship endured until they both entered military service and I had entered college. For many years, we saw little or nothing of each other, but after a time, I'm happy to say, we reestablished the friendship, and it continues to this day!

I can't resist writing about two interesting and rather exciting experiences during those high school years. The first incident occurred sometime after the end of World War II and the atomic bombing of Japan. It was a time when the collective fears in the U.S. were turning toward our former allies, the Russians, who had developed their own nuclear capability. That forms the setting of incident #1.

I had recently obtained an interesting little gadget by mail order from an ad in a comic book! It was a small microphone which could be wired to a radio. Pressing a button on the "mike" would cut out the radio transmission and allow the person with the 'mike' to speak into it with his voice transmitted through the radio speaker. The possibilities of this gadget were endless!

Clif, Dick and I had run a wire from a wardrobe in my parent's bedroom through a doorway into the living room where there was an old floor mounted combination radio-phonograph. We had a lot of fun interrupting radio transmissions with our own voices. Then we conceived "the grand idea." We wrote a script, of an imagined newscaster interrupting a program with an "emergency news bulletin!" *"We interrupt this program to bring you a special bulletin! We have received a report that an atomic bomb has been dropped on San Francisco!! Stay tuned for further reports. We now return you to the program in progress."* And back over the radio would be heard the real program. Then we composed a second "news bulletin" "confirming" the earlier report. It still wasn't clear what we intended to do, but we thought it would be great fun to "fool" some unsuspecting person, and then let them in on the trick demonstrating how clever we were.

Then we happened to spot a neighbor boy, Jim Warren, a year younger than myself. Jim was outside of his home across the street, busily dribbling a basketball on the sidewalk. Now the stage was set! Clif concealed himself in the bedroom wardrobe, with our "news bulletin" scripts and a flashlight to read them by and I tuned the radio to a station broadcasting music. Dick and I went outside and called to Jim, inviting him to come over. He was a bit reluctant, and I can't really remember what "bait" we used to get him into the house. But once inside, the stage was set!

Suddenly, the radio music stopped in mid-song, and a voice cut in with the announcement of a report of an atom bomb dropped on San Francisco! *"We interrupt this program to bring you a special bulletin . . ."* Dick and I acted with well-feigned alarm, and included Jim in our questions. I suggested that it had to be a big mistake, while Dick said he thought it might be "for real." Then Clif's voice cut into the music again, as he intoned the 2nd of our scripted "news" bulletins "confirming" the earlier report. This did it with Jim. With great excitement, he ran out the front door, shouting that he had to go home and tell his parents this earth-shaking "news!"

Now it was the turn for Dick and I to panic! We suddenly realized the gravity of what we might have done. I had a fleeting vision of the entire town erupting into full-blown hysteria. Dick and I ran after Jim and caught him before he could spread the "news," trying to explain that it was all a hoax. It had been so realistic, that it took a lot of persuading! We only succeeded in convincing Jim, when we practically dragged him back into the house and showed him Clif, ensconced in his little nest in the wardrobe, and then demonstrated for Jim how the microphone contraption worked.

We all began to realize that we had nearly created a possible disaster of our own, not as serious as an A-bomb being dropped on San Francisco, but serious enough that we might have gotten ourselves into some rather serious trouble. We never tried to repeat our little game!

The 2nd experience that will never be erased from my memory happened like this: I've mentioned being a Chicago Cubs fan, as were Clif and Dick, but by the end of my Junior [3rd] year they had graduated and had gotten jobs and then entered military service. During that summer I was approached by a student from Milton Junction that I knew only slightly, but well enough to know that he was also a fervent Cubs fan. His name was Arthurmurray Robertson, [his mother was an ardent admirer of the popular ballroom dancer of those days named Arthur Murray!], and he was probably the only Union High School male who was shorter than I was!

Arthurmurray approached me one day and wondered if I'd like to attend a Cubs game with him. Silly question! Of course I would! The Janesville YMCA would usually sponsor a bus trip once each summer to a Cubs game and I'd taken two or three of these 100-mile trips to Chicago. But I jumped at a chance to see another game. Arthurmurray had come up with a complicated but exciting plan which he proceeded to explain to me.

His father worked for the Chicago Northwestern Railroad which ran through Milton Junction, and his family members were eligible for free passes on the train as passengers. Arthurmurray had a younger brother so he could get a pass for himself and one for his brother for expense-free trips by train to Chicago for two. Since he was smaller than I, his plan was for me to pretend I was he, and he would pretend to be his little brother. How in the world he managed to get his parents to go along with this plan, I couldn't imagine, but he did. Actually, I'm not sure how I managed to get my parents to agree to let me go, either, but they did.

All went well, as we boarded the train, and made the uneventful trip to Chicago. As soon as we arrived, however, a slight problem confronted us. We suddenly realized that we had no idea how to get from the train station to the ball park! Well, we could ask someone. We spotted a well-dressed gentleman wearing a suit and carrying a briefcase, went over to him and asked if he could tell us how to get to Wrigley Field where the Cubs played their games. The man was obviously in a hurry, but he said, "Just follow me, I'm going right by there." So we followed our "leader".

What an experience! The gentleman had a transit pass and he paused long enough for Arthurmurray and me to get passes. [A 50 cent transit pass was good for any form of public transportation in the city and was valid for a month from the date of purchase.] We proceeded to follow this total stranger on his hurried journey to . . . we knew not where. From the train to a street car, then from the streetcar to the elevated train. Off the El and down stairs to the subway, then up the stairs to a city bus, off the bus and back to a street car! I think we rode on every means of public transportation that Chicago had to offer, several of them twice! During the entire trip neither the man we were following nor either of us exchanged a word to each other. We had no way of knowing where we were going. At last, as we climbed down from a city streetcar headed we knew not where, the man turned and pointed down a side street saying, "There it is, boys!" And there it was!!! We turned to thank the man, but he'd already disappeared!

Looking back on the experience I can hardly believe it. I never told my parents about it, until I was much older. They would have had a fit! In today's world Arthurmurray and I would probably never have been heard from again! We went to the Cubs game [I have no memory of the score or even which team won], and as we left the ballpark, we suddenly realized that now we had no idea how to get back to the train station!! Fortunately, we had no desire to try the same approach again. We counted up the money we had and decided that between the two of us, we had enough to take a taxi, which we did! We arrived home safe and sound the beneficiaries, I think now, of several small miracles.

INTERLUDE

A Good Man [Part I]

Without fully realizing it, I think I always held my father in very high regard. As a youngster, people would frequently ask me, "What are you going to do when you grow up?" [I wonder if there has ever been an American child who has not been asked that question?] According to my mother, I had a stock answer: "Gon'na 'hmoke an' go to college!" My dad was a heavy cigarette smoker and he was the Registrar at Milton College. How better to tell people that I wanted to be just like my dad?

Fortunately, the resolve to be a smoker did not endure. I tried it a few times as an older boy and young man, but never got "hooked" on it. Cigarettes just left a bad taste in my mouth that I instantly disliked. One of my most enjoyable childhood memories was a camping vacation we took at Devil's Lake State Park, when I was 6 or 8 years old. During that trip, my dad had switched—or was trying to switch—from cigarettes to a pipe. The fragrance of pipe smoke, associated as it was with a delightful camping trip to an enchanting locale, had a magnetic attraction for me. Two or three times as a young adult I experimented with smoking a pipe, but it always left a burning taste in my mouth and never smelled like I remembered, so I never kept it up more than a few days. I should mention that I don't remember my dad ever encouraging me to smoke, nor do I remember him ever expressing a hope that I <u>wouldn't</u> take up the habit. He left it up to me, and I've always appreciated the trust in my judgment which that implied.

I don't ever remember my dad spanking me either, or striking me as punishment for misbehavior. That certainly does not imply that I never misbehaved! He never punished me physically, but he was a master at administering a verbal chastisement, always delivered calmly and without anger. Even so, I was in great fear of those times and a "bawling out" by my father was far more effective, I think, than any physical punishment would have been. I sought his approval above all else.

One example stands out in my mind to this day. One afternoon when I was 6 or so, I was playing baseball across the street in the yard of my friend Windy with several other friends. Windy had two older brothers and during the game he gleefully confided to the rest of us that he'd just learned "a new swear word" from one of his brothers! We were all delighted with this news, as this was a sure way to help us along the road to adulthood, so we eagerly added the new word to our vocabularies. The word was "fart." Not only was it new to us, but Windy said that his brother had assured him that the word was totally unknown to adults, including parents! Perfect!!

My parents, living upstairs in the Studio found it easier to summon me when it was time to come in, by opening one of the upstairs windows and calling my name when they wanted me, usually due to the arrival of mealtime. On this occasion, it was my dad calling my name. I was due up to bat and not at all ready to go in for supper. I hollered back my negative reply. My dad was insistent, so I picked up my baseball glove and started across the street, but still feeling put out, it suddenly occurred to me to express my unhappiness at being called home, by trying out the new word! So I shouted back, in tones that could be heard throughout the neighborhood, the word that I was positive would be totally unknown to him! "Fart, Daddy!!" "Fart, daddy!!" I yelled it twice.

When I got in the house, I discovered to my amazement, that my father WAS familiar with that "secret" word! I received a thorough "bawling out" administered as if meant to end all such scolding. From that day on I was quite ready to believe that there was nothing in the world that my dad didn't know! I can't deny that I often curse or swear under my breath, or in my mind, but I very seldom use "4-letter" words within the hearing of others. It was a lesson I learned early in life: If you swear at someone, they just might know what the words mean!

CHAPTER 10

Giving It The Old College Try

If my life ambition to smoke soon vanished, the expectation of going to college did not. I don't think it ever occurred to me that I would not go directly from High School into college. Nor was there any possibility that the college would not be Milton College. This certainty was no doubt enhanced by the fact that children of faculty members received free tuition. My dad, as registrar, was considered a member of the faculty. So, college for me was not a great change. I didn't have to worry about raising extra money, as my tuition was free, and I could still go on living at home!

I'd learned in High School to avoid classes that I didn't like or found especially difficult and I employed the same tactic in college as much as possible. I stayed completely away from anything related to mathematics, or foreign languages, and concentrated on subjects that I enjoyed and didn't have to study too hard for.

I would take every history, geography, sociology, political science and English course that was offered. Normally this would lead to a BA [Bachelor of Arts] degree, rather than to a BS [Bachelor of Science] degree. But a BA degree would also require Speech and foreign language courses, all of which I also wanted to avoid. At least one full year of a science or math course was required for a BS degree, and I thought I could take the one required science course and then pick up enough history, social science and English courses to earn a BS degree. My rationale was getting the most difficult course out of the way as quickly as possible. So as a freshman I chose a chemistry course and results were predictable. The first-year chemistry course was taught by a young recent graduate of the college, Wil Hurley. He knew my family and had married a 2nd cousin of mine, Mary Babcock. It appeared promising, but I quickly got off on the wrong foot.

I had a lab partner, whose last name was Dahl, [I seem to have repressed his first name], but we didn't help each other. He was a kind of "class clown" and I quickly fell into that approach to the study of Chemistry. When we worked as lab partners, we developed the practice of referring to each other as "Dr., Ein" and "Dr. Stein," and the lab part of the course became a kind of "goof off" time. At the end of the first semester Wil passed me with a "D" grade. I think he did so because he felt, as a friend of the family, he had to. My lab partner, "Dr. Ein," received an "F" and dropped out of college after that one semester!

Seeing the handwriting on the wall, and the grade on my report card, I dropped Chemistry after that one unseemly semester, and switched to Biology to fulfill my year's science requirement. The second semester offering of the Biology Department was Botany. I found the study of plant life to be both interesting and understandable, nor did it require me to cut up dead animals, so I was able to buckle down enough to earn a "B" grade. From then on I chose classes that I could handle.

My favorite professor in college was William "Bill" Cornell who taught sociology. I found that subject interesting and understandable and I took every sociology course that was offered. I especially enjoyed Prof Cornell's lectures. He made a practice of interjecting quotations from well-known scholars, writers and others into his lectures as a way of illustrating points that he wanted to emphasize. A fun hobby of my dotage is collecting quotations, and I'm sure my inspiration for that was from Bill Cornell. Prof Cornell was a bachelor and a particular friend of my dad, and used to drop by our house for an evening visit from time to time. I felt quite privileged that they would include me in their conversations. It made me feel quite "grown up"!

I also took all the history courses that were offered by the two professors of that subject. Dean of the College, John Daland was quite elderly and legally blind. If he wanted to digest a new book or refresh his memory in regard to a certain subject, he would have students in to read to him. I felt very privileged to be able to perform that task on many occasions. It was a humbling experience to realize that he and I were learning together. I still enjoy reading aloud to anyone who may be willing to listen to me.

H. H. James was the other history instructor. I liked him, but did not consider him to be what I would regard as a good teacher. His lectures were rambling discourses on just about any subject except what we were supposed to be studying. Long narratives about where he'd gone and what he'd done on his last summer's vacation, or on something in the previous day's news, were commonplace. What any of us learned about history in his classes was obtained from the assigned reading.

Fortunately, Prof James was aware of this and always emphasized to students that his tests or exams would be strictly on the assigned reading he'd given us. So if one did the reading, there would be few if any problems in getting a passing grade. And by reading the assignments we learned from them. I still love reading history.

Prof. James always delivered his "lectures" while sitting on the front of the desk in the classroom, rather than standing at a lectern. One of my mother's jobs as Assistant Registrar was to assign the classes to the various classrooms available. She once related how Prof James had on one occasion, come into her office to complain about his class schedule. This was at the beginning of the 2nd semester, in the middle of an especially cold Wisconsin winter. His complaint was that he had three consecutive early morning classes, each one in a different classroom. My mother asked why this was such a major problem, as they were all in the same building. "Well," huffed Prof. James with a straight face, "the problem is that with your schedule I have to warm up three different desk tops in this cold weather!" My mother, for one of the few times in her life that I'm aware of, was speechless! She said that Prof James, obviously enjoying the moment, just gave her a wink of his eye, and turned and left!

I was still painfully shy around girls and my self-confidence was as cold as Prof. James' desk tops. It wasn't until my senior year that I finally developed a "love interest." Kathy K. was a music major and lived in the Women's Dormitory on campus, as her hometown was several hours distant.

I don't really have any memory of how this romance first developed. Neither Kathy nor I were into the college social life so perhaps we recognized each other as "kindred souls."

We "went steady" for most of two years, until we realized that our lives would be taking different paths and our relationship sort of "faded away." This photo is her graduation photo from the college Yearbook.

Our relationship was probably doomed from the beginning, as Kathy was quite religious and I was not. For most of the time we were going together, I made a concerted effort to accommodate my thinking and activities to match or at least co-exist with hers, but in the long run it was no use. I even joined the Student Christian Association, a nondenominational organization on campus, and served, rather awkwardly, for a year as its president! But my motivation was an attempt to please Kathy, rather than from any conviction on my part.

The photo at the bottom of page 66 is the only picture of Kathy that I have, other than her graduation photo from the Yearbook. My mother took this picture of Kathy and I, with the college gymnasium in the background, on the day of my graduation in 1952. As the expression on Kathy's face indicates, she was totally surprised by the click of the camera.

Milton College was founded as a church school by a very small protestant denomination, known as Seventh Day Baptists [or SDBs]. The denomination still exists, but the number of members has always been very small. Most people that I've known in adult life have never heard of it! My parents had both been raised as SDBs, but as a family we attended church somewhat irregularly and more as a social activity than from deep religious convictions. [In her later years, and after my dad's death, however, my mother became VERY religious.]

The college had a well-deserved reputation as having an outstanding music department, and Kathy was a music major, singing in the *a capella* choir and playing the oboe in the orchestra. She also earned a little spending money by performing as an organist in several churches in the area. As indicated earlier in this treatise, I was hopelessly inept at any and all musical instruments, but I enjoyed singing and sang in the college choir for three years.

At one point three or four of us male students began singing in multiple church choirs on weekends not, in my case, for religious reasons but just because I liked to sing. There were Seventh Day Baptist churches in both Milton and Milton Junction. The Milton church choir was large [and good!] and the congregation took an inordinate amount of pride in it. The "Junction" church was small and barely had enough singers to make up a choir, male voices being especially lacking. A classmate at the college who intended to become an SDB minister was acting as a student minister for the latter congregation and one day he mentioned this problem to three or four of us fellows who were singing in the Milton Church choir.

The services at the two churches we discovered were such that we could go to the "Junction" church, and perform the choir number, then slip out the back, drive the mile or so to the Milton church and get there in time to sneak in the back door and into the choir loft in time for the choir's number. At one point we also sang in the Milton Congregational Church choir on Sundays! It was a fun thing for us, but it lasted only for part of one year.

Kathy played the organ for a Methodist Church in a nearby town and I would sometimes drive her there and sit in the congregation. The young minister there was very "liberal" so I enjoyed his sermons, while I found most church sermons to be rather insipid and irritating to sit through. I got well enough acquainted with him, that on one occasion, when he found himself with a schedule conflict, he asked me if I would conduct the next week's service! I did, delivering a VERY liberal, anti-war sermon and choosing hymns like "Oh Young and Fearless Prophet" and "Once to Every Man and

Nation" that also reflected my liberal religious and anti-war views. It was kind of fun! [For me, at least!]

Milton College had a long-standing tradition of presenting to the public a Shakespearian play at commencement time each year. Remembering my enjoyment of being in a couple of stage plays in high school, I got up enough courage to try out, and was accepted for a very small part in the production of "The Merchant of Venice" my Sophomore year. I played the part of Stephano, a servant, and had two very brief speeches in the course of the play! I enjoyed the experience, however, and it gave me confidence enough to try out and perform in three additional Shakespearian productions. I never tried out for a major part, but had slightly larger parts as the years progressed.

I played one of the "villains", Borachio, in the "Merchant of Venice", Fabian in "Twelfth Night" and my favorite role was as Grumio, in "The Taming of the Shrew." I also acted in a non-Shakespearian play as a policeman in a production put on by a student drama group called The Satellite Drama Guild. Years later I became very active in community drama groups while living in British Columbia, both in White Rock and in Kamloops. [See **Appendix A** for a complete listing of my theater involvement.]

CHAPTER 11

"My Radicalization"

My last years at Milton College were a time of political, social and religious radicalization. I'm really not sure of the motivational source, and probably there were several. Seeds of it may have been there all my life. Politically, my Dad had been associated with the Progressive Party founded by Wisconsin's U.S. Senator, Robert M. LaFollette. A former Republican, LaFollette broke with that increasingly conservative party, and founded a new, distinctly left-leaning Progressive Party. "Fighting Bob" LaFollette, Sr. (June 14, 1855-June 18, 1925), served as a member of the U.S. House of Representatives, as Governor of Wisconsin, and as a U.S. Senator from Wisconsin (1906 to 1925). In 1924 he ran for President of the United States as the nominee of the Progressive Party, carrying the state of Wisconsin and 17% of the national popular vote.

The bushy-haired, craggy-faced LaFollette died in 1925, five years before I was born. My dad was not alone in his admiration of this outspoken reformer, who has been called arguably the most important and recognized leader of the opposition to the growing dominance of corporations over the government and is one of the key figures pointed to in Wisconsin's long history of political liberalism.

The online encyclopedia, "Wikipedia" notes that, "He is best remembered as a proponent of progressivism and a vocal opponent of railroad trusts, bossism, World War I, and the League of Nations." In 1957, a Senate Committee selected LaFollette as one of the "five greatest U.S. Senators", along with Henry Clay, Daniel Webster, John C. Calhoun, and Robert Taft. A 1982 survey asking historians to rank the 'ten greatest Senators' in the nation's history based on "accomplishments in office" and "long range impact on American history," placed LaFollette first, tied with Henry Clay.

After his death his widow and two sons, Robert M., Jr., and Phillip carried on in his place. Bob, Jr. was elected to replace his father in the U.S. Senate and "Phil" served several terms as governor of Wisconsin. So, it was perhaps natural that I grew up sharing the admiration my father felt for these men and the party they founded. I remember that my parents subscribed to two different daily newspapers: *The Janesville Daily Gazette*, provided local news and most everyone in Milton subscribed. But, Dad also subscribed to *The Capital Times*, published in the state capital, Madison, and which presented a staunchly LaFollette/progressive viewpoint regarding state and national news, in contrast to the rather conservative *Gazette*.

I'm sure that I was influenced in my thinking from an early age in the direction of Progressive politics from reading *The Capital Times*. This outlook was enhanced by the hours that I spent as an avid listener at frequent evening discussions between my father and Bill Cornell my college sociology professor, who shared political outlooks and which I, not unexpectedly, also learned to share. My first ever vote for U.S. president was for Norman Thomas the Socialist Party candidate, in 1948!

It was Thomas' anti-war stance that first attracted me to his candidacy, but I soon found many other Socialist concerns that matched my own developing ideas. Socialism meant the emancipation of the working class and its transformation into the middle class; it championed universal not-for-profit medical care, social justice and a progressive tax system, all of which appealed to me. I've basically considered myself a Socialist ever since, although the weakness and fragmentation of the Socialist political party of the U.S. has found me voting primarily for Democratic Party candidates. I never affiliated with the Democratic Party, however, always registering as an Independent. During my 15 years in British Columbia and after obtaining dual citizenship, I supported the Canadian New Democratic Party an avowed socialist party.

It was Prof Cornell who first interested me in the Society of Friends [Quakers], not so much in a religious sense as in regard to their "social testimonies". Non-violence, simplicity, decisions by consensus and social service were all concepts that were basic to Quakers and that appealed to me. Prof. Cornell also told me of the American Friends Service Committee. I was impressed favorably enough to sign up for an AFSC sponsored workcamp in the summer of 1951 following my junior year of college.

Held at Rapid City, South Dakota, it involved doing recreation work with Native American children of the Lakota [Sioux] tribe, who were trying to cope with off-reservation, city life. It was an exciting and satisfying experience and ignited my interest in social service, and also in semi-communal life as part of a group of equals. I'll have more to say about workcamps and Quakers further on in this story, as I participated in 3 AFSC workcamps over a period of 4 years, plus spending a week visiting another. And, along the way, I became an "official" Friend by joining the Madison, Wisconsin, Quaker Meeting!

On the religious side, as well as the social, I was also very favorably impressed with Friends, as more than any other religious group or church that I'd come in contact with, they seemed to more closely practice the teachings and example of Jesus Christ himself. I began to view most other Christian denominations and their parishioners as rather hypocritical in claiming to be followers of Jesus. That continues to this day. The Seventh Day Baptist church in Milton, that I attended, was quite ornate and this clashed with my belief that "simplicity" should be a hallmark of Christian living.

The SDB congregation in Milton was, inordinately proud of its beautiful church building and its choir, and I thought that pride was supposed to be not only one of the "seven deadly sins" in Christian belief, but in almost every list, pride is considered the original and most serious of the seven deadly sins, and the source of the others. So I was feeling uncomfortable  about our family church. This is not a good photo of the church, but is the only one I could lay my hands, or mouse, on.

As a college student, at the same time, I was drawn toward more progressive, if not radical, views in other areas. I was impressed by Garry Davis, a former WW II bomber pilot, who renounced his U.S. citizenship in 1948 and declared himself a "World Citizen." I even signed on as a World Citizen [I wasn't required to renounce my U.S. citizenship] and for years carried in my wallet a certificate documenting me as a World Citizen. By January 1949 over 750,000 individuals, including a number of prominent persons, had signed on as World Citizens. One of them, Albert Einstein, wrote of Davis: "Mark my words, this boy, Garry Davis, has grasped the only problem which deserves the devotion of contemporary man, the problem to which I, myself, am determined to devote the rest of my life . . . to the survival of the species.' It is a question of knowing whether mankind . . . will disappear by its own hand, or whether it will continue to exist."

I also became involved with a group called, at that time, United World Federalists, and tried to organize a student chapter at Milton College. With somewhat similar objectives, it didn't come to much or last long at Milton, as there were only 2 or 3 other students who shared the aims and objectives of what was also a movement favoring a "world government." The presence of the United Nations as a kind of pseudo World Government was enough, I think, to doom those and other efforts in that direction.

I suffered from asthma as a young boy and through my teens, but it was not anywhere near as debilitating as my dad's affliction. It was, however, just bad enough to earn me a 4F [physically unfit] rating for the military draft. I'd actually gone to the U.S. Navy enlistment office in Janesville sometime shortly after I turned 18, and when

I was still suffering from a fairly severe case of adolescent patriotism. They turned me down, primarily because, at the time, I was still slightly less than 5'2" in height, the Navy's minimum requirement at that time. Not long after that, Dr. Vogel, certified me as "unfit" due to asthma, when I came up before the draft board. So I had escaped military service. By the time I reached my senior year in college, I'd become a convinced pacifist.

This was a major reason for my gradual disaffection with the Christian religion and the majority of their churches including the SDB denomination. At first I naively thought I could influence our church in the direction of pacifism. The Youth Group had begun publishing a monthly tract, due to a distant cousin of mine, Don Gray, who owned and operated a small printing business in Milton. I wrote a series of articles for that publication, mostly critical of Christian churches for not following the example and teaching of the man they regarded as God's Son. My Monthly polemic essays, under the collective title, *Pro Bonum Causae,* were generally ignored and I gave up the effort after a few months. [The title was Don Gray's incorrect attempt to translate "For the Good of the Cause" into Latin!] I enjoyed writing them and still feel that they were well-founded and well-reasoned! I got a few—very few—compliments from individuals to the effect that they thought I'd stated my position very well, but no indication that they would embrace those positions themselves!

INTERLUDE

A Good Man [Part II]

I took part in my first AFSC workcamp during the summer between my 3rd and 4th years at Milton. It was following that experience that much of the "radicalization" just discussed took place. It was all interrupted by a sudden deterioration in my father's health that winter, midway through my Senior Year at Milton College. Everything had been going well for me. I was taking courses that I enjoyed and Kathy and I had resumed our relationship, after a summer hiatus.

For years my Dad had controlled his asthma by fairly frequent self-administered hypodermic injections of adrenalin. That winter he suddenly went "adrenalin fast" which meant that his body had built up immunity to the drug so that it was no longer effective. His doctor tried a variety of other treatments including epinephrine, but nothing seemed to help. Finally the doctor said that the only way he could think of for my Dad to find relief would be to try going to a drier climate. After much discussion Mom, Dad and I finally reached a decision.

A "dry climate" meant one thing to us: the American Southwest, and specifically, Arizona. It was near the end of the 1st semester at the college and Dad was granted a leave of absence from his job as registrar. The plan was that I would drive him to Arizona and stay with him for a time to see if the climate change helped. I was doing well in my classes and it was arranged that my semester final exams, due in a couple of weeks, would be mailed to my father who would monitor my taking them and return the results to the college.

The drive to Arizona took 4 days. We stayed nights in motels and Dad's asthma improved enough so that there were no problems on the trip. We chose Tucson, rather than Phoenix, as our destination, partly because it was a smaller city but mostly because the University of Arizona was located there. Being near a college or university was important to my dad. We were lucky in finding a small [2 rooms plus bathroom] apartment for rent that was within walking distance of the University of Arizona campus.

I'm not sure if it was the drier climate that made the difference, but Dad's asthma seemed better as a result of the relocation. We located a doctor who would supervise his condition. I remember only once that an unusually severe attack necessitated a visit to our apartment by the doctor, but he saw dad in his office every week. My semester exams arrived, I took them under Dad's supervision, and he returned them to the College. I passed all of them.

There was a weeklong semester "break" before classes resumed. Dad, Mom and I all thought it was important for me to complete the 2nd semester so that I could graduate in June as planned. Dad was feeling better and after a few weeks, thought that he could take care of himself and that I should return and graduate with my class. I left the car with him, and took a bus back to Wisconsin, and resumed my classes.

By spring Dad was feeling better and getting very homesick, so my mother went by bus to Tucson, picked up my dad and began driving home. *En route*, they stopped in Lincoln, NE, to visit Dad's mother, and his siblings Edwin, Art and Katharine for a few days. Resuming the trip back to Milton, as Mom was driving through Omaha, Dad suddenly developed a severe headache and within a few minutes lost consciousness. Mom spotted a police car, stopped and asked for directions to a hospital. The officer said, "Follow me," and escorted her to the nearest hospital.

My mom later remembered that Dad regained consciousness only once. That was only long enough for him to recognize that he was in a hospital and to murmur, "Thank God for Blue Cross." They were his last words, as he was pronounced dead the next morning. The cause of death was a ruptured cerebral aneurysm that the doctors believed had been present since birth!

That evening I received a phone call from Uncle Edwin, telling me of Dad's death. It was a definite shock to me and I was feeling pretty low. I needed someone to talk to and went over to the Women's Dorm just a few blocks from our home. Kathy came down to the lounge and I explained what had happened. She walked back to the house with me and we spent a couple hours just talking. It was a great relief to me. The curfew for Kathy was 10 PM but I called the dorm and spoke to the Matron, Mrs. Kidder [readers may remember her as my former 8th grade teacher]. I told her about my father's death and asked if she would let Kathy stay out past the curfew hour. She was sympathetic and said that Kathy could stay out until midnight, so we had a couple more hours together.

After the funeral at the Milton SDB Church, my Dad was buried in the Milton cemetery. I went on to pass my final exams and graduate with my class. My mother held up very well, although I knew that she'd been through a very difficult time. She and I were both grateful that Dad had that last family get-together in Lincoln with his mother, sister and two brothers, and that their support was available to my mom when she most needed it.

The College's Semi-Annual Yearbook, *Fides,* was published that spring and contained a very moving full page tribute to my father, written by his colleague and our neighbor, Dean John N. Daland. I've reproduced it here. It's very meaningful to me and, I believe, presents a very true-to-life word portrait of my father. I can't think of a finer or truer tribute, and I'm happy that I'm able to share it here. In today's [2012] political climate, with its intense debate over what constitutes fair policies of taxation, I find Dean Daland's comment on "the ultimate test of good citizenship" to have a particularly cogent significance. **I believe my father was, truly, a man of profound courage, rectitude, tolerance and honor.** I experienced his rather sudden death as a very significant loss. He had gone through a great deal of suffering during his life, due to his health problems, and I was glad that his death came quickly, with a minimum of suffering. I'll post here Dean Daland's very moving memorial statement and well-deserved [to me at least] tribute. I don't think anyone could have captured better my father's character.

R.I.P. Dad!

In Memoriam

Oscar T. Babcock was a friend to everybody, and was universally and affectionately known as "O.T." His legal training and close association with his father, a thinker and broad-minded lawyer, brought out his natural talent for logic. O.T. was preeminently a clear thinker and correct reasoner.

Each man has his own attitude towards life, and O.T. inclined in politics and religion to the liberal point of view. He was one of the most fair and open-minded men I ever knew, always reading and considering both sides of every public question. I never discussed these matters with him without benefit to my own thinking.

O.T.'s interest in national and local affairs is well known. In his own community he was an ideal citizen, serving faithfully and intelligently in school and local offices.

He met the ultimate test of good citizenship: he believed in paying taxes and never complained of the taxes he was called upon to pay.

In his educational and administrative work at the college for the last twenty-seven years, O.T. displayed not only intellectual attainments, but qualities of a fine human texture.

As registrar he came in contact with more students than any other teacher, and he was courteous and agreeable to everyone. He understood the student point of view and listened patiently to all complaints. Yet he was firm in giving good counsel and in explaining the necessity for upholding the rules of the curriculum.

All that he accomplished, and it was a considerable contribution, was done against the background of ill health and inadequate physical strength. Herein lies one of his great qualities. It took courage to come back after each attack and plunge again into his work with never a complaint.

Strict himself in the path of rectitude and honor, he was tolerant of the weakness of human nature, and was constantly seeking excuses for his fellowmen. In his frail body dwelt a high and noble spirit, intelligent, independent, liberal. He exemplified in his life the celebrated words of Terence: "I am a man and whatever concerns my fellow man is my concern."

—Dean John N. Daland

CHAPTER 12

Wandering and Wondering

I finished my final semester and was able to graduate with my class in June of 1952, with a degree of Bachelor of Science *cum laude*. The "Science" is a bit misleading, and was due to that one semester of chemistry and one semester of botany I took as a freshman. Those were the only science courses I took and really didn't deserve a passing grade in chemistry. To earn a Bachelor of Arts degree I would have needed courses in Speech and a foreign language and I'd taken neither!

I graduated, but wasn't through with college yet. As my graduation approached, I realized that I wasn't really qualified for anything resembling a career, and I had no great interest in spending my life as a common laborer. In High School, I'd worked during summers at jobs like de-tasseling corn in the fields and two summers working in a canning factory in Janesville. I cordially disliked both. I'd graduated from college, but what was I going to do with myself now??

Suddenly I had a brainstorm. I could go back to college for a 5th year, take Education courses, which I'd avoided up until then, qualify for a teaching certificate, and become a High School teacher! That seemed, [from a comfortable distance] like something that might lead to a career that would at least be tolerable. Since I knew that I could perform successfully as a student, maybe I could perform successfully as a teacher also.

So I went back to Milton College for a 5th year. My mother still worked there, so tuition was still free, I had our family home for living quarters, and after all I <u>had</u> enjoyed going to school. Oh, yeah, and Kathy would still be there for her Senior year. So that's what I did. All went pretty much as planned until it came time to do my "Practice Teaching" as it was then known, or "Student Teaching." I was assigned to a Social Science class for High School sophomores [10th graders], in the nearby town of Edgerton. It was pure misery.

I got through it OK, but didn't enjoy it a lick! I felt more like a policeman than a teacher, and endured a very miserable 6 weeks. I spent more time and effort trying to maintain at least a modicum of discipline than I did in teaching subject matter. Suddenly the notion of teaching High School, or any sort of school where students were there because they HAD to be, was very repugnant to me. Is that how I really wanted to spend my adult life? No way, Jose!! To make matters worse, Kathy graduated and got a job teaching music at a high school quite some distance away, and there seemed to be no way of continuing our relationship. We knew that neither of us was ready to get married, so our relationship ended with sad feelings, as we decided we must go our separate ways. It had been a good two years.

The summer after Kathy graduated, I went to my 2nd summer "workcamp" sponsored by the American Friends Service Committee. I'd become very interested in the history of Native American tribes, and this camp was on the Pine Ridge Reservation in South Dakota working with the Oglala Lakota [Sioux] Tribe.

Our major activity was building what we referred to as "bus shelters". Actually, they were wooden box-like structures to be placed along roads where children had to wait for school busses to pick them up and take them to school. The winters there were VERY cold and before our shelters, school children had to stand in the open,

waiting for the busses, often in blizzard conditions, and often running late! The photo here shows me [*sans* shirt] along with two other work-campers putting the finishing touches to a "bus shelter." [Really "children shelters", but we called them" bus shelters."]

In addition to building "bus shelters" in Pine Ridge, we also held recreation programs for Sioux children. Some of these were held in the community of Pine Ridge, but groups of 5 campers were sent to two outlying communities on the reservation. One group to a small settlement called Allen, and the other to a little town called Porcupine. I was a member of that group. We would go to Porcupine for 3 days at a time staying while there with an older Lakota couple who had a spare one room log cabin where we just spread our sleeping bags on the floor and for the most part prepared our own simple meals using a camp stove when needed.

I'll never forget an incident that took place the first day after we arrived in Porcupine. The couple we stayed with, a Baptist minister and his wife, had invited us to join them for dinner that first evening. They had a granddaughter about 6 years old staying with them and while Froy, Mary and I were waiting on the porch steps for our evening meal the granddaughter was playing happily with a small puppy. Intent on making friends we began telling the child what a fine handsome puppy she had. Unfortunately, our admiring compliments were over-done and, worst of all, misunderstood. Suddenly, with tears welling in her eyes, the little girl picked up her puppy, hugging it tightly and said in the saddest voice I've ever heard, "I'll ask my grandma to cook it for you!" It took us several minutes of profuse apologies and explanations to convince her that we were admiring the pup only as a pet and a playmate, and <u>not</u> as a potential meal! We had forgotten a comment from our orientation, that dog meat was considered a very special gastronomic delicacy by many Native Americans. Fortunately, we overcame this rather awkward misunderstanding and the rest of our time in Porcupine went by with no more cultural *gaffes*.

The entire summer was another highly enjoyable experience for me. In addition to building "bus shelters" and doing recreation programs with Lakota children, we "work campers" got to help tribal members prepare for and then join them in their traditional summer Sun Dance. During our time at Pine Ridge we met sons and grandsons of some famous Sioux leaders such as Red Cloud and American Horse, and also enjoyed camping trips to the Black Hills and Badlands.

My interest and admiration for Quakers was greatly enhanced. I also enjoyed a brief romance with one of the work campers, a lovely blond girl named Ellen "Froy" Hammar. The relationship continued as a friendship afterward, which saw us both get married, just not to each other! We still exchange Christmas letters. Here's lovely Froy at lovely Roughlock Falls in the Black Hills.

Back in Wisconsin that fall, with nothing better on the horizon, I got a job working at the General Case Company, a small factory in Milton Junction that manufactured plywood cases for medical instruments and things like film and slide projectors. It was bearable, through the winter, mainly because my good friend, Clif Boehm, was working there, too. In fact it was he who arranged for me to get the job, as the company belonged to an uncle of his. But, I knew from the experience that I didn't want to spend my life doing that sort of work. By spring I'd had enough, and the summer of 1954, I signed on for a 3rd AFSC Work Camp! I'd saved enough money from the job to make it possible.

Again, I chose a workcamp with Native Americans, but this time with Navajos in the Southwest, a part of the country I had already fallen in love with and had been eager to visit more extensively. Our location was in a community called Crownpoint in northwest New Mexico. Navajos make up by far the largest Native American tribe in the U.S. and they have organized local governing "Chapters." This summer our task was to construct a building—a Chapter House—as a place for the Crownpoint area chapter council to meet.

The building was to be constructed of native sandstone and we started from "scratch." We began by quarrying sandstone from an outcrop in the desert and hauling it to the site that had been selected, using a flatbed truck belonging to a young Navajo who, along with his brother and father, were part of the Navajo work crew working alongside of us.

A concrete foundation was poured and we got a rough sub-floor in place and the sandstone walls up to the windows in the 8 week long period that we were there. The Navajo stone mason, Tom Yazzi, who built the walls was a real artist! The building

would be finished by another workcamp the following summer and the finished building was indeed a work of art. Our camp had another great group of participants, and we made friends with a number of the Navajos who worked along with us.

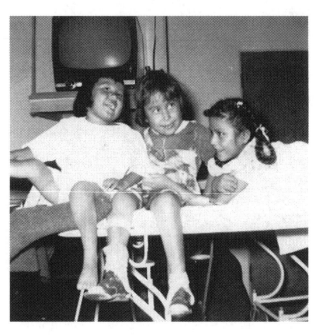

We had time for hikes and several of us campers made friends with the Anglo owner of one of the two trading posts operating in Crownpoint. Don Walker took us in his in jeep on several off-road excursions to isolated Anasazi ruins and other places of interest. [The Anasazi were the prehistoric native people who had inhabited this part of the Southwest centuries earlier.]

There was a hospital in Crownpoint and several of us made weekly visits to the crippled children's ward, which I found very gratifying. Such sweet children and so de-lighted by our visits! But it was something of a "downer" when we had to say goodbye when the camp closed. Here are Mary Anne, Shirley Barbara and Betty Largo, three of the sweetest!

I want to relate a story that I'll never forget. We attended a Chapter meeting in a nearby community, attended by Chapter representatives from several outlying Navajo communities, and also by the Anglo architect and several Anglo employees of the

Bureau of Indian Affairs [BIA]. During the meeting the architect was asked how the building we were erecting would be heated as there was no indication of a fireplace or wood-burning stove. He explained [in English] that it would have an automatic heating system with a thermostat. Most of the Navajos there had no idea what the architect was talking about.

Questions were asked and detailed explanations were attempted through bilingual interpreters. Still, several of the Navajos shook their heads as they failed to understand the concept being discussed. Finally Paddy Martinez, the chapter representative from Bluewater, who was bilingual stood up, and spoke a single sentence in Navajo. All the Navajos who had been so mystified nodded their heads and signified their understanding and the meeting continued.

I was curious and after the meeting ended I went to a BIA man who I knew spoke the Navajo language and asked, "What did Paddy Martinez say that they were able to understand what an automatic heating system was?" He smiled and said, "Paddy Martinez told them that an automatic heating system was like a good wife who turns the blanket down when it's too hot and pulls the blanket up when it gets too cold." Clear as could be!

After the workcamp ended several of us participants wanted to see a bit more of the southwest. One of the fellows had a car and offered to drive 4 or 5 of us on a brief camping trip. But where to go? I think I mentioned earlier that I love maps and study them whenever curiosity prompts, or whenever I'm about to venture into an area that's new to me. I'd seen on a map a place in Arizona, somewhat off the beaten path, called Verde Hot Springs. Not too far distant was a National Monument called Montezuma Castle. I suggested that it might be a fun destination worth visiting. My suggestion was eagerly accepted.

The hot springs turned out to be reached over about 25 miles of little used dirt roads, out of a small town called Camp Verde. We learned that there had once been a secluded resort at the hot springs, but it had burned down a number of years before and never rebuilt. We found ourselves in a very isolated spot on the banks of the Verde River, with no humans in evidence anywhere around. We had little camping equipment, but just spread sleeping bags out on the ground and dug a shallow campfire pit. We were beginning to feel that we'd made a poor choice, when a couple of us waded out into the river and suddenly felt the upwelling of very warm water.

We discovered several vents of very warm water in the otherwise rather cold river, and rejoiced at having this delightful spot all to ourselves. We stayed three nights and made day trips to visit the National Monuments in the area, Montezuma Castle and a detached section, Montezuma Well. The Castle featured a large pre-Columbian Indian ruin high in a cave. Early settlers had incorrectly guessed that it had been built as a refuge by the Aztec chief, Montezuma, after fleeing from Cortez and his Spanish conquistadors. A totally incorrect assumption, but the name had stuck.

All in all, it was a delightful experience. Clayton, our driver drove us back to Flagstaff where the nearest bus and railroad service could be found, and from there we all made our separate ways homeward. I even received a grateful "thank you" from the group for having suggested the hot springs destination. It was a satisfying and captivating end to an extremely enjoyable summer.

[Unfortunately, this idyllic place would undergo a rather sad metamorphosis over the years. It probably began in the 1970s when, as Bob Dylan noted, the times they were a-changin'. By the time I moved back to the area in 1989, a cruel fate had overtaken the Hot Springs area, and paradise had been lost. The old Childs PowerStation near where we camped had been abandoned, and an invasion of the area by the more undesirable element of the "hippy culture" had taken place. A little campground had been established by the National Forest Service, near the spot where we had camped. It had, however, been appropriated by a sizeable number of "Hippies." Quantities of trash, loud music, nudity and even violence had become commonplace. Although the campground area was a little downstream and across the river from where we camped in 1954, the semi-permanent hippie settlement effectively blocked access to our location. One quick look and I never went back again.]

The summer at Crownpoint had been the best work camp experience yet, but when I returned home I was once again faced with the dilemma of what I was going to do with myself next. Then I had another brainstorm. College students were in school because they <u>chose</u> to be, not because it was mandated by society. If I went to graduate school, and got a Master's Degree I could perhaps get a job teaching at a college! Or, a second choice beckoned as well. With a Master's Degree one could also become a Social Worker, a fact of which my favorite professor at Milton, Bill Cornell, often reminded me. These choices sounded promising and, besides, I enjoyed going to school more than working!

So I entered upon my **sixth** year [!] of post-secondary education by enrolling the fall of 1954 in Graduate School at the University of Wisconsin in the State Capital city of Madison, just 40 miles from Milton. Prof Cornell knew the Baptist Minister who operated the Baptist Student Center, a rooming house just off campus, where living expenses would be reasonable. The minister, "Shorty" Collins was a confirmed pacifist, and the Madison Monthly Meeting of the Society of Friends met there at the Student Center on Sunday mornings. All this I learned from Prof Cornell. "Shorty," who stood at least 6'6" on a lanky frame, and I hit it off immediately and I quickly booked a room!

During the semester break, "Shorty" took 6 of us on a "field trip" by car to visit the United Nations in New York City and the Capitol and Congressional offices in Washington, D.C. all of which was a very enjoyable experience. One event, in particular, was stamped into my memory. I've mentioned the Wisconsin tradition of progressive politics under the La Follette father and sons. It came as a surprise, shock and great embarrassment to many of us when in the early 1950s the state had elected probably the most malicious and invidious U.S. Senator in history, Joseph McCarthy. It was during that period of history known as the Cold War, when "communist" was the most pejorative word in the English language, and McCarthy loudly and profanely applied that label to anyone he didn't like or who disagreed with his extreme right-wing views. In doing so, he ruined the careers of many good people.

When our little group visited the Senate office building we found that body to be in the midst of its Christmas recess and only a few Senators were present. We did find Sen. Herbert Lehman of New York in his office, however, and stopped to greet him. Now, Sen. Lehman was one of the most liberal members of the U.S. Senate. Just prior to the recess the Senate had passed a bill bringing into existence the South-East Asia Treaty Organization [SEATO] the far-east equivalent of the NATO pact. Only two courageous Senators had voted against the bill, Wayne Morse of Oregon and Herbert Lehman of New York.

As we were leaving Sen. Lehman's office I told him that I was happy to meet one of the two Senators with the courage to have voted against the SEATO treaty to which I was also opposed. Sen. Lehman, looked surprised and then asked, "Where did you say you were from?" I answered, "Wisconsin." The Senator said "Thank you." Then, as he turned away, I heard him add, "That state never fails to amaze me!" I knew that I'd just received a very heartfelt compliment. The state that had produced the progressive champion followed by the arch political mountebank still harbored some progressives!

Back in Madison, I attended the Madison Friends Meeting and, after a couple months, applied for membership, and was accepted. So, now I was a "real" Quaker. For recreation that year I attended all the UW football and basketball games, which I enjoyed greatly!

My experience as a student, while enjoyable in most respects, led to a kind of personal epiphany. My major educational field was looking into the effects of U.S. government policies toward Native American tribes. One of my classes was a seminar group of 6 students. I made good friends with two of them and we enjoyed many a pleasant hour or two after classes drinking coffee in the Rathskeller lounge in the Student Union building. But one member of our seminar, whose name is long forgotten, became a kind of object lesson for me.

I discovered that he had been in graduate programs at the University for 5 or 6 years, and every time he approached getting his degree, he'd decide to change his field of study, in effect starting all over again. He'd become a "professional student," and as such cut an extremely pathetic figure, spending his evenings and weekends drinking heavily and going absolutely nowhere in life. Gradually I began to fear that I might also be in danger of turning into a "professional student!" It was a realistic concern, as I was then in my sixth year of post-secondary education! The prospect scared me enough that I decided to drop out of the Masters' program, which I did at the end of my first semester.

I still didn't know what I wanted to do with myself. While trying to figure that out, I got a job in a Co-Op gas station, pumping gas and changing oil, and audited a single course at the University that looked interesting. It was a course on the philosophies of Mohandas Gandhi and Albert Schweitzer. It was fascinating, and it gave me time to do some "soul searching." My pacifist convictions were strengthened as I studied Gandhi's practice of non-violence and Schweitzer's concept of "Reverence For Life."

I was also getting more and more interested in what, at that time, were referred to as "Intentional Communities." These were small groups of people who were trying to practice an alternate life style, centered around a way of life that stressed self-sufficiency, simplicity, and co-operative living as differentiated from the standard economic and social patterns.

I learned of the existence of a half-dozen of these groups in the U.S. [There were also groups in other countries.] They were mostly rural and tried to be as self-sufficient as possible while also attempting to practice simple living, non-violence, and a degree of communalism. [This was still in the 1950s. By the early 1970s, the concept had undergone changes and discontinuity and one offshoot had morphed into the hippy/commune movement.]

These groups seemed to me at the time to be something like ongoing, more permanent Friends' workcamps! I'd greatly enjoyed those experiences with groups of people working and living together cooperatively with a high degree of sharing and these Intentional Communities seemed to offer the possibility of that type of life on a more permanent basis. I was ready to move on from academic life and venture out into a new world. New, at any rate, to me.

CHAPTER 13

Bus Stop [And Go!]

But I wasn't <u>quite</u> ready yet! The open road was also calling and I had to scratch that itch before I could really start an almost totally new phase of fiddlefooting through life. I was, at the time, footloose and fancy free, but had no <u>clear</u> idea of what I wanted to do. Two notions were loose in my brain. One was to try out the "intentional community" way of life I've just described, but another was a desire to visit a part of the country that I'd fallen in love with, still largely unseen except through photographs.

I'd seen parts of the southwest in the times spent in New Mexico and Arizona. Somewhere along the way I'd also seen the magnificent photographs of this part of the country in magazines like Arizona Highways and National Geographic. So, in the spring of 1955, I mapped out a trip by bus [partly via Greyhound and partly by Trailways] that would enable me to see more of this enchanting country at first hand. After the pleasure trip, I could check out the Intentional Communities.

I traveled west across Nebraska and southern Wyoming to Salt Lake City, most of the time managing to obtain a front seat where I could chat with the drivers and pick their brains about the places we were traveling through. I rode nonstop to Salt Lake City, where I had to change from Greyhound to Trailways. I stayed overnight after seeing Salt Lake City on a city bus tour, and then headed south planning to visit Bryce Canyon and Zion National Parks.

The Salt Lake City bus tour was interesting and the highlight of it was the best and most deserved "put down" I've ever heard. Again, I managed to get a front seat opposite the driver. Across from me just behind the bus driver was a rather portly and extremely obnoxious lady from somewhere in the East. She kept up a steady barrage of negative comments and complaints aimed at the driver about anything and everything imaginable. The driver, demonstrating a patience that would have done credit to Job, kept doing his best to answer her seemingly endless and inane questions, which she asked in a voice so loud that it carried all through the bus. As we neared the end of the tour it was evident that the driver's patience was wearing thin.

We had just driven around the city square where the Mormon Temple and Tabernacle stand. The driver, as part of his spiel mentioned that the stone used to build the magnificent Temple had been quarried in the Wasatch Mountains and that it had taken over 40 years to complete the building. At this point, the lady snorted in disgust and exclaimed, "40 years!! Well, all I can say is you Mormons must be the slowest people on earth!" I think the driver bit his tongue to avoid an impolite rejoinder.

Just at that instant we turned a corner and there directly ahead of us was the Utah State Capitol building. Seeing it the lady immediately exclaimed, "Driver! Driver! What's that building up ahead?" The driver paused a beat and answered, "Darned if I know lady. It wasn't there yesterday!" I saw a slight twitch of the driver's lips as the busload of passengers erupted in laughter. The obnoxious lady did not say another word the rest of the tour. I handed the driver a dollar tip as I got off the bus, and said, "You made my day!" He let a slight grin cross his lips and gave me a wink of his eye.

The next morning I boarded the Trailways bus heading south. The town of Panguitch, Utah, was the closest the bus got to Bryce Canyon, so I stopped there, having told the driver of my desire to see both Bryce Canyon and Zion National Parks. It lead to an incredible stroke of luck. As I got off the bus in Panguitch, the driver suggested that I check out the Cameron Hotel, saying that the owners were in the business of taking tourists to "see the sights" of the area. It was one of the best pieces of advice that I've ever received. [Since that summer bus drivers have been among my favorite people—along with firefighters!]

The Hotel was actually a large three story brick home that had six or eight rooms that were rented out to overnight guests. Mr. Cameron, the husband and father, owned and operated the business and his wife was the cook and served meals to guests. Best of all, Mr. Cameron was not only a long time area resident, but a professional photographer. Many of the photographs in Arizona Highways and National Geographic that had drawn me to this country were photos that he had taken! Every evening, he presented a slide show in the parlor for hotel guests.

In addition, I learned that the family operated a tour service available to guests for an additional, but very reasonable, fee. The usual tour guides were Mr. Cameron, two grown sons and a son-in-law. So, I wanted to see Bryce Canyon and Zion National Parks did I? They could give me a personal, full day tour to each, at reasonable prices, if I could stay two days. Could I?? I thought I'd gone to heaven!

The next day Mr. Cameron himself, took me around Bryce Canyon, and also to a very scenic, off-the-beaten-path area just outside the park that he had "discovered" and named "Kodachrome Flats" while doing a photo shoot there for National Geographic Magazine a few years earlier. The next day, the younger son took me to Zion National Park, bringing along two girls that he knew [after checking with me if that would be OK. Of course it would be OK!] After a drive around the floor of the Virgin River Canyon, we took a couple of hikes up out of the canyon, one to a place with a clear stream flowing into a series of natural "tanks" eroded out of the sandstone, where we enjoyed a quick refreshing "dip." No, not a "skinny dip" but an almost as scandalous "underwear dip!" After each of these day excursions I'd enjoyed different slide shows at the hotel after dinner.

I'd intended to leave the next morning, having visited and seen both Bryce Canyon and Zion, my targeted destinations, but after the slide show that evening, Burnett Hendricks, the son-in-law, approached me with an offer I couldn't refuse. He was scheduled to take a couple from "back east" who were staying at the Hotel, on a longer tour the next day. They were going to drive via dirt roads, up to a town called Escalante where there was an Anasazi ruin being excavated and then on to another town called Boulder which would include a side trip over "Hell's Backbone." Burnett said he was impressed with my knowledge, appreciation and interest in the history and geology of the area, and if I could stay an extra night and day, he would take me along as an extra passenger on this trip at no cost to me! How could I refuse?

It was a GREAT all-day trip. Hell's Backbone turned out to be a place where the narrow dirt road ran along the spine of a ridge which got so narrow that at one point a platform of logs had been laid across it to make it wide enough for a car to cross! This platform or "bridge" was 50 or 60 feet long, with no side rails and a nearly vertical drop-off of several hundred feet on both sides! And that was only one highlight!

It was an awesome, never-to-be-forgotten trip!! The Anasazi Ruin was later developed into a State Park and the Hell's Backbone "bridge" had been widened and side rails added. [Years later, while driving back-country "jeep tours" for the Rimrock Inn, I would cover some of the same areas.]

This whole experience was far more interesting and exciting than anything I'd dreamed of and was easily the highlight of the entire trip. I'd made a friend in Burnett, and we corresponded for some months after my visit to Panguitch. However, all good things must come to an end. Fortunately, though, more good things were still ahead.

Back on Trailways, leaving Panguitch that evening, my next destination was the Grand Canyon in northern Arizona. The bus did not go out to the Canyon itself and I had to get out, early the next morning, at a tiny desert road junction very appropriately named Cameron. [I wondered if the name indicated a connection with the Hotel family in Panguitch, but I never found out.]

It was about 30 miles to the National Park boundary and another 25 miles along the South Rim to the Park headquarters. There was only one way to get there, other than by shank's mare, and that was to hitch-hike! I'd never really hitch-hiked before, but I guess the old Anasazi Gods were continuing to smile on me. It was about dawn and within about 15 or 20 minutes a car stopped! It was a young man driving a convertible coupe' and he picked me up. He was not only there to see the Canyon, but intended to drive through the park and leave by the other entrance and then drive on to Flagstaff. Exactly what I'd wanted and hoped to do! [Love those old Anasazi Gods!!]

We made stops at <u>all</u> the overlooks and interesting places along the drive through the Park, from the Watch Tower at Desert View to Hermit's Rest and got into Flagstaff just about dark, where I managed to get a room at the YMCA. The rest of my circle trip was anti-climactic in some ways, but I enjoyed it all.

I rode buses south through Arizona to Tucson, then turned east across southern New Mexico to El Paso, Texas, making a few more stops along the way. Then headed back by the most direct route to Janesville, WI, where my mother picked up her very tired, but very happy son.

End Part II

PART III

Go West, Young Man . . . [A Search For Community]

CHAPTER 14

Tuolumne

For want of anything better, I'll refer to the second notion that had gotten loose in my mind as "a search for community." I had not only enjoyed my experiences at the three Quaker Work Camps that I attended in 1951, 1952 and 1954, but I'd become interested in the idea of a total "way of life" that roughly incorporated some of the Work Camp practices and ideals. In my spare time I began a search to discover if any such thing existed.

Somewhat to my surprise, and to my utter delight, I discovered that there were several such groups in the U.S. Collectively, they were referred to as "Intentional Communities." Most of them tended to be rural in terms of location, and consisted of small groups of families and single persons. I wrote letters to several that sounded the most interesting and received invitations to visit and learn firsthand what life was like in such a community.

This coincided with my decision to take an indefinite hiatus from the academic life that I'd pursued up until then. I was still living at the Baptist Student Center in Madison, had been working for several months in a Co-op gas station and had bought a used Willys Jeep complete with a removable canvas and plastic "cab" over the drivers' and passenger seats. I was ready for a fairly drastic change in my life. I would follow the advice of an unnamed wit and "grab the bull by the tail and look him straight in the eye!"

My mother was secure in her job as Assistant Registrar at Milton College to which she had returned after my dad's death, and had no objections to my plans. I'd been living on my own in Madison for the past year, and Kathy and I had gone our separate ways, so there was nothing to hold me back from this new phase of life.

Several different "intentional communities" sounded interesting. One, called Macedonia, was led by an interesting sounding man named Art Wiser. I thought seriously about going there. Another, called Koinonia, was interesting but seemed a bit too religious for my tastes. Both of these communities were located in the state of Georgia, and the southern U. S. was not an area that appealed to me. Another group had started in Germany and had several communities in Europe, Latin America and the U.S. These groups were known collectively as Brüderhof, or "Society of Brothers" communities. The one in the U.S., Woodcrest, was near Rifton, in New York State. Brüderhof communities had a rather strict religious orientation also and that, plus the near urban setting of Woodcrest, caused me to cross it off my list of possible destinations.

After an exchange of several letters, and an invitation from the families there, I decided on Tuolumne Cooperative Farm, near Modesto, California, as my destination. Knowing that I was about to embark into what for me was unknown territory in the West, I felt a kinship with the Lewis and Clark expedition and how they had been aided in their westward venture by the young Shoshone girl, Sacagawea. Conscious of how I'd be relying on my little jeep, the name seemed a natural "fit" and I christened my vehicle, "Sacagawea" and painted the name on the side.

I loaded my few belongings on the back of "Sacagawea" and set out for California early in the summer of 1955. You can see me with Sacajawea [above] and with Mom, Grandpa and Grandma Vincent [below], ready to see me off into the wild blue yonder.

Of course I would do a bit of sightseeing on the way. I remember stopping at a place called Massacre Canyon in the southwest corner of Nebraska. There was not much to see there except a tall stone monument on top of a low, steep-sided hill. I was particularly interested in stopping there as I knew that my great-grandfather Whitford had visited the site shortly after a major battle was fought there in

1873 between members of the Sioux and Pawnee tribes. He had found a cavalry-type sword on the battlefield and had kept it. I never learned any more about it, whether it

had been carried by an Indian, or had belonged to one of the U.S. Army soldiers who arrived shortly after the battle. The sword came into my mother's possession after her grandfather died and for many years hung under the mantle of our fireplace in Milton. Unfortunately, I don't know what happened to it after my mother died.

That site was on my route west, but one reason I remember that isolated monument is that as I got in my jeep to leave, the motor would not start. I was able to let Sacagawea roll down the steep slope and fortunately she started and I was able to continue my journey. Since my visit, the huge granite monument has been moved and is no longer located on that steep little hill. I'm just glad that it hadn't been moved at the time of my visit! I didn't realize it then, but Sacagawea had developed a chronic ailment.

The following day I had driven off US Highway 50 to visit Black Canyon of the Gunnison National Monument in western Colorado. After stopping at a scenic overlook, Sacagawea again failed to start. Luckily for me two National Park maintenance men happened to drive by in a pickup truck and stopped. They discovered that the problem was that the starter was "locking." They showed me how to get at the starter, open it, [fortunately I had the requisite wrenches] and "unlock" it. I was especially lucky to learn how to correct the problem, as it happened again the next day when I stopped along the main street of Ouray, CO. I was now able to perform the "operation" myself and continue. It happened a fourth time just after I arrived at my destination, Tuolumne Cooperative Farm a few miles west of Modesto, CA. I got the starter unlocked one last time and promptly had the troublesome mechanism replaced.

Tuolumne Co-op Farm was the start of an entirely new life for me. First let me describe "the Farm." TCF had been in existence for a number of years. Four families had agreed on the ideas behind it, and had combined resources to purchase a 160 acre farm along the north bank of the Tuolumne River about six miles west of the city of Modesto in California's San Joaquin Valley. Two of the families would move to and operate the farm. The husbands, Wendell Kramer and George Burcham were both Methodist ministers. Two other families joined them a short time later, Ted and Vi Klaseen and Ken and Dorothy Stevens.

George Burcham, who was to become my father-in-law, had left the farm after a few years, eventually joining another cooperative community, and will reenter this narrative. My own thinking is that two strong-willed preachers trying to live and work together was asking just too much of human nature! The large Stevens family [5 or 6 children, if I remember correctly] also left TCF after a few years and bought a farm of their own a few miles away, but remained close friends with the TCF families.

The Kramers were also a large family with five children. The youngest daughter, Vonnie, had married George Burleson and they and their young daughter made a third TCF family joining the Kramers and Klaseens. The Kramer's two older daughters and eldest son were married and living elsewhere, their second son was away at college and only the youngest, 12 year old Stanley, remained with his parents. The Klaseens had a young daughter, Theo, and two sons, Sven, and Nels. So I found myself a member of a community of three families, which included five children. From time to time other families, couples, and single persons would be residents of the farm for varying periods of time, and both the Klaseens and Burlesons would add additional children to their families.

The photo shows the farm family after Carol and I arrived, minus the Burlesons who were absent at the time of the picture;

Back row: Bryce, Carol, Wendell Kramer, Stanley Kramer.

Middle row: Ted Klaseen, Vi Klaseen, Ruth Kramer.

Front row: Sven, Theo & Nels Klaseen.

The farm community operated both a cow dairy and a goat dairy, and much of the 160 acres was devoted to growing hay and corn for livestock feed. A small peach orchard was being developed with plans to expand the orchard into a producing economic unit.

Ted Klaseen was in charge of the cow dairy which consisted of between 20 and 30 head of milk cows, Jersey, Guernsey and Holstein. The Burleson's were in charge of the goat dairy, with between 40 or 50 female goats of several breeds including Alpine, Saanan and Nubian plus a couple male "billy" goats for breeding purposes. Ted used milking machines with the cows, but the goats were milked by hand. I was at first assigned to work with George and Vonnie in the goat dairy and learned the fine art of milking goats by hand.

Later, in my second TCF episode [more on that later] I worked with Ted in the cow dairy. Milking in both dairies took place twice a day, early in the morning and again in the late afternoon, seven days a week. General fieldwork occupied much of each weekday. Weekends were "rest days" except that the two dairy herds still had to be milked and fed. The farm had two tractors, a huge I-9 machine, and a smaller Ford-Ferguson. I learned to operate both, and how to plow, cultivate, and harvest the crops, mostly hay and corn. It was all new to me but I found that for the most part I enjoyed the work.

Each family or single person was paid a modest monthly wage based on the number of people and their ages, in each household. Breakfast and lunch were prepared by the women and were communal meals, held in a large community dining room/auditorium-like building. Each family had their own house and took their evening meals in their own homes. Single persons, like myself, would take our evening meals with the various families in rotation, an arrangement that worked out very well. All this, and much more, had been explained to me and discussed in letters prior to my decision to join the TCF families.

There was a small, presently unoccupied, "pre-fab" house, which I could live in. At one point I had a roommate for several weeks. Herb and Ellie Foster, a Quaker couple, were close friends with the TCF families and Herb was a youth probation officer with the state of California. It was during the spring of 1956 that Herb needed a temporary home for Ron, a boy of about 17, one of his probationers. Herb asked the farm families if they could provide a home for this boy until a more permanent living arrangement could be found. I agreed to share my little two bed-room house with him. There were no major problems, but I was not sad when he left. Our lifestyles were quite different!

As I said, milking the cows and goats had to be done seven days a week, but otherwise weekends were free. The Kramers and Klaseens were both Methodist families, while the Burlesons and I attended Delta Friends Meeting [Quakers]. These Meetings were rotated through three neighboring cities, Modesto, Stockton, and Tracy. The name Delta came from the fact that all three communities were located around the delta of the San Joaquin River and geographically formed a triangle like the Greek letter Delta.

The Klaseens and Burlesons were part of a group of like-minded families from Modesto and the surrounding area that met every Saturday evening. It included Sam and Carol Tyson, Olin and Betty Tillotson, Rudy and June Potochnik, and Howard and RubyTen Brink. Known to participants simply as "The Saturday Night Group" it was an informal gathering with no fixed agenda, and included the families' numerous children, about 14 in all as I remember! Each week a different family would host these get-togethers. I was invited to join the group which I did, finding it a comfortable, relaxing time for visiting after a week's hard work.

I really enjoyed my time at TCF and found farm work to be more enjoyable than I might have expected. There seemed to be a satisfying sort of rhythm to the daily routines as well as those of the seasons. I was to spend two separate periods at TCF, first as a single person and again as a newly married husband. Two particular events during this first period left indelible impressions on me and merit some comment.

The first was the "Great Christmas Flood" of 1955 which occurred on Christmas Eve the first winter I spent at TCF. It resulted from a week or more of torrential rains in the San Joaquin Valley and Sierra Nevada mountains to the east, the source of the Tuolumne River. It was evident by the day before Christmas that the Tuolumne would be out of its banks in some areas that evening.

At least the rains in the Valley had stopped. Most of TCF's 160 acres were on low land and subject to occasional flooding. Fortunately, one corner of the property consisting of a few acres formed a low knoll, where all the farm buildings, houses, barns and livestock corrals were located. These we knew were not in danger from the immanent flood.

Into the base of the knoll, however, was a large elongated pit or trench measuring about 12 feet across and perhaps 40 feet long, that we had dug in which to store corn silage for the winter. I mentioned, in Part I, the silos in Wisconsin which served that purpose. For some reason, unknown to me, silos were pretty much unknown in California's San Joaquin Valley, and this pit, or trench arrangement was used instead. The silage, formed by a machine which chopped not-quite-mature corn [stalks, leaves, ears—the whole shebang] into one or two inch pieces, was an important source of food for the dairy animals during the winter, and if the flood waters reached our silage it would be ruined and feed for the animals would have to be purchased elsewhere and trucked in—a very expensive proposition.

It was vitally important to save the several tons of silage if at all possible. The trench-like pit was covered with waterproof canvas, but the lower end was open so that, each day, silage could be removed, forked onto a small trailer and hauled up to the barns and feed lots, either by the small farm tractor or by Sacagawea. There was only a single option available to keep the flood waters from entering this open end. Perhaps we could build a kind of dam across the open mouth of the trench that would keep the flood waters out.

It was a race against time. All four of us men, Wendell, Ted, George and yours truly, set to work. Taking turns, one using the smaller tractor, with a scraper blade attached, and three with shovels, we began building our dam, stomping the dirt firmly with our feet. The flood waters were rising slowly, but soon night had closed in. The ladies rigged up a flood-light [no pun intended] so we could see what we were doing. Later a neighbor, who lived nearby on higher ground came to help us. It was a touch-and-go proposition as the flood waters crept higher and higher, and we frantically kept building our dam higher, barely keeping ahead of the flood.

Finally, near morning, we noticed that the flood waters were no longer rising, and then finally beginning to slightly recede. Our battle with the elements was won, and as morning dawned we were able to leave the dam and collapse into our various beds. It was a Christmas Eve that none of us would ever forget! As for Christmas Day, it would not be remembered! We all slept around the clock.

The second notable event of my first stay at Tuolumne was a cross-country trip in the early summer of 1956. At this time there existed in the U.S. an organization called the Fellowship of Intentional Communities [FIC]. It was a loose-knit group, the function of which was to enable intentional community groups to share experiences, problems, and ideas. The group held yearly conferences, rotating among the member communities.

At TCF a "community meeting" was held, usually once a week, to discuss . . . . well, anything that needed to be discussed! The FIC Conference that year was scheduled to be held in the early summer at a community called Gould Farm in western Massachusetts. It was decided at a community meeting that George Burleson and I would attend as TCF's representatives.

We came across a newspaper ad by a man who was moving "back East" and had a second car that he needed to have delivered to his new location in western New York State. An arrangement was worked out that George and I would drive east-bound and deliver the car to its destination, and then make the rest of the trip by bus or by hitchhiking. The trip, itself was pretty uneventful. Actually, so was the conference. Quite a lot of interesting talk, but no actions of significance.

The organization, or an offshoot, still exists under the name of Fellowship for Intentional Communities. I believe that the only links today from the time of the conference I attended are Koinonia Farm in Georgia and Gould Farm. Woodcrest Bruderhof is no longer extant, but other Bruderhof communities exist in several countries. I still believe that the underlying ideas of these communities are positive and feel sad that the promise behind them has never been fulfilled.

Probably the thing I remember most vividly about the FIC conference of 1956 was that one of the attenders was Dave Dellinger, who at that time was involved in establishing an Intentional Community at Glen Gardner, a little town in New Jersey. Dave was far and away the most dynamic person at the Conference. I'm not sure what happened to the embryonic Glen Gardner Community, but Dave went on to an impressive career as one of the country's most influential radicals. He was an outspoken pacifist, socialist, and activist for non-violent social change, was co-founder and editor of Liberation magazine, and also co-founder of the Committee for Non-Violent Action [CNVA], an organization which will appear later in my story.

Dave Dellinger was probably best known to the American public for his arrest, and trial years later, as one of the "Chicago 7" for their non-violent protest regarding the Viet Nam war at the Democratic Convention in that city in 1968. No one, I think, summed up Dave's life and activities better than American writer Noam Chomsky, who wrote: *"Before reading [his autobiography], I knew and greatly admired Dave Dellinger. Or so I thought. After reading his remarkable story, my admiration changed to something more like awe. There can be few people in the world who have crafted their lives into something truly inspiring. This autobiography introduces us to one of them."* My own impression of Dave mirrored that of Chomsky.

George and I decided not to go through the uncertainties of hitch-hiking and took a bus, or actually several busses, on our return to California.

During the period of the mid-to-late 1950s a number of rural cooperative community groups formed or attempted to form, including at least one more in California. Known informally as the "Gridley group", one such community was started by Marvin Crites just outside the small Sacramento Valley village of Gridley, near Marysville. Marvin owned a farm and operated a cow dairy, but was also a licensed surveyor. He had the dream of turning his farm into an "intentional community," and two families had moved onto his property to join Marvin and his family in this effort.

One family was that of George Burcham, the retired Methodist minister, who had been one of the founders of Tuolumne Co-op Farm.

Marvin had visited at TCF and I had met him and decided to leave TCF and move to the unnamed Gridley community. I really don't know why I made this decision. I was not unhappy with life at TCF. Perhaps, it was just a case of wanderlust. I guess I was still in a "search" mode in regard to what I wanted in life. So, in the fall of 1956, I loaded up Sacagawea, bid farewell to the TCF people and moved north to the Crites' farm near the little town of Gridley in the Sacramento Valley. The decision was to have a major impact on my life.

CHAPTER 15

The Times They Were A-Changin'

The families at Tuolumne, were sorry to have me leave, but wished me well. Three families, with a combined 6 children occupied the three homes on the Crites' property so Marvin cleaned up a small camp trailer which became my living quarters! The tiny trailer—too small even for me to stand erect in—had been used as a chicken coop, and required a major clean-up! It had been well fumigated, cleaned, and given several coats of paint, so it was adequate for me as I used it primarily for sleeping only. A small mattress on the floor on which I spread my sleeping bag, was the main furnishing. I took all meals with the other families on a rotating basis.

Marvin's wife, Beulah, and their 3 children, pretty much took care of the dairy, with some help from Marvin. But most of his time and that of the other males were devoted to the business of agricultural surveying which was the primary source of income for the nascent Community. The Sacramento Valley was mainly devoted to two types of crops, both utilizing flood irrigation which necessitated surveying.

Fruit and nut orchards were common. Apples, peaches, pears, apricots, almonds and walnuts were plentiful. The most common method of irrigation was to run surveys to mark contour lines at elevations a few inches apart. Then low dikes or levees would be plowed up along the contour, so that each section of the orchard could be flooded in sequence. The highest section or "check" first, then the water would be allowed to flow into the lower areas in succession through "check gates" built into the dikes. The other major crop, rice,

required flooded "paddies" which were leveled and would be kept flooded until just prior to harvest time.

The photo on p. 99 shows two rice paddies under flood irrigation. Levees separating the two paddies can be seen as dark lines across the photo. For running contours only two people were required, one sighting through the telescopic level, or "instrument," and one carrying the "rod", a pole with calibrated markings and a metal "target" that could be raised or lowered. For staking out fields that needed to be re-leveled or areas not previously leveled, we needed a larger crew, usually a half-a-dozen people, and used both men and women. At times, if not enough community residents were available, we would stop by a migrant labor camp and pick up some extra help.

Some of the work would involve re-surveying previously surveyed land that needed updating. We also surveyed land that was being leveled for the first time. For this we would also stake out the area. Marvin usually manned the telescopic "instrument" through which he would follow the progress of a "rodman" carrying the long wooden rod. Earlier, rows of lath [stakes] would have been placed in the ground in straight lines, at intervals of 50 feet. The rodman would stop at each stake and the instrument man would take a reading which he would note in a small book. Marvin would then compile a map to show how much soil removal or how much fill would be needed at each stake in order to create a gently even slope.

The amount of fill or re-moval would be marked on each stake, in red for fill and blue for removal. Usually we would need to go through this procedure two or even three times, as the big scrapers, like the one pictured here, that were used to move the soil were large and not meticulous enough to get everything just right the first time.

Surveying was not difficult work, although it could get extremely hot in California's summer sun. It could also get a bit boring at times, especially the staking process. I much preferred carrying a rod, while running contours, although Marvin would occasionally trust me to operate the instrument.

A major change in my life was, however, about to take place. I mentioned that our little community was made up of three families when I arrived. One family was that of the owners, Marvin and Beulah Crites, and their 3 children, a daughter and two boys, all of school age. An older couple, Louie and Nancy Neumann were living in the old original farmhouse. Louie worked regularly on the surveying jobs while Nancy helped Beulah and the Crites' kids working mostly in the dairy and in the garden.

I need to introduce the third family in a little more depth. I mentioned earlier in this narrative, George Burcham, who had been one of the founders of Tuolumne Co-op Farm. He had lived there briefly but had moved on with his wife, Margaret, and two daughters, Carol and Wilda.

Margaret had passed away, and George had remarried and sired two more daughters. He had been inactive as a Methodist minister for some time. For a number of years the family had operated a Youth Hostel in the Sierra Nevada foothills near Sequoia National Park. With his second wife, Evelyn, and the four girls the family eventually found their way into this more recent experiment in "community living."

When I arrived in Gridley, George, Evelyn, George's daughter, Wilda, and her two step-sisters, Betty and Kerry, were living in the third house on the Crites' farm. [It was a rather new and interesting building that everyone referred to as the "Tie House" as it was constructed from used railroad ties!] George's eldest daughter, Carol, was away for the summer attending an "Interns in Industry" program in Lynn, Massachusetts. These programs were operated by the American Friends Service Committee [AFSC], the same Quaker organization that had sponsored the Work Camps I had attended during three different summers.

The Intern groups shared living and eating activities, but each participant had to find employment in the community. Carol had found work in an ice cream manufacturing plant! She returned home at the end of that summer of 1955 after a brief visit at Woodcrest, the Rifton, NY, Brüderhof. I think you can probably guess where this is leading.

The temptation is to announce that we "fell in love." At least, as two single people in their 20s, we began a relationship. Neither of us was involved in a "love relationship" with anyone else, and it wasn't too long before we began "going out" together and from that it was not long before we began to think and talk about getting married. It was a decision that we were both drawn to, and by spring, 1956, we had decided to marry. Neither Carol's parents nor my mother in Wisconsin voiced any objections and, I think, all welcomed the decision.

Carol and I were married June 9, 1956, on the front lawn of Elwood and Ruby Johnson [neighbors and friends of Marvin and Beulah] who lived across the country road from the Burchams.

Carol's family was there, of course, and my mother flew out from Wisconsin for the wedding of her only child. Carol and I both wanted a simple Quaker-like ceremony, built around silence, and without the usual trappings that accompany most church weddings. Carol's father still had a valid license as a Methodist minister and signed the official document that made the ceremony a legal marriage!

Carol and I planned and designed our marriage ceremony. We used as a center-piece part of the Apache Indian marriage ceremony as set forth in a book we had both read recently. The book was a novel by Elliot Arnold called "Blood Brother" and the part we used goes like this:

"Now for you there is no rain,
For one is shelter to the other.
Now for you there is no sun,
For one is shelter to the other.
Now for you nothing is hard or bad,
For the hardness and badness is taken by one for the other.
Now for you there is no night,
For one is light to the other.
Now for you there is no cold,
For one is warmth to the other.
Now for you the snow has ended always,
For one is protection to the other,
It is that way, from now on, from now on.
Now it is good and there is always food,
And now there is always drink,
And now there is always comfort.
Now there is no loneliness,
Now, forever, forever, there is no loneliness."

I still think it is the most beautiful description of what a marriage <u>should</u> be. Sadly, the "forever" did not prove to be forthcoming for us, but that was not apparent at the time. Here is a picture of the wedding party: Front row, left to right: Wilda [Carol's sister], Evelyn [step-mother], George [father], Carol, me, and my mother. In front are Carol's step-sisters, Kerry and Betty.

Carol and I decided that for a honeymoon we would undertake a backpacking excursion in Yosemite National Park. Carol had been backpacking there a few years before, but it would be an entirely new experience for me. As it was, we made just about every mistake that two relatively inexperienced backpackers could make, but somehow we managed to survive and look back on that week with a mixture of pride, wonder and relief.

To fully grasp the situation, one has to first understand the topography we were to encounter. It was not as if we were unaware of that little factor. We had both been to Yosemite before. I suppose the novelty of being there as a newly married couple caused us to forget things that we should have taken into consideration. We knew that we would make our base camp in Yosemite Valley and that the hike we had in mind would involve negotiating a trail up out of the narrow valley.

The problem was that we didn't realize how poorly equipped we were for what lay ahead, our minds being elsewhere, I guess. We would leave behind our tent, pitched at a campground in the valley and would hike out carrying a sleeping bag and knapsack each, the latter packed with extra clothing, food, water and sundry other items that we imagined would be useful or needed. It never entered our minds that our equipment and supplies were designed for camping, but not for hiking and carrying. Our sleeping bags were not light, down-filled backpacking bags, but just ordinary bags. Carol's was, if I remember correctly, of homemade construction. Nor did we take into consideration that Carol's previous backpacking trip had been with a group that had employed mules to carry most of the camping gear!

We had two packs, one fairly small and one a good deal larger. We did have sense enough to pack lighter things like clothing in the larger pack. Carol would carry that. My pack was smaller, but contained things like canned goods [!] and other foods including a large salami sausage that was at least a foot long. Cooking and eating utensils, including a 12" cast iron frying pan were also part of my load! Now I think you have the idea.

For a destination, we had decided on a trail that led out of Yosemite Valley, switchbacking steeply up the almost sheer rocky walls to where Nevada Falls carries the waters of the Merced River over the cliff edge and down to the valley below. The trail from the campground in the Valley to Nevada Falls is about 3 miles in length and the gain in elevation is close to 2000 feet! Before we had climbed halfway we were exhausted! By that time, we were walking 50 feet or so and stopping to lean against the rock wall alongside the trail to catch our breaths. At one point we met a portly middle aged couple coming down the trail. They were the image of a stereotypical New York Jewish couple, the husband wearing a garish Hawaiian-style shirt. As they passed us on the trail our exhaustion must have been obvious. They didn't stop, but the husband murmured, his encouragement, "Poiservere! Poiservere!"

By the time we reached the falls, darkness was rapidly falling. We had no tent, so we laid out our sleeping bags on the ground in a little meadow off the beaten hiking trail, placing the backpacks side by side at the head of the bags, and walked a few hundred feet or so to view the falls where the water surged over the cliff edge, while there was still enough light to see. Then we headed back to where we'd laid out the sleeping bags. Due to the ensuing circumstances we forgot entirely about an evening meal! WE forgot, but someone had not!

As we approached our campsite [such as it was] the first thing I noticed in the gathering dusk was that there was an empty space where the small knapsack had been. It was gone! Carol and I began looking around, though it was fast growing dark. Then I spotted the pack over near the edge of the little meadow. I had taken only a few steps towards it, when I noticed two other dark objects nearby. Suddenly, I realized what they were: A large black bear and her cub!

Without thinking, I did a really stupid thing. I continued walking towards them to retrieve the knapsack! When I reached it, the first thing I noticed was that the flap had been pulled back revealing an open space just the size of a large salami sausage! The flap of the pack was wet from mama bear's saliva. For some unknown reason, instead of adding me to their salami supper, the two bears moved back into the trees. I quickly scooped up the packsack and returned to where our sleeping bags were laid out on the ground.

What had transpired during our look at the falls was obvious. Mama bear had scented the salami, dragged the pack across the meadow and then with her mouth pulled back the flap of the pack and neatly removed the salami.

Mama bear and her cub were busily enjoying their pilfered meal when I approached them. Fortunately, they seemed satisfied with a supper of salami, exhibiting no immediate need or interest in a second course of newlyweds, and had disappeared into the trees. I returned the pack to its place at the head of my sleeping bag. By this time it was almost fully dark, and both Carol and I were beginning to realize the danger of our situation. We climbed fully clothed into our sleeping bags and armed ourselves with matches and several rolled up newspapers that we had brought for starting fires. We hoped with the naivety of two babes in the woods that if the bears approached us during the night that lighting and waving crude newspaper torches would deter them from a search for dessert.

Be assured that we didn't get much sleep that night, although, somehow, we did get <u>some</u>. Whether or not it surpassed the allotted forty winks, or not, I can't be sure. We were rather fortunate, I believe, that Mrs. Bear and her cub had apparently been satisfied with their salami snack and did not return. We were so clueless that the next day we hiked on ahead to what's known as Little Yosemite Valley and spent another, and reassuringly uneventful, night before returning back to our base campsite, tent and trusty Sacagawea.

Whenever I think now of that entire experience, I marvel at our naivety and pure dumb luck.

CHAPTER 16

TCF Reprise

We had decided before the wedding not to remain in Gridley. There were two primary reasons, I think. One was that there was no place there on the Crites' farm for us to live! My little chicken-coop trailer was totally inadequate. The other reason, I think, was a mutual feeling that it would be wise not to be living in such close proximity to Carol's parents. And, yes, I believe the feeling was mutual. [Carol and her step-mother had their differences.]

Both Carol and I had positive memories of times at Tuolumne. Carol had ties there from her childhood, and we knew the small house where I had stayed before was again unoccupied. In advance of our marriage, we had written to the TCF families and they assured us that we would be most welcome to begin our married life as additions to the TCF community. So, immediately after the honeymoon hike, we returned to Gridley, packed our few possessions in reliable Sacagawea and back to TCF the farmer took his wife. Hi-ho, the derry-O.

We were warmly welcomed by the families at TCF. The small two-bedroom "pre-fab" house, empty since I had last moved out, also welcomed me back with my bride. The house was small, having a living room, kitchen/ diningroom, two small bedrooms, and a bathroom, plus a closet. The TCF ladies had cleaned it thoroughly in anticipation of our arrival.

The main change for me was that I began working with Ted Klaseen in the cow dairy. Ted and I got along very well together and I enjoyed working with him. The goat dairy was no longer in existence. The closing down of that operation had been made before Carol and I arrived. It may have been due in part at least to an incident that had occurred during my earlier stay at the farm. There were very probably other factors, but I believe the incident may have played a major role in the decision to abandon the goat dairy and is worth mentioning here.

A bit of background is required. For both goats and cows to lactate, which is the object of a dairy, they must be bred and produce offspring. For the cow dairy, female calves were kept and raised and usually added to the herd at some point. The male calves were, when the calving season ended, shipped off to feed lots and eventually most ended their earthly sojourn as steaks or hamburger or, perhaps, fertilizer or something even less appealing. But it was all done "out of sight and out of mind" as the saying goes, and some use was made of them. Those of us on the farm were not directly involved and the actual slaughter of the animals was carried out at a distance and in relative anonymity which made it easier to ignore, overlook, or accept.

With the goats the story was somewhat different. The female goat kids would be kept and added to the herd when grown, but the male kids, were simply knocked on the head and killed, then thrown into in a mass "grave" right there on the farm! They would live only until the last adult females had given birth. The difference was that the "mass murder" of the male goat kids was done right there on the farm, "in both sight and mind," if you will. And no use of any kind was made of the male kids. Wendell Kramer was the "Lord High Executioner", but everyone knew perfectly well what was happening and "looked the other way," so to speak.

My feelings about this were illogical perhaps, but sincere. I was, I think, as negatively affected by the factor of <u>waste</u> as much as by that of mass slaughter. So at one of our regular community business meetings, I spoke up: If the male goat kids must be killed, and there seemed no alternative, the least we could do would be to use them for food, rather than just knocking them on the head and dumping the bodies into a hole in the ground!

The matter was discussed and my perhaps curious logic seemed to strike a chord. From then on, it was agreed, the male goat kids would, like their bovine counterparts, still be condemned to the death penalty, but the meat would be used for our own human consumption, instead of just wasted.

From that time on, goat kid became the staple meat consumed by the Farm residents. Frozen for storage and then eaten. The whole matter may now seem somewhat illogical in a way, but at the time it made me feel like I'd accomplished something worthwhile.

After Carol and I joined the farm community, she and I decided that we needed to go further down the road to vegetarianism and we decided to forego eating meat altogether. We never really knew what the other TCF residents thought, but they accepted our decision. The illogic of shaming the farm families into eating food that we refused to eat never occurred to us at the time! We saw ourselves not as total vegetarians, or "vegans," but as non-meat eaters. No one else at the farm joined us in our decision and we abandoned the practice after we left TCF.

As a newly married couple, Carol and I had discussed the matter of children. We decided that we would not consciously try to have children, but neither would we actively try to prevent a pregnancy from occurring. We would just allow Ma Nature to take her course. It seems rather ridiculous now, but that was our decision. Not surprisingly, Carol told me two or three months later that we would be adding to our family. She had an uneventful pregnancy and our first born, a boy, arrived on St.Patrick's Day, March 17, 1957, not quite a year after we "tied the knot." Taavi was born in Memorial Hospital in Ceres, a "satellite" suburb of Modesto.

One of the Kramer's married daughters, who visited the farm periodically, was horrified when she learned that Carol was not eating meat during her pregnancy, and kept attempting to "smuggle" meat dishes to Carol every time she visited. Carol would graciously accept the "offering" and feed the meat to Perro, our dog. Regardless of Carol's meatless diet she had a normal pregnancy and a healthy baby.

Far in advance of Taavi's arrival, we had discussed names and decided that we preferred something a bit unique. One name I recalled was that of an exchange student from Finland who had lived at the Baptist Student Center in Madison when I stayed there. Carol and I both liked the name, Taavi, and decided on that for the name of our firstborn. [My early childhood trauma over MY somewhat unusual name was completely forgotten, or ignored!] We chose Kirk as a middle name simply because we liked it.

I mentioned "our dog." No, Taavi was not the first addition to our family. I've totally forgotten where our canine pet came from but some time long before Taavi's birth we had acquired a puppy. I gave him the name Perro, the Spanish word for "dog." [It seemed a logical name.] Showing off my limited knowledge of Spanish, I used to tell people who inquired about the name that sometimes I called him Perro Caliente, which meant hot dog, and sometimes I called him Perro Frio, which meant that he was a real cool dog, but his real full name was Perro con Pulgas, which meant "dog with fleas."

Perro actually never, to my knowledge, had fleas, but it wasn't long before I realized that some training was required, as there were farm chickens that ran loose around the farm homes. I worked hard training Perro not to chase chickens, birds or any other animals. I'd never tried to train an animal before, but somehow, I succeeded beyond my wildest expectations.

This became evident one winter evening, prior to Taavi's birth, as Carol, and I sat reading in the living room of our little house. To set the scene, I need to explain that Carol and I were both trying hard to be complete and total pacifists. "Live and let live" was our "golden rule." This was put to the test when we discovered one day that we were sharing our abode not only with a human baby soon to arrive, and a now nearly full grown dog, but also with MICE. Well, we would reaffirm our "live and let live" philosophy, and what harm could arise from a mouse in the house? It was not long before we learned the answer and realized that we were providing accommodations for more than one of the furry little rascals. Gradually, we came to understand that our original mice tenants were inviting friends, relatives and offspring to join them in their new-found domicile.

We stuck by our pacifist beliefs until one day during her pregnancy Carol discovered that some of the bed sheets in our closet had acquired several raggedy holes. There was only one possibility. Mice were taking unwarranted liberties with our peaceful philosophy. Regrettably, we decided that our philosophy of life had a flaw. We needed to put aside our well-meant willingness to share hearth and home, at least as far as these rascally rodents were concerned. We began setting out a mouse trap.

We had made encouraging headway in ridding the house of the varmints, when one evening as we sat in the living room reading [no TV in those days] we heard a loud SNAP from the kitchen where we had a set our baited mouse trap. "Ah ha!" I thought. "We got another one. When I finish this chapter, I'll go and empty the trap," I told Carol.

What I'm going to relate next may stretch a reader's credulity, but is the absolute, unvarnished truth. My training of Perro in canine pacifism was about to be put to the test! He was stretched out in the middle of the living room floor, relaxed, and on the verge of dozing off, when his low whine made me look up. Staggering, along a zigzag course as though drunk, through the open doorway from the kitchen came a mouse. Its head was bloody and it appeared to be at least partially blinded. We both realized immediately that it had set off the trap and the bar had struck it across the head but had neither caught nor killed it.

The mouse, half stunned and at least half blind, was staggering directly towards Perro, albeit with a number of zigs and zags. Perro, as I had trained him, remained absolutely still! Hardly believing our eyes, Carol and I watched as though mesmerized, hardly daring to breathe, as the wounded mouse bumped against Perro's side. Then—and this is the honest-to-God truth—staggered alongside the dog, climbed onto his tail, made its way hesitantly along the tail and across Perro's back, until it reached the top of his head. There it stopped and didn't move for a moment or two. Perro lay perfectly still, except for an involuntary trembling and a nervous rolling of his eyes! After a moment or two the mouse turned and retraced its uncertain steps, at last leaving the dog and staggered back into the kitchen!!

Carol and I, maintaining a breathless silence, were almost choking in our efforts to keep from laughing out loud but didn't move from our chairs. The whole business was both amazing and absolutely ludicrous. With the mouse retreating back into the kitchen and out of sight, we erupted in gales of laughter and exclamations of wonder at what we'd just witnessed. I hugged Perro telling him how proud I was of him for his forbearance.

A couple of days later we found the mouse had learned nothing from the experience as it had attacked the reset mouse trap again, probably due to the odor of the cheese bait. This time it mercifully met its demise. We knew it was the same mouse as the evidence of its head injury from its previous appearance was obvious. In retelling, the whole episode sounds unbelievable, but I'd be willing to swear on a stack of bibles to its absolute truth. I'm sure Carol would back me up entirely.

CHAPTER 17

Logging In . . . Logging Out

I hadn't thought that the itching of my feet was contagious, nor am I sure whether Carol caught the malady from me, or if she had already been afflicted before we met. We had enjoyed living at TCF for the most part and liked the other members of the community but were still feeling an urge to learn if there might be something we would find even more satisfying. Perhaps there was just a wanderlust virus in the air that spring, or perhaps it had been carried by a pair of visitors to the Farm! Whatever the cause, we were smitten with the urge to discover . . . . what, I'm not sure! But we couldn't resist the thought that the "promised land," might be lying just around the next bend in the road or over the next hill of our life's journey.

Shortly before Taavi's birth a couple about our age, Don and Mildred Shaw with their son, Sam, just 3 or 4 years old, had stopped at TCF for a visit. The Shaws had recently purchased a quarter section of land in Oregon, in the foothills of picture-perfect Mt. Hood. The property included three small, neglected, mature pear orchards, and their dream was to start an "intentional community" of their own using the pear orchards as an economic base. At some point during their visit at TCF, they invited us to join them after our child was born.

Carol and I had caught the wanderlust infection blowing in the wind, or for which the Shaws may have been carriers. Whatever the cause, we decided that after Taavi was born we would leave TCF and move to this romantic-sounding mountain top near Hood River, Oregon. Sacagawea had performed nobly for our off-farm transportation, as well as serving as a kind of miniature tractor on the farm given her 4-wheel drive, but in anticipation of the growth of our family, I finally traded her in for a Ford coupe'. It was only slightly larger but offered the prospect of more comfortable travel for a family of three with one an infant. We had no room for Perro, so we left him with the TCF families.

So with Taavi only a month old, warmly ensconced in a padded box between us on the seat, Carol and I set out with only a hazy notion of what lay ahead. Don and Mildred had told us that there was an unused two room cabin on the property which, we confidently assured them, would be adequate for us. It consisted of a kitchen with a table and two chairs, plus a wood burning cook stove, and a bedroom with enough space for a double bed and a crib. Wired for electricity, each room had a cord and light socket hanging from the ceiling. Between the two rooms was a small closet and an unfinished washroom containing a totally useless non-operational toilet. Meanwhile, a small outhouse stood nearby. So our home was wired for electricity, but was without running water.

There was, however, a spring on the mountainside above us and the water from it was piped to a stand-pipe about six feet tall with a curved top and spigot, just outside the cabin. Good enough for hardy souls like us! I fashioned a frame box about 2 feet square, covering the open sides with wire screen and then Carol helped in covering the entire box with several layers of burlap. It had a tin roof and the front panel of the box was hinged so that it could be opened or secured shut by a hook and eye fastener. Thus made virtually varmint-proof, we suspended the box in mid-air where the steady flow of icy cold spring-water from the always open spigot at the top of the standpipe kept the entire contraption always wet and everything inside cool. It made a very serviceable storage box in which to keep otherwise spoilable foods.

Mildred had a wringer washing machine that she let Carol use which, with Taavi in diapers, was not viewed as a "luxury." We had no complaints, and even my mother who visited for a week, primarily to see her first grandchild, expressed [at least verbally] no complaints.

The pear orchards had to be pruned, but would produce no income until harvest time in the fall. For income until then Don's solution was that he and I become loggers. Most of the 160 acres was in pine and fir forest, and most of the acreage was mountain-side. Don was young and strong, standing over 6 feet in height. He had an

old flatbed truck, a chainsaw, a couple of axes and two peaveys. He would fell trees using the chainsaw, and cut them into 8 foot lengths, while I would trim off the branches with an ax. The Shaw's owned two horses, and they would be used alternately to drag the logs to a wooden ramp that some previous loggers had built on the mountainside, some years before. Backing the flatbed truck up to the ramp the two of us together could manhandle the logs onto the truck using the peaveys.

For those readers who may not have experienced the pleasure of working in the logging industry, a peavey is a steel tipped wooden pole about 5 feet long with a hinged metal hook-like device attached. Here's a drawing of a man using a peavey. We would use a horse to drag the logs to the ramp, then, using the peaveys, we could roll the 8-foot logs onto the loading ramp. The flat-bed truck would be backed up to the ramp and we would manhandle the logs onto the truck, again using the peaveys. It was back-breakingly difficult work and because of my small stature, Don had more than his fair share of these tasks.

My primary job was to drive the loaded truck down the mountain on dirt logging roads and sell the logs to a stud mill in the little town of Dee in the valley below. There, the 8 foot-long logs would be cut into 2X4 studs to be used in the building trade. This was a job I could handle, although I found it extremely stressful psychologically. Why, you ask? As Don explained just before my first drive down the mountain, the truck's brakes were defective and I was to use them as little as possible to avoid burning them out completely!

Those logging roads, or more accurately "tracks," were rough, narrow, winding and STEEP! As instructed I would drive the entire distance of some 15 miles in the truck's lowest gear, depending on the low gear plus very judicious use of the emergency hand brake when the truck approached a speed which threatened to send truck, logs and terror-stricken driver careening down the mountain totally out of control! I always found myself to be a nervous wreck by the time I reached the mill! I don't know how many of these trips I made that summer. In all honesty, I believe I was afraid to count them. Don and I split the income from the sale of the logs. I have no recollection of what my income was that summer, either, but it was fairly miniscule.

I was delighted when the pears were ready to harvest early that fall! But before that I got a break from the logging when I took a week off in August to participate in a protest demonstration against the testing of nuclear bombs in the Nevada desert. The protest was organized by the Committee for Non-Violent Action which I mentioned earlier in this story. This was 1957 and there was a growing concern nationally over health risks from radioactive fallout from these atmospheric, above-ground, nuclear tests . . . . and Carol and I had a son less than a year old.

Don was not particularly happy over my taking the time off, but didn't try to prevent my going. The fact that he also had a young son may have played a part. [I'd be lying if I tried to deny that I welcomed the opportunity for a "vacation" from logging which sorely taxed my strength, endurance and emotional stability!] Carol assured me that she could cope in my absence.

I took a bus to Las Vegas, Nevada, and joined in the protest. I was pleased to find friends that I knew well among the protestors. Ted Klaseen from TCF and Sam Tyson, from the Saturday Night Group, would both be my companions in the protest. Ted's wife, Vi, accompanied him. Sam came alone and he and I shared a room at an inexpensive motel. Transportation was arranged by CNVA.

The following **INTERLUDE** is an account I wrote of that experience, a good many years later after we moved to Cottonwood, AZ. I wrote the piece for a lady in Sedona, AZ, who put a notice in the local newspaper to the effect that she was preparing to write a book about the "downwinders" of Nevada, Utah and Arizona who had suffered from the radioactive fallout effects of the aboveground nuclear tests. I never heard back from her, and don't know if she ever wrote the book, or not. My story was not particularly pertinent to her aim, but I wanted to leave a record of my experience anyway, and this was a good opportunity to do that.

INTERLUDE

Civil Disobedience
Nuclear Tests Protest 1957

I'd become a member of the Society of Friends [Quakers] and an avowed pacifist. My wife, Carol, shared my feelings. We had moved to Oregon from California shortly after our first child, a son, was born in March 1957. We knew of the above-ground nuclear tests that were being conducted near Las Vegas, NV, and were aware of the dangers of the radioactive fall-out from these tests. As parents of a newborn child we were particularly concerned.

During the summer in Oregon we had learned, through Quaker contacts in California, of the plans of an organization called the Committee for Non-Violent Action to hold a protest in Nevada, against the nuclear bomb tests scheduled for August of that year [1957]. I knew personally, some of the CNVA organization people, and many others by reputation. I had joined the CNVA and decided that I wanted to be a part of that protest.

I travelled by bus to Las Vegas to join the protest. There were 50 or more people there who had come to participate in the protest and I joined a group of 12 other CNVA members who planned to enter the Camp Mercury test site on the morning of Aug. 6, 1957, when a nuclear test was scheduled. We thought that date was particularly appropriate as it marked the 12th anniversary of the nuclear bombing of Hiroshima.

We publicly announced to the authorities and through newspaper and radio our intention of peacefully entering the fenced-in site through the main gate as a protest against the exploding of nuclear devices, emphasizing that radiation from these tests posed a health threat to people living downwind of the test site. We were told that if we entered at any point, we would be subject to arrest. We said that we would proceed with our non-violent protest and that we would enter through the main pedestrian gate the next morning. On the evening of August 5, about 50 of us gathered and maintained a silent vigil just outside the main gate. Shortly after dawn the next morning the 13 of us proceeded to the main entrance. We couldn't believe what we saw.

In spite of having clearly proclaimed that our protest would be entirely non-violent and that 13 persons intended to enter openly through the main gate, the authorities obviously did not believe us and seemed to have prepared for an armed invasion! Two ranks of barbed-wire barricades stretched as far as we could see about 100 and 200 ft. inside the main high outer chain-link fence. There were, as I remember, three ranks of armed, mostly uniformed, men from the U.S. Army, FBI, Atomic Energy Commission [AEC], plus Nevada State Police, spread out as far as we could see on either side of the main gate! We could hardly believe the paranoia which seemed to have gripped those inside!!

The thirteen of us walked in single file up to the gate where several armed guards stood. One at a time we stepped up to the narrow entrance gate. As each person moved up, one at a time, we were told that we could not enter and that if we stepped through the open gate we would be arrested. One at time we stepped through the narrow entry and were placed under arrest by a uniformed armed guard. It didn't take long.

We were immediately herded onto a waiting bus, and told that we were going to be taken to the Nye County Seat about 150 mi. away [!], to be tried for "illegal entry" to a restricted site. A noted Civil Rights attorney, Francis Heisler, who had volunteered to represent us, was allowed to board the bus with us. The "trial" was somewhat of a farce. After arriving at the tiny hamlet of Tonopah, the County Seat, we were taken to the local jail, and then told that we could, on our own, go down the street to a little restaurant for lunch.

It was about noon by then and we had had no breakfast. The rest of the group went for lunch, but I said that I was fasting as part of my protest, so I remained alone in one of the two [unlocked] cells in the "County Jail." The authorities had, apparently, become convinced by now that we were telling the truth about conducting a non-violent protest and were not intent on staging an armed "invasion."

When the others had finished lunch and returned to the jail, we were all conducted to a small building that served, I believe, as the County Court House, and arraigned before the local Justice of the Peace who acted as Judge for our "trial". [In "real life" the Justice of the Peace owned and operated the town's only gas station!]

The noted civil-rights lawyer, Francis Heisler, had offered to represent us at no cost and advised us to plead <u>nolo contendre</u> [no contest, that is, neither guilty or not guilty]. After consulting with several men that I believed to be federal lawyers, the gas-station-attendant-judge pronounced us guilty and sentenced each of us to one year prison terms. Having determined that none of us were Nevada residents, he then announced that he would suspend our sentences, as long as we did not reenter Nevada during a year from that date. If we should be found in the state during that time we would be subject to a year's incarceration. We all returned to Camp Mercury, rejoined the other protesters and sat with our backs toward the test site as the nuclear blast was set off, delayed for a number of hours by our "invasion."

The CNVA protest got quite a lot of publicity in the Las Vegas newspaper, but I'm not sure about the rest of the country. It must have had some effect on the policies of the AEC and the federal government, however, as the following year, 1958, the above-ground nuclear tests were moved to the vast Pacific Ocean.

One of the group of 13 who were arrested in the Camp Mercury protest, Albert Bigelow [a U.S. Navy Captain during World War II] set out to sail his 30 ft. ketch the Golden Rule, into the Eniwetok Proving Grounds where the 1958 tests were to be held. The Golden Rule was detained near Hawaii and Bigelow and his 4 pacifist crew were detained as the AEC hastily issued an injunction making it illegal to sail into the Proving Grounds site. Bigelow and his crew ignored the injunction and set sail again, only to be intercepted by the U.S. Coast Guard in Hawaiian waters, arrested, charged with contempt of court and given 60 day jail sentences which they served. [As a footnote, Albert Bigelow and his wife, through arrangements made by the American Friends Service Committee, had provided a home for two of the severely disfigured A-bomb survivors known as the "Hiroshima Maidens," who had been brought to the U.S. to undergo plastic surgery in 1955. The experience made him into an ardent pacifist. Bigelow continued to take part in non-violent activities including the Freedom Rides sponsored by the Congress of Racial Equality [CORE], into the 1960s. I feel privileged to have known him personally.

Hearing of the plight of the Golden Rule, another CNVA member, anthropologist and Quaker Earle Reynolds, who had visited Hiroshima to study the effects of the atom bomb, sailed with his wife, Barbara, in their yacht "Phoenix of Hiroshima", into the test site at Bikini Atoll later that summer. Earle was arrested and served six months in jail.

So, although, I was never a victim of radioactive fallout from the nuclear testing in Nevada, as were so many "downwind" residents of that state, and of Utah and Arizona, I have at least some satisfaction that I may have played a part, however small, in perhaps preventing additional harm to larger numbers of people.—Bryce

CHAPTER 18

California Here
We Come... Again
OR
"You May Fire When
Ready, Gridley!"

Following the events described in the foregoing, I returned by bus to Hood River. Carol and I helped Don and Mildred with the pear harvest. The Shaws would not be staying on their ranch over the winter, as their property would be deeply snowed in, and neither Carol nor I really wanted to return to that life the next summer. It had been an interesting experience, but the work was harder than I wanted to continue with [I think Don realized that] and both Carol and I were ready for a change in scenery. California seemed like "home" to both of us and so in October, 1957, we headed back to more familiar surroundings.

Carol's family had left Gridley and moved to a nearby community, Grass Valley, in the lower reaches of the Sierra Nevada. After sampling "Intentional Community life" at TCF, Gridley and Hood River, I think Carol and I were both a bit disillusioned by that time, and ready to take a break from that hope, and experience life more on our own. The "community" dream was not dead, only dormant. But for now we felt drawn to renew contact with friends and family. Grass Valley was an attractive community and we ended up going there.

Through Carol's father, we found a lovely old house for rent a few miles out of Grass Valley. The owner, a sweet older widow, Mrs. Wheeler, had lived there until a new home was built for her on the same property. She agreed to rent us the old home for a ridiculously low price. It was nothing fancy, but very comfortable, especially when compared to the cabin in Oregon! It had most modern conveniences with one partial exception. The telephone line that served the house was part of a small, localized, private line and had an old-fashioned wooden wall phone with a small crank on the side which when turned would access an operator. A caller would, then, tell this live operator the number and she would make the connection. Making a telephone call was like stepping back in time. It had been many years since I had last picked up a telephone receiver and heard a human voice ask, "Number, please?"

George, Carol's father, was working at the time for a friend named Mervin Baker, who owned a planing mill on the outskirts of Grass Valley. A planing mill took various types and dimensions of rough-cut lumber and planed them smooth, ready for carpenters to work with. George arranged for me to work there also, so for the first time in several months Carol and I had a regular income. I found the work, however, to be fairly hard and <u>very</u> boring. During the winter we had visited Marvin and Beulah Crites in Gridley. No longer trying to host and develop an "intentional community" on his farm, Marvin offered me steady employment working with him on surveying jobs.

I'd done this work before, and decided that I'd prefer it to working in the mill. So Carol and I decided to move back to Gridley. It was partly the job, but neither Carol nor

I enjoyed living in close proximity to her step-mother, so we decided to accept Marvin's offer. The other homes on the Crites farm were all rented out, but we had saved up enough money to purchase a small house-trailer, or mobile home, and there was space to park it and hook-ups available for water and electricity.

After we moved in I built on a small porch and entry room where Carol is standing in the photo holding Taavi. So in February of 1958 we were on the move again, this time out of the mountains and back to the Sacramento Valley. The Ford coupe' was traded in for a used Studebaker pick-up truck, needed to pull the house trailer.

I was familiar with the surveying work so I was able to slide effortlessly back into the various duties of the job. I enjoyed it, probably as much as any job I'd had up until then. Marvin was using a neighbor, Cecil Catledge, as one "regular" member of his surveying crew, but needing another full-time crew member, seemed pleased to have me back. Carol's and my peripatetic life style hadn't ended, but had leveled off temporarily, and we actually settled down and remained in one place for all of 19 months! That was long enough to welcome two additions to a growing family.

Our *laissez faire* approach to family planning had already resulted in a second pregnancy for Carol even before our move back to Gridley. It had been another reason for the decision to make the move, added to the fact that I had enjoyed the work on a surveying crew more than that of the planning mill. Our daughter, Talitha was born July 22, 1958.

We were, as always, looking for an unusual name, but one that we liked. I found the name Talitha in a paperback Western novel and we both liked it. Later, Carol's dad, the former Methodist minister, told us that the name was also found in the Bible and, appropriately enough, meant "little girl." Carol chose Karlin as a middle name, from a source I never knew.

The other addition to our family was by "adoption" and was an addition of the canine variety that joined our family about a year later. Here's how the "adoption" occurred. Marvin's other survey crew member, Cecil Catledge owned a home and peach orchard nearby. Cecil and his wife, Bonnie, were near our own age, had 3 small children, and we became close friends. One day while visiting them we noticed the 5 children playing happily in the yard with a dog.

We were struck by the behavior of the young female dog. She let the kids climb all over her, wrestle with her and even pull her tail and ears with never a growl or bark. The dog would just accept everything and play happily with the children. Cecil and Bonnie already owned a large German Shepherd dog and we asked how they had acquired this new pup. Cecil explained that he'd had a crew of migrant workers harvesting his peach crop the week before. The dog had been with them, but for some unknown reason they'd left it behind and had since left the area. Not wanting two dogs, Cecil added that he intended to take this abandoned spaniel-looking creature to the pound.

Carol and I were so impressed with how well behaved this little dog was, and how much the kids enjoyed playing with her, that we wondered if we might take her instead. Cecil and Bonnie and their 3 boys were delighted by our offer, and so we added another female to our family. Now it was time to play the "name game" again.

On my drive from Wisconsin to California I'd stopped in Ouray, CO. The town was named for that famous Ute Indian chief and while there I visited a small historical museum which contained an exhibit on his wife, a rather remarkable woman named Chipeta. I suggested Chipeta [with a long "e"] as a name for our new family member. It stuck, although our kids usually shortened it to "Petey."

Appearing to be some kind of Spaniel mix she would be a valued and much-loved member of our ever-growing family for some 10 years! I love the photo on the preceding page of our two "girls", Talitha and Chipeta.

We would remain in Gridley for about 19 months, which would be our longest stay in a single location since our marriage. All in all, it was a comfortable and relatively stress-free period. However, the old longing for some kind of cooperative community living had not died and gradually began to reassert its fascination. Or was it a recurring infection? How can one be sure?

End of Part III

PART IV

Land of Enchantment

CHAPTER 19

Off the Deep End
[Or Life on the Edge]

After trying "community" living at Tuolumne, Gridley [twice each] and Hood River, the Brüderhof [for Carol] and AFSC workcamps [for me], I think both Carol and I were becoming somewhat discouraged with the realities of that as a permanent kind of lifestyle. We were still enamored, however, with the notion of rural, self-sufficient, simple living for ourselves, and even the possibility of sharing this vision with another couple if possible. Unfortunately, we had only the vaguest notion of what this kind of life would entail.

On her previous flight to visit us in Hood River, in 1957, my mother had met a retired widower from Chicago on the plane and they had maintained contact afterwards. His name was Paul Kaase and their relationship deepened, culminating in marriage that December. Paul, who was a retired Lutheran minister, moved into mom's home in Milton. I was happy that my mother had found a congenial partner with whom she could share her so-called "declining years."

During the winter of 1958-59 at Gridley we'd read about very low-priced farms that could be purchased in the Ozark country of northwest Arkansas. We had corresponded with an Illinois couple, Gene and Corinne Kreves, who were interested in buying land in the Ozarks, and also with a family who had "homesteaded" in northern New Mexico. During the summer of 1959 we made a family trip back to Wisconsin to visit my mother, and her new husband, Paul. We also made plans to swing south to visit the Kreves, then to look over the cheap farms in the Ozarks, and, lastly, visit the Grant family in New Mexico on our way back to California.

Headed back to Gridley, we stopped to meet the Kreves, at their home in a Chicago suburb. They were pleasant and friendly, but we felt no real bonding of plans or personalities. Swinging south, we spent a couple of days looking around the Ozarks and checking out farms for sale. Low prices of farms was very much a reality, however neither Carol nor I felt that it was an area in which we wanted to live . . . cheap land notwithstanding.

Our visit to New Mexico was quite a different story. Bob and Carolyn Grant seemed very much like "our kind of people". A year or two before, they had moved to the tiny village of El Rito in the mountains of northern New Mexico, about 50 miles north of the state capital of Santa Fe. They were not interested in communal living, but were convivial and friendly and indicated that they would very much enjoy another congenial "Anglo" family in this little Spanish-American village.

Let me set the scene presented by "The Land of Enchantment," to use the somewhat contradictory motto that the state of New Mexico has taken to itself. The LAND **is** enchanting, but conditions of life there can be crude, squalid and even a bit grim. Poverty is rife in northern New Mexico. We were to experience both positive and negative aspects first hand but, overall, my feelings still tilt very positively toward "The Land of Enchantment."

People of Spanish origin or descent had explored and settled the area that is now New Mexico and their descendants, even today, make up the majority of the population in the mountainous northern part of the state. As far as these present majority residents are concerned they are not and never have been "Mexican." They think of themselves as "Spanish-American", and to refer to them as "Mexican" is regarded as an insult. The population of the little settlement of El Rito, where the Grants lived, was 99% Spanish-American. Many spoke little or no English. Non-Spanish-speaking Americans were, and are, referred to as "Anglos." In 1959 there were probably no more than 25 or 30 "Anglos" in this little community of perhaps 700 people.

Carol and I both liked the Grants, and fell in love with the scenery and "laid back" life-style of the northern New Mexico area. We visited the Grants for two or three days and then drove back to Gridley after telling them that we were interested in a possible move to El Rito. After returning to California we continued our correspondence and Bob sent us several typewritten pages containing detailed information about climate, living conditions, crops, housing, employment opportunities and just about anything that might be of interest to someone considering a move to the area.

We told Marvin of our interest in leaving Gridley. He was not too surprised. Then, not long after our return, Bob wrote mentioning a house for rent in El Rito at a very low rate. That was enough to push us "over the edge" and into making somewhat of a snap decision to leave Gridley and start a "new life" [more or less] in New Mexico. We sold our little mobile home, which provided a small financial "nest-egg," bought a small second-hand trailer we could tow, loaded it and our pick-up truck with belongings and children and in September, 1959, headed for a new life in "The Land of Enchantment" as the alluring state motto of New Mexico promised.

The physical layout of El Rito involved being at the end of a paved road at about 6,800 feet above sea level. Unpaved roads branched off from there in three directions:

north, up the canyon of El Rito, the "Little River," south to loop back to the paved road, and east over a low mountain range to another valley and stream near a little settlement called La Madera. The house Bob had told us about was up the canyon alongside El Rito, perhaps a half-mile from the town "center" where the pavement ended. In fact the house was on the very edge of town and on the far side of the stream and could be reached only on foot over a narrow foot-bridge.

The house and lot belonged to an artist acquaintance of Bob, named Tom Dryce. Tom had been building a home for himself and his wife, but she had suddenly left him and Tom intended to move to Santa Fe, instead of living alone in the only partially completed house he'd been building for his "dearly departed" wife. He would rent us the unfinished house for $20 per month!

Tom and his wife were each owners of <u>enormous</u> Siamese cats! She took her female cat when she left. Now, Tom decided that he didn't want to take his cat, a huge tomcat named Simon, to an apartment in Santa Fe. He offered to drop the rent by $3 per month if we would keep and feed Simon, whose diet, he explained, had to be fish, not commercial cat food. We agreed. We bought frozen fish for Simon once, and then he went on a diet of packaged cat food, and never once complained! Several months later Simon got severely mauled by some wild creature. Not knowing what else to do, we took him to the animal shelter in Santa Fe, and left him there. We wrote to Tom telling him of Simon's whereabouts, but never heard further about the matter from either Tom or Simon.

The house, unlike most homes in El Rito which were constructed of adobe bricks, was a large frame structure shaped something like _/ with the "open" side facing southwest where it would catch the afternoon sun. Most of the walls had no interior paneling with exposed insulation between the wall studs, and the floors were <u>dirt</u>. Not hard packed adobe which were the most common floors in El Rito homes and were almost as hard, smooth and durable as concrete. The floors in Tom's house, except for a wood floor in the kitchen, were still just semi-packed ordinary DIRT. We were beginning to understand why Tom's wife had left him.

The two wings of the house were pretty much unfinished. The one on the right was intended to be an art studio and could be shut off by a door. We hardly used it. The left-hand wing, as seen in the diagram, served as a bedroom and contained our box-spring and mattress bed, plus a small bed I'd made for Taavi after Talitha was born, and Talitha's crib, inherited from her brother. The central section of the house was a combined kitchen on the right and living room on the left in the diagram, although there was no structural division between them. An outside front door opened from the living room and a back door from the kitchen.

In the living room, near the front door was an Ashley stove. Ashley stoves were wood burning stoves, opening from the top and equipped with a control damper mechanism. They were far superior to more conventional wood burning stoves. You could add wood before going to bed, turn down the damper, and the fire would smolder all though the night giving off some heat. In the morning the damper could be opened and the remaining wood would re-ignite. You didn't have to get out of bed in the morning to a cold stove and cold room and build a new fire from scratch. The Ashley stove was a godsend as the winters at an elevation of 6,800 feet were both LONG and COLD!

The kitchen was equipped with a modern cookstove that could be hooked up to bottled gas, or used as a wood burning stove. We couldn't afford gas, so we used wood. Outside the back door was a hand pump which supplied both our drinking water and wash water. The water from the pump contained a quantity of rust particles, and Tom explained the purpose of a large basin or kettle that rested on a stool just inside the back door. If you filled the kettle with water from the pump, the rust would settle to the bottom after an hour or so, and you could skim off the clear water for drinking or cooking!

In hindsight, it all sounds rather complicated, but actually everything worked out quite well. Yes, it WAS cold during that winter, but we wore layers of clothes when necessary and got along quite well. I don't remember any colds or illness affecting any of us during the winter. Taavi did lose his balance and fell off the picnic-style kitchen table once and reaching out, attempting to break his fall, put his hand on the hot Ashley stove and suffered a rather severe burn to the palm of his hand, which necessitated a trip to a doctor in the nearest city, Espanola, some 32 miles away. Taavi recovered quickly and there were no lasting after-effects.

In the front wall of the living-room section of the house Tom had installed a picture window of sorts. It was composed of multiple rectangular panes of glass, rather than one large pane, but stretched from floor to ceiling. Catching the low winter sun from the southwest, it made for a pleasant warm area in which to sit and read. It also gave me a sudden idea!

As I mentioned, our floors were just dirt. On more than one occasion we found Taavi and Talitha sitting in the middle of our living room floor digging in the dirt with spoons! That gave me the idea and as the weather warmed I loosened the soil of the floor inside the big window and planted lettuce and radishes! They came up and we had a good laugh over eating fresh vegetables grown in our living-room floor in mid-winter. Here's the "garden" window from the outside with Carol, Taavi, Talitha and Chipeta.

There was a U.S. Forest Service station in El Rito, but the employees kept pretty much to themselves. I don't remember meeting any of them in the three years we spent there! The postmaster, John Goddard, was a survivor of the World War II Bataan "Death march". The owner of the larger of the two "General Stores" [that also sold gas and oil] was Tom Martin. Both John and Tom were bilingual Anglos and had families.

We had frequent contact with Tom and John during our years there but only had passing contact with their families.

At one point Tom hired me to put in a flagstone patio behind his house. He'd purchased the flagstone and I leveled the soil, fitted and laid the stones, filling in the gaps with cement. The photo shows Main Street in El Rito, Martin's store, in the distance, has the white false front. The Coffee House described on the next page, would be to the lower left, just out of this picture.

An elderly Anglo couple lived near the Grants on the dead-end side street located between the Coffee House and the little El Llano store just beyond it. The white-bearded old patriarch, named Foster Jewell, was a wood carver whose avocation was a full time job. He excelled at this work and we found the couple to be friendly and interesting to visit with. Since neither Carol nor I spoke Spanish, our contacts with other El Rito residents was limited. No one was unfriendly, but we were always virtual "strangers."

Bob and Carolyn had three young children. Both parents were artistically inclined, Carolyn as a painter and potter, Bob as a writer and painter. They were renting a house set back from the paved main street. The house belonged to a man named Peter Van Dresser and in front of it, right on the community's "main street" was another building, seen here, formerly a small barn, that Peter had converted into a cozy little restaurant, with a sign out front reading "COFFEE HOUSE". This is looking down the street in the opposite direction from the last photo.

Peter had worked at designing and building cabins for yachts and other small boats, and he was an artist at carpentry work within small, cramped spaces. The Coffee House was fully furnished and quaintly attractively, but was sitting empty and unused. The building beyond the Coffee House is Garcia's little EL Llano general store. The Grant's home is just out of sight to the right, set back a bit from the street.

It's a fitting time to interrupt my story and introduce readers to this interesting man, Peter Van Dresser. At this time Peter and his wife, Florence, were living in Santa Fe. [Florence, incidentally, was a sister of Jeff Corey, a highly respected Hollywood character actor of that era.] Peter had become single-mindedly consumed with the possibilities of solar power, which at that time was in its infancy in the U.S.

Peter had purchased two pieces of land in and near El Rito. One was the property I've just described. The other was a property, called "The Potrero," in a small, isolated, side canyon off El Rito Canyon a mile or two north of town. There he had built a large home with out-buildings. The attractive stone and frame home was designed to be powered and heated by solar energy, but, sadly, it had failed and the whole complex now stood empty and abandoned. Peter had taken a step back, moved to Santa Fe and was then working on converting to solar power a small two-room adobe building he had purchased there.

Peter had rented his home in El Rito to Bob and Carolyn Grant, generously allowing Bob the use of his large war-surplus truck, a jeep pick-up truck [with 4-wheel drive], a chainsaw and other belongings. Peter was also looking, until now unsuccessfully, for someone who would open and operate the trim, tidy little Coffee House. Bob mentioned this to us.

I'm not sure if Carol and I were naïve, stupid, foolish, overly optimistic, or a combination of all those things, but we had moved ourselves with two small children [and a dog] to this small, isolated, economically depressed little community that embodied a quite different culture from anything we were familiar with, without a place to live or a job offer or income source of any kind! Through good fortune and the perspicacity of Bob Grant, we'd stumbled into a solution of the housing question. That solved one problem, but what could we do to generate enough income to sustain ourselves?

Peter was so anxious to have his little Coffee Shop open for business that he would not even charge us rent for the use of the facility if we would undertake to open and operate it! So, with no other source of income in sight, we elected to give it a try. Carolyn volunteered to look after Taavi and Talitha along with her own kids while we were tending to the Coffee House. Bob had a small printing press [also belonging to Peter!], and Carol and I wrote and printed a menu, consisting of things we thought we could both afford to make and, perhaps, sell. A cup of coffee we priced at 5 cents, a hamburger at 30 cents, a bowl of soup [canned!] was 15 cents, *et cetera*.

We had no inventory to speak of, but purchased a few things that we thought we might be able to use, and *voila*, we were open for business! The photo shows the inside with Carolyn Grant [holding baby Paul] and Carol [with Taavi on her lap] by the wall, and Bob Grant at the counter flanked by his daughter Beata and son Theo with Talitha on the far right.

"Business", however, was slower than slow. We couldn't keep an extensive inventory of edibles on hand, so on the few occasions, when someone came in and asked for something that we didn't have [most anything not in a can!] I would duck out the back door, run across the side street to Garcia's El Llano Store and buy what we needed, then run back to let Carol do the preparation and serving. Actually, we sold mostly coffee, and because of that raised the price to a dime after a few weeks!

We did have one "specialty" rush! Bob knew the owner of an apple orchard in Velarde, about 40 miles away who told Bob that we could pick a few bushels of apples FREE! So we and the Grants each obtained several bushels of free apples. Carol promptly began making fresh, home-made apple pies which we sold for 15 cents per slice. Even that resulted in few sales, until two big strapping black loggers rented rooms across the street. They knew what a Coffee House was and became our best customers for the few weeks they were in town. They loved Carol's apple pies and would come in every day, and buy a whole pie for $1.00. Unfortunately, after a few weeks they moved on to another job, and our business plummeted back to previous levels.

CHAPTER 20

Miracle on Main St.

As winter tightened its grip, and fine fall days disappeared, so did our few customers. Our tiny cash reserve was rapidly disappearing as well. Christmas 1959 would soon be upon us and the outlook was bleak. Let me set the scene for the "miracle" that bailed us out: It was a cold, blustery day, with flurries of snow. We'd had no customers all day and as the afternoon crawled by, I checked our cash on hand. We had no cash register, but kept what money we had in an empty coffee can behind the counter. It's difficult to get a sinking feeling when you're already depressed, but I remember the feeling I had as I counted our remaining cash. We had precisely $1.72.

[Disclosure: For its dramatic effect I like to tell that story: That we were, literally, down to our last $1.72! It wasn't exactly true. Soon after our arrival in El Rito, I'd taken $100 from our funds and hidden it away. Not even Carol knew of this. It was my "emergency" reserve in case we found ourselves in totally desperate straits. So, we did have a thin "cushion" against "starvation." I was just then at the very cusp of realizing that we might have arrived at that desperate time—when the "miracle on Main Street" occurred.]

It was just about two weeks before Christmas. It was cold, snowing harder with little chance of any customers dropping in as darkness was rapidly approaching. I put the lid back in our coffee can "bank" and said to Carol, "We might as well close early, get the kids from Carolyn and go home." Carol quickly agreed, but at that instant the Coffee House door opened, and in out of the snow and gloom stepped three wise me . . . uh . . . three figures. A male voice intoned, "We were driving by and saw your light. Can we get some hot coffee?" That was the one thing we COULD offer, so I quickly told them, "Sure!", and Carol served up 3 cups of coffee. A conversation ensued as they warmed themselves with coffee sitting around the store's little Ashley stove, and soon fortified themselves with refills.

Our visitors were an older, white-haired man and woman and a younger woman. Their name was Atterberry, and they were from San Diego, California, driving a rental car. The wife was an MD and the husband was an avocado grower. They were obviously not poor! The younger woman was their 30-something bachelor daughter. This woman [I've repressed her name] wanted, more than anything else in life it seemed, to be a cowboy! So the doting parents had just purchased for her a 640 acre ranch near La Madera in the next valley east of El Rito! They'd taken an alternate route on their way back to civilization, and found themselves seeing a light and a sign that read Coffee House, so had "knocked on our door," so to speak.

As we conversed, they mentioned that they had to fly back to San Diego the next evening. The daughter would be moving onto her new ranch in the spring. Mr. Atterberry mentioned that he hated to leave the ranch unattended until then and wished that he could have found someone to act as "caretaker" in the meantime. Ideally, a person who might stay on as a hired hand.

As he said those words, I looked at Carol and Carol looked at me. Then I looked at Mr. Atterberry, cleared my throat and said, "I might be interested in something like that." "Really?" he said, "Have you had experience in ranching?" "Well," I said, "I've worked on farms for several years in northern California." There followed a discussion of my work at TCF. "We've got to be on our way, but I'll make you an offer," Mr. Atterberry said. "I'll pay you $200 a month to look after the ranch until our daughter gets settled in. If all is well you can stay on after that. There are two houses on the property, you can move into the old house and stay there rent free. How does that sound to you?" Hardly believing what was happening, I said, "That sounds just fine to me."

"I know you won't be able to move over there until spring, but I'd appreciate it if you could go over there occasionally, just to keep an eye on things, until you can move in," said Santa Cla . . . uh. . . I mean, Mr. A. "That will be no problem," I said. Mr. Atterberry pulled out his check book, saying "First month's pay in advance," and wrote out a check to me for $200. I was still staring dazedly at the check, when I heard Carol call "Goodbye." The "three kings" having delivered their wondrous gift, had disappeared into the snowy night.

Carol and I sat there in a kind of stunned silence, for several minutes. Then we closed up the Coffee House [for the last time!], picked up the kids and went home. The next day, I told Bob about our "windfall," then Carol and I drove to Espanola, the nearest city, to cash the check. That $200 in cash was the most money I'd ever seen at one time in my entire life! We felt like we were rich. And in a way, we were.

The checks kept coming every month in the mail. Carol and I drove over to check out the ranch nearly every week. Only about 12 miles from El Rito and our friends Bob and Carolyn, it was a lovely place. Land on both sides of a paved highway with a perennial stream flowing alongside. Two houses, one a modern home where Miss Atterberry would live when she arrived, and the original ranch building, a two-story adobe home, that we would soon occupy. There were wood-burning stoves for both cooking and heat, and cold water piped into the kitchen sink from a nearby spring. Best of all there were several hot springs on the property!! To us, it seemed like paradise. In early March we moved in, making two trips with our loaded pickup truck and small trailer.

Unfortunately, it wouldn't last. Everything was, I thought, going well. I had the irrigation system working and pastures under irrigation, and had plowed and planted two fields of corn, when Miss Atterberry arrived with her "herd" of 6 head of cattle and several horses and moved into the main house. Within a couple weeks she'd gotten acquainted with the former ranch foreman that her father had fired when he purchased the ranch. This man wanted his old job back and began badmouthing me to Miss Atterberry. Under his prodding, she was critical of everything I did. One day, I was irrigating some pasture land, and she came by and began ragging me about something I'd done or hadn't done. It was the last straw for me. I'd had enough. I handed her the shovel and said, "I quit!" And I did.

When he heard about it, Mr. Atterberry came all the way out from San Diego and tried to persuade me to change my mind. But I knew he'd be heading back to California in a day or two, and I'd had all I could take of that shrewish harridan of a daughter. I got along fine with old Mr. Atterberry, but the daughter and I just could not make peace with each other. Still, I might have changed my mind had it not been for a piece of news I'd recently received from Bob Grant.

INTERLUDE

"Father" in More Ways Than One?

One doesn't have to spend much time in north-central New Mexico to realize how prevalent is the surname Martinez. It almost seems like out of every 3 or 4 people you meet, there will be at least one named Martinez. Bob Grant explained this phenomenon to us, with the comment that the prevalence of the name was due to the presence in the area over many years of a charismatic Catholic priest, Father Martinez. Bob's comment was, "Padre Martinez was a Father to his parishioners in more ways than one."

I've tried, since then, to explore the matter more deeply, but facts are not easy to come by. There <u>was</u> an influential and popular priest, born Don Antonio Jose Martinez [1793-1867] who had been a prominent citizen of the community of Taos and in all of north-central New Mexico. He also achieved some notoriety, being excommunicated from the Catholic Church in 1858. During his lifetime, he entered several "marriages" and probably fathered a not insignificant number of children from other liaisons as well. Many of whom he acknowledged as his offspring. If these children, in turn, produced offspring in quantity, which is not unlikely, it would, perhaps, explain the phenomenon. Martinez <u>is</u> an unusually common surname in north-central New Mexico.

Most of the details of Padre Martinez' life are obscure and learning all the facts surrounding his life is difficult and would require more time or inclination than I'm ready to invest here. He played a prominent role in the history of the part of New Mexico in which we found ourselves, and to a lesser extent, beyond. He appears in Willa Cather's well known novel, "Death Comes to the Archbishop" although not the title role. In our brief three year residence we certainly came in contact with a great many persons who bore the surname Martinez.

CHAPTER 21

"Oh, Give Me a Home...
and a Job"

Just a week or two before my abrupt blowup at the Atterberry ranch, Bob Grant had come by for a visit and mentioned that he'd heard about a fine house for sale in El Rito. The price and terms were almost unbelievable and the house, on the unpaved Placitas road, about ½ mile south of "downtown" El Rito, was on an acre of land with a fine mature orchard. I think I must have had this in my mind when I made the snap decision to quit the La Madera job.

I had immediately asked Bob to take us to see the place and meet the elderly owner, Jose Martinez. It was a lovely place. On the acre of fenced land was a six room, one story adobe house, painted a bright yellow.

There was a large, somewhat dilapidated, barn/garage, an out-house, a big garden area, and an irrigation ditch flowing across the back of the property with a gas driven pump to get water to the garden and to the most notable feature of the property, the orchard, which covered half or more of the acre.

The majority of trees were apple trees, but there were also a few peaches, pears and plum trees. We fell in love with it at first sight. The picture shows part of the orchard, with the apple trees in bloom. Taken in 1962 the photo shows me with baby Kemet and Chipeta.

The house had six rooms, of which two at the end of the house nearest the road, were separate from the others with no inside door between. As it turned out, Jose would like to live in those two front rooms until his daughter and son-in-law who lived a short distance down the road, could finish the required remodeling of their home in order for Jose to move in with them. We were happy to oblige.

Our living space would consist of a living room and a kitchen with a wood-burning cook stove and a sink with cold water supplied from a well with an electric pump just outside. Down a couple of steps from the kitchen were two side-by-side rooms which would serve as bedrooms. One bedroom for Carol and I and the other would be a children's bedroom.

Sort of like this: **J J = Jose's 2 rms. L = Living rm. K = kitchen OB = our bedroom; CB = children's bedroom.** [graphics not to scale!]

				OB
J	J	L	K	CB

We would soon add a third child. This photo of the house looking toward the road, with me, Taavi, Kemet and Talitha was taken [obviously!] after Kemet was born in 1961. A porch extended all along the south and west sides of the house and the outside doors opened from the porch.

Jose was asking $1,500 dollars for the property, which we could hardly believe. He wanted $500 down, and two other payments of the same amount at 6 month intervals. We jumped at this opportunity. We had the $500 down, from what I'd earned from the Atterberrys, but I would have to find another job to pay off the balance, which didn't seem to be an unmanageable problem. We closed the deal, paid Jose $500 and moved in our belongings the beginning of June of 1960. So far, so good!

I can't resist adding another picture of our El Rito home taken shortly after we moved in. Talitha and Taavi are shown here in a view looking toward the road and the narrow "pedestrian" gate.

We owned our first real home and had moved in, but now came the most difficult part. I had to find a job. There were no jobs available in El Rito, at least none for which I had the requisite talent, skill or ambition.

Once again, Peter Van Dresser would supply a temporary and partial answer. He offered to give me part-time work helping him in his attempt to convert his small "Casita" in Santa Fe to solar power. We worked out an arrangement that I would drive to Santa Fe each week and work with Peter for 3 days, then return to El Rito. In the meantime I would look for a fulltime job.

With no hope of finding such work in El Rito, my only option was to check out Espanola, a smallish city 30 miles south of El Rito and about 20 miles north of Santa Fe. Small as it was, it was the largest community, population-wise, in our county of Rio Arriba. As such, it promised more employment resources than any other community within reasonable driving distance.

I had, however, not the faintest idea where to begin my job search. I felt up against the proverbial stone wall, but on the first day I discovered the obvious answer. Walking along Main Street I saw a sign that identified the New Mexico State Employment Office! I metaphorically kicked myself! Why hadn't I thought of that before?

I went into the rather bare, apparently uninhabited, office. Then a youngish Pueblo Indian girl, perhaps in her early 20s emerged from a back room and asked if she could be of help. I said that I was looking for a job! [Duh!] She asked a few general questions, and then came the crucial one. "Do you have a High School diploma?" she asked. I assured her that I did, and then added almost as an afterthought, "I also have a college degree." The girl's eyes grew as big as saucers, as she managed an astonished, "Oh."

Suddenly, I realized that I was probably the first job-seeker that she'd ever encountered that had more than a high school education. Without another word, she picked up a kind of clipboard with a thick pile of employment notices, blew the accumulated dust off the top sheet and began thumbing through them. After a minute or so, she looked up from one of the notices and asked, "Would you be interested in a job as a social worker?" I could hardly believe my ears! Thoughts of Prof. Cornell urging me to consider going into social work, and all the sociology courses that I had taken in college flashed through my mind. Then "reality" set in.

"Yes," I replied, "but becoming a social worker requires a Master's Degree." She looked again at the job notice, frowned and said, "Not according to this," and showed me the sentence indicating that beginning social work positions with the New Mexico Department of Public Welfare required a Bachelor's Degree. Slowly it dawned on me that in more heavily populated and more prosperous areas, a Master's Degree might be required. But this was backward, impoverished northern New Mexico! A Bachelor's Degree was gold!

I said that social work seemed like a perfect fit for me, and asked where I could go to apply? She directed me to the Rio Arriba County Welfare Department office only a few blocks away, and instructed me to go there and ask for [you guessed it!] Mr. Martinez, the County Director. New Mexico, the young lady explained, had a State Welfare Department with subordinate County Offices, but each county had authority to hire their own staff.

Happy as a clam, I proceeded to an interview with County Director, Eddie Martinez. It was a cordial and professional type of interview. When it was over, Mr. Martinez said that he thought I'd make a good social worker, and that he was expecting a staff vacancy the following month. Since I had no telephone, I should check back with him at the beginning of the next month. I was driving on "cloud 9" as I returned home with that encouraging news.

To my great disappointment when I returned as instructed, it was to be told that the vacancy had already been filled. Another vacancy was imminent, however, so come back next month, Mr. Martinez told me, and I should be able to be taken on then. Unbelievably, to me, this exact same scenario occurred again, the following month. I was both baffled and discouraged.

My disappointment was exacerbated by the news that Carol had given me at about the time this whole charade had begun. I'm sure you can guess what that information was. Carol was pregnant again! Bob and Carolyn urged Carol go to a Dr. Pijuan in Espanola to see her through the pregnancy as he was, in their opinion, by far the best doctor in the area. So we followed their advice, which turned out to be one of the best decisions either of us ever made.

We didn't know it at the time, but Dr. Pijuan was very well known and highly respected, not just by medical professionals, but by lawyers, teachers, politicians . . . just about anyone who knew him. He agreed to take Carol as a patient and she had gone ahead and provided him with the lowdown on our family situation, including the financial picture.

On one of her early visits Dr. Pijuan inquired how my job hunting was going? Carol explained about my quest for a job at the Welfare Department, and how I'd repeatedly been getting the "runaround" being led to expect a job only to have it go to someone else. Without a word, Dr. Pijuan tore off a sheet from his prescription pad, scribbled a message on it, put it in an envelope and gave it to Carol with the words, "Tell your husband to go to the State Welfare Office in Santa Fe and give this to the State Director." We had no idea what was in the message—but we would find out!

I was planning a trip to Santa Fe the next day, as part of my work with Peter on the Casita. With such an important meeting, with such an important person in the offing, I thought I should wear something a little more "dressy" than my usual jeans and T-shirt. My only other clothes were one pair of grey slacks and a maroon corduroy sports jacket that had belonged to my dad, plus a couple "button-down-the-front" shirts. So I took them along. I had no necktie, but hardly anyone in northern New Mexico wore a tie, so I figured I'd be OK.

Two mornings later I prepared for my "interview" with the State Director of Public Welfare! As I dressed, I discovered that my dad's slacks were too big for me around the waist **. . . .** and I'd forgotten to pack a belt! In desperation I found a length of clothesline rope at the Casita, threaded it through the belt loops, tied it in a knot and buttoned up my maroon corduroy jacket to conceal the "evidence."

I found my way to the State Director's Office downtown in the State Office Building near the Capitol. I had no appointment, so after a moment's hesitation I knocked on the closed door. I heard a voice say, "Come in", so I entered. It was a huge room. In the center near the back wall was the largest desk I'd ever seen, and behind it sat a little man.

With some trepidation, I approached the desk and the little man. I didn't know what else to do so I held out Dr. Pijuan's envelope and said, "Dr. Pijuan, in Espanola, asked me to give you this." The little man read the note, then looked up and said, "Go out and down the hall to your right. You'll see a sign that says, 'Department of Child Welfare.' Go in and ask for Miss Young." That was all. The only choice I had was to follow instructions, so I did, even though it all seemed very mysterious. After traversing the long hallway, I entered the open door beneath the sign.

A rather tall lady of perhaps 40 or 45 greeted me. "I'm Hazel Young," she said, "Come in." Over the next half hour all was made clear to me! Miss Young explained that she and the State Director had each been briefed by phone calls from Dr. Pijuan and were expecting me! Proceeding to evaporate the clouds of mystery, she gave me the story in a nutshell.

The New Mexico Department of Social Welfare had two major divisions, Public Assistance and Child Welfare Services [CWS]. Employment in the Public Assistance Division was within the realm of County Directors. Eddie Martinez, Miss Young explained, had his personal quota system for his staff. He would not employ more than two Anglo Social Workers on his staff at a given time. He was simply hiring Spanish-American applicants to replace Spanish-American employees. I had been both discriminated against and lied to, by Eddie Martinez, but there was not much that could be done about it.

Well, actually, there was, and it had already been done! At her most recent visit to Dr. Pijuan, he had asked Carol if that husband of hers had finally gotten a job, and Carol told him about my experiences with Mr. Martinez. The good doctor grasped immediately what was going on. He knew something else as well. Staffing for Child Welfare Services was under the jurisdiction of the State, not the County! Miss Young, as the director of Child Welfare Services, had the hiring authority for personnel in that department.

After a brief interview about my academic background, Miss Young informed me that there were two Child Welfare Services positions allotted to the Espanola office and there was currently a vacancy. Miss Young, who was an Anglo, did not have a quota system. Did I want the job, she wondered?

That was probably the easiest question I've ever been asked. "Yes. I want it!" I said. "You've got it," said Miss Young. It was with the greatest feelings of relief I think I've ever experienced, that I left. Once again I found myself on "Cloud 9", but this was not an insubstantial ephemera, but a down-to-earth reality! I not only had a job—it would be the best paying job I'd ever had or even dreamed about, and a job I felt eminently suited for—and not once had my tightly buttoned sports jacket revealed the length of clothesline rope that was holding up both my trousers, and my dignity!

CHAPTER 22

Hi-ho, Hi-ho,
It's Off to Work I Go

For the first time in four years of married life, Carol and I would enjoy a period of smooth sailing with only—if I may mix my metaphors—a few minor bumps in the road ahead. It was, I must admit, a relief to have a steady job and an adequate income. For the most part I found that being a social worker was satisfying, and interesting. Best of all, the knowledge that financial worries were behind was an immense relief. Especially, with another family mouth to feed!

Our second son was born May 28, 1961. The usual search for a name had been going on for some time. Then one day as I was reading a book of mine called "*An Encyclopedia of World History*" [I was a glutton for light reading!] I came across the name Kemet. Carol and I both liked the sound of it and decided to bestow it on our innocent babe. If you must know, Kemet was the ancient name for Egypt's Nile valley which translated as "the dark land." [Look it up if you doubt my word. Top of page 21.] But our new son could have cared less. I don't remember why we picked Reid as a middle name, except that we liked the sound of it and it fit a pattern of a middle name that was one syllable shorter than the first name, which we thought gave the full names a pleasing lilt when spoken.

The hospital nearest El Rito was in Espanola, a 30 mile drive, and that's where Kemet was born. Dr. Pijuan was out of town when Kemet decided to enter this world, so Carol was attended by a doctor, whose name I've repressed. He annoyed me, because he refused to believe that Carol was ready to deliver almost immediately after we arrived. As a result, he was late making his appearance in the delivery room, and Carol had actually given birth before the doctor got there. *No problemo*, and no harm done, but his casual attitude annoyed both Carol and I!

That 30 mile commute between El Rito and Espanola was the only real drawback as far as my new job was concerned. The staff in the Espanola office was friendly, and

I even got along with Eddie Martinez, perhaps because I had virtually no contact with him. My immediate supervisor, Miss Mary Tenney, came by about once every two weeks. She was a very pleasant lady and we got along exceptionally well. I soon learned that Miss Tenney and Miss Young were long time conjugal partners. I liked them both, and they both treated me with friendly professionalism.

The "Welfare Office," as it was usually referred to, consisted of the two divisions, one of which dealt solely with financial assistance and was by far the largest, with probably a dozen "case workers." The major programs of this division were Old Age Assistance [OAA] and Aid to Families with Dependent Children [AFDC]. [When the public speaks negatively about "welfare", their criticisms are almost always aimed at the latter program.] They were supervised by Eddie Martinez.

There were just two of us Child Welfare caseworkers, and our primary job was to conduct studies and approve [or disapprove] of families who applied for or had been recruited [another of our tasks] to become foster parents, and to place children in need of foster care with an appropriate foster family. The other Child Welfare caseworker was a Spanish-American lady named Emma Writtenberry who was married to an Anglo. Emma and I got along splendidly, and each of us supervised a group of 12 or 15 foster home placements.

We also worked with the parents, or parent, of children we deemed to be in need of foster care services. The children we placed in foster homes might be neglected, abused or abandoned. Occasionally, children were placed in foster care at the request of police or courts when a child was considered to be in need of foster care due to abuse or danger of abuse. One of our goals was to work with the natural family, if such existed, towards a return to them of the children in foster care. The two of us in the Espanola office were supervised by Mary Tenney who worked out of the State Office in Santa Fe, and stopped by to see Emma and I on a weekly basis.

Another category of our clientele consisted of unmarried mothers. If an unmarried mother planned to give up her baby for adoption, the child would first be placed in a foster home until a social work specialist [one with a Master's degree!] located a suitable adoptive family. Foster care was always expected to be temporary, while adoption was intended to be permanent. Most of the time the placements that I supervised were fairly routine, but occasionally a situation could present a more complicated problem.

One early case involved a 17 year old girl I'll call Mary, just beginning her senior year in High School. She was a very pretty girl, something of a "teacher's pet" and an honor student who had gotten pregnant and had given birth just before the beginning of the school year. An orphan, she lived with an elderly grandmother, and had immediately made it clear that she wanted to keep her newborn child.

Several of her teachers and the school Counselor, were adamant that Mary should put the child up for adoption, so that she, a "straight A" student, could stay in school and complete her final year of High School. They finally got Mary's grandmother to agree and the baby had been placed in a foster home. That's when I entered the picture, being totally unaware of the preceding facts. The reason for my being called in was that a disappointed, frustrated and very angry Mary had expressed her frustration by getting pregnant again! She <u>wanted</u> a baby!

There was no point in going through the same old tug-of-war. The well-meaning but misguided school personnel, perhaps realizing their previous error, and confronted with Mary's determination to retain custody of her baby, seemed willing to let me attempt to deal with the situation. With Miss Tenny's approval, I arranged for Mary's first baby to be returned to her custody, with the understanding that Grandma would act as baby sitter and that Mary would return to school and complete her final year of High School, her pregnancy notwithstanding. The frustrated school personnel seemed to at last give up their attempt to exercise control over a very willful and determined teenager. Mary <u>did</u> go on to graduate.

Lesson learned. Never try to pressure people to act against their own wishes. You can try to persuade and even argue, but in the final analysis, they need to make choices that they will be happy with. I hope Mary was happy with her decisions. She had considerable potential.

There was a large boarding school on the outskirts of El Rito. An uncle of Bob Grant had once been the principal there. Among the High School age students were five or six teenage girls who were under the care of Child Welfare Services. Since I lived in El Rito, they were assigned to my caseload. I also had an older boy in my care. Rosendo Moya was about 16 and refused to stay with his elderly surviving parent, his father, any longer. At the same time he adamantly refused to go to a foster home.

I didn't really know what to do with him, as he was pretty much existing on the streets of Espanola. He was a likeable and resourceful teenager. Then, suddenly, his father died and the city somehow found a way to condemn and tear down the ramshackle little building he had called home. As a result and as the only heir, Rosendo found himself eligible for monthly payments from the city which had destroyed the only property the father owned. I was able to persuade the court to allocate part of the money to Rosendo as a monthly stipend, and to set up a bank account for him for the surplus. I also found an Aunt who agreed to keep in touch with him without trying to control him. A very un-orthodox arrangement, but one that worked out reasonably well, for a surprisingly resourceful teenager.

For the most part I enjoyed the work that I was doing. I had just one scary moment when I was asked to transport "Bobby" to the State Mental Hospital in Las Vegas, New Mexico, about a 90 mile drive from Espanola. Bobby, in foster care, was 18, a husky six-footer, borderline mentally retarded, and reputed to have occasional outbursts of violence. His Foster parents felt they could no longer handle him and finally a court ordered him to be placed in the Mental Institution. Bobby had not been a part of my caseload, but his regular worker was a lady who was currently on a medical leave of absence. As the only male caseworker then available I was asked to undertake the task.

Bobby and I had never met and we were both rather suspicious of each other. Bobby knew where we were going and had repeatedly expressed his fear and dislike of being taken to a mental institution. I tried to show Bobby concern and understanding and it seemed to take some of the "edge" off his feelings and demeanor. But as we neared our destination he lapsed into a sullen silence. Then, just as we were approaching the Hospital, Bobby reached into his pocket and pulled out a large jack-knife. My heart almost stopped, but Bobby just handed the knife to me, saying, "I think you'd better take this." He walked with me to the admissions desk and we said "goodbye."

I told Bobby that I hoped his stay at the hospital would be short and wished him "good luck." Then I handed the knife to a hospital attendant, told him it was Bobby's and asked him to return it when he thought it was safe to do so. This was shortly before I left my job so I never knew what happened to Bobby. I've often wondered.

I'll mention just one other rather unusual experience I had as a Child Welfare Worker in the backwater of Rio Arriba county of New Mexico. One morning at work in Espanola, a call came from the State Police asking for someone to pick up three small children and transport them to a foster home. I happened to be the person available. The children, it developed, had been living with their father in Tierra Amarilla, the tiny County Seat, up near the Colorado border about 70 miles north of Espanola. The mother was not in the picture at all, and the father had just been arrested and thrown in jail. He was probably going to be transferred to the State Penitentiary and there was nowhere for the children to go. I was to drive to Tierra Amarilla, pick up the three children, bring them back to Espanola and find a foster home that would take them in.

It was around noon by the time I got to the small community of Tierra Amarilla. I saw the father in the jail and explained that I would be taking the children to Espanola, place them in a foster home where they would be safe and well-cared for. He'd been given a two year sentence, and accepted the plan when I explained that the kids, two boys and a girl, ages 6, 4 and 3, could be returned to him after his release. The children were brought to the jail to say goodbye to their father and told that they were to go with this total stranger. Me.

The children were, quite understandably, confused, and scared. No, actually they were VERY confused and VERY scared! Not knowing where they were being taken, and only that they were being taken away from their father by a total stranger, they all began crying. No, they began bawling! They wouldn't get in my station wagon, and as I tried to help them inside the bawling turned to screaming. I tried to comfort them and ease their fears. So did the father. So did the neighbor woman with whom they'd been staying that morning. So did the sheriff and his deputy.

Nothing helped. The screaming and fright only seemed to intensify. Finally, I got in my station wagon and started the engine. The others picked the kids up, screaming and kicking, and deposited them on the back seat, quickly shutting the door . . . and off we went. After about 20 miles down the road, the crying and screaming began to abate and finally stopped. They were, in fact, too exhausted to continue their protests and soon fell asleep.

I'd headed back toward Espanola, but by then it was late in the afternoon. I realized that by the time we reached Espanola it would be dark and there was no way I could locate a foster family to take even one child, let alone, three! We were just about to where the road to El Rito turned off from the Highway. I made a snap decision. I'd take them to my home for the night. Carol had no idea that I would be arriving unannounced with 3 small children, but she was resilient, and took this small surprise in stride.

It looked then that I'd made a great decision. Carol was unfazed, fixed supper and the three waifs were put to bed. By morning the three little tykes had gotten used to Carol and our kids and had settled down. I think the fact that they were with other young children helped. Leaving the children with Carol, I hit the road for Espanola, conducted a search and by noon had located a foster home that would take all three of them in. I headed back to El Rito to pick up the children and transport them to their temporary new foster home.

For some reason I hadn't expected it, but as soon as the poor little creatures realized that they were going to be uprooted from another sanctuary where they now felt safe, it all began again!

With the three little tykes kicking and screaming once more, Carol and I finally managed to bundle them into the station wagon and we were on our way. This time the tantrum duration was, mercifully, shorter. By the time I got them to another strange home and more strange people I think the poor little lost bairns were too tired to go into their standard routine, and we got them installed this time with a minimum of protests.

When I related the incident to Miss Tenny, she was sharply critical of my decision to take the children home with me before dropping them at the foster home. Her reprimand faded quickly when I asked her what she would have done under the circumstances.

CHAPTER 23

Meanwhile, Back In El Rito....

Chapter 22 provided a somewhat inaccurate snapshot of my job as a Child Welfare social worker. When all is said and done, it was not all that fraught with difficulties. For the most part it was fairly routine and sometimes quite rewarding. The abject poverty of the area was an eye-opener to me, however. I remember visiting the home of an elderly grandmother and her three young grandchildren. The home was as bare as Mother Hubbard's cupboard. There was a table and one straight-backed chair in the living room. But on the wall was fastened a wooden crate which contained a full set of brand new Encyclopedias. [In English, which no one in the family could read!] Inquiry on my part revealed the fact that the little community had been visited by a smooth-talking, unscrupulous, Anglo salesman a few months before, who had conned the grandmother into a purchase that she had no possible use for. It was not the only such sale in the community.

Meanwhile, life in El Rito went on. Like the job, there were some difficult times, but there were plenty of good, enjoyable times. A new Anglo family had moved to El Rito. Wilfred Lang was an artist [a painter] and he and his wife, Marcia, and family of four children became our close friends. The two older children were girls. Sonia, who was about 20, and Tina, about 19 as far as I can guess. Then there were two boys, Stan who was perhaps 18 and Pete about 16. We enjoyed the presence of another Anglo family in El Rito, and found them all to be friendly and congenial. Years later, in British Columbia, Stan would turn up again and our path and his would cross once more.

Another Anglo family also made a brief appearance. A rather strange couple, we had known just in passing in California, Hudson and Madge Kimball. They were trying to live a life of "voluntary poverty," I guess, and we had encountered them only briefly at a "Rural Life Conference" in California, where they excitedly informed everyone of a great place to get cheap food. It was a place in the Bay Area that processed fish, and they were able to obtain "fish heads" free of charge! Fish heads!!! Carol and I found the notion rather disgusting, and the Kimballs definitely a bit "strange."

They were the most innocent and gullible people I've ever encountered. How or why they turned up in El Rito one summer I have no idea. They didn't stay long, and we were not sorry when they left. They had with them their rather sensuous teenage daughter, Ariadne, who was about 15. I remember one evening we encountered the somewhat distraught parents outside Martin's store. It was getting late in the evening and they asked if we knew where the "drive-in theater" was? It seems that Ariadne had met a boy who asked her to go to a movie, "up the canyon at the drive-in theater." The theater, of course was non-existent, totally imaginary. But the parents were so clueless that they'd fallen for the story, hook, line and sinker. Soon after that encounter, the family disappeared from El Rito, and we were neither surprised nor disappointed. We never saw them again.

Fortunately, the Grants were still there, and Bob and I combined our talents [or lack of same] in getting firewood. Probably 99.9 % of the homes in El Rito depended on wood-burning stoves for both heating in winter and cooking the year around. Bob had the use of Peter Van Dresser's 4-wheel drive jeep pick-up truck and chain saw, so getting firewood should not have been a major problem. We would take the truck up into the National Forest where it was legal to cut and remove any "deadwood" that could be found. Deadwood was fairly plentiful, so getting enough firewood to last us through the winter should be a breeze we thought. We should have thought twice.

We planned to load the pickup to capacity and split the firewood between us. The lower elevation forests were mostly piñon pine and juniper trees, both of which were excellent as firewood, and could be reached only a few miles up the canyon above El Rito. Piñon was the wood of choice as it burned slower and longer than juniper.

Unfortunately, there was a problem with our plan. Bob and I liked to talk far more than we liked to cut firewood. Invariably when we went out to get firewood we would work diligently for two or three hours or so, wielding the chainsaw and axes. When we got a little tired, we'd decide to take a "10 minute" break. Most often, we would get totally engrossed in our discussions, no matter what the subject. After a couple hours we'd realize that it was getting late and we'd better start back, even though we had only half a load of firewood on the pickup. This did not just happen once or twice. It happened just about every time we went to get firewood.

Of course firewood gathering needed to be done before the snows came. The National Forest land where it was legal to cut dead trees or branches was higher in elevation than El Rito and would accumulate snow both earlier and deeper than where we lived. As a result, the Babcock's, at least, were almost always short of firewood. One time I remember that Bob and I were so desperate that we drove the truck up to the Potrero, Peter's solar fiasco. The Potrero's elevation was not much higher than El

Rito, and there was a road in to it, so it was reachable with four-wheel drive, when the roadless forest was not.

Bob and I tore down a half-collapsed, snow covered log shed on the property, cut up the logs and hauled the wood back. Unfortunately, the structure was constructed of aspen poles, not piñon or juniper. Aspen is a very soft wood, and gives off very little heat, so is practically useless as firewood. Still, in the state that we were in, it was better than nothing,

CHAPTER 24

Carrying Coal to El Rito

Our last winter in El Rito we thought we'd found a solution to our perennial firewood shortage. Coal. Bob had learned that there was a small coal mine just outside the town of Cuba, a small community some 70 miles west of El Rito. It was a privately owned family operation of a "slope mine" located in the side of a low hill. Trucks could be driven under the lip of a loading platform, or ramp, located outside the mine adit on an off-road "cut" at the base of the little hill.

The father and 3 grown sons who operated the mine would dig out the coal at the end of a shaft dug back into the hill, load the coal into a large open "tip-cart" on train wheels mounted on a short, homemade length of railroad track. Then the 4 men would manually push and pull the loaded cart along the rails through the nearly level shaft and out onto the specially built ramp where the load of coal could be dumped into the buyer's truck parked below the ramp.

The coal [definitely bituminous or "soft" coal] was priced at a ridiculous sounding $8 a ton! Bob and I figured that if we each got a ton to supplement our supply of firewood, it would carry us through the winter. In addition to Peter's jeep pickup truck, he also owned, and had put at Bob's disposal, a big army-surplus truck capable of easily holding two tons. It would be well worth the drive to Cuba and back, a round-trip of about 140 miles. And we'd come back with a ton of coal each!

With Bob driving, we started out about 8 AM, arriving at the mine site around 11 o'clock. The first crimp in our plan was the discovery upon arrival that there were 4 or 5 other customers in line ahead of us! Fortunately, they were all pickup trucks capable of carrying only ½-ton loads. Still, the 4-man mining crew had to stop for their lunch break so it was after 2 PM before our turn arrived.

Each load of the tip-cart carried a half-ton of coal. After two loads had been deposited in our truck, I happened to notice that the rear tires were showing ominous-looking bulges. Bob and I hastily decided that we'd better not risk a heavier load and called a halt. A flat tire and we'd be in deep doo-doo. There was no spare! Quickly, we decided to settle for the single ton of coal rather than double the load and risk one or more flat tires. Besides, it was getting late and we hoped to get home before dark. We paid for the ton of coal and headed home, Bob again behind the wheel.

There were several small villages along our route and we were getting close to the town of Gallina, about 1/3 of the way home, when a strange noise from under the hood and a quick look at the temperature gauge caused us to stop. Inspection revealed a broken fan belt! What to do? We didn't dare risk overheating the engine and cracking the engine block of a truck we didn't own. What to do, indeed! It was time for improvisation.

Both Bob and I were wearing ankle high "clod-hopper" shoes, and each shoe was laced with leather "boot laces." After finding the broken belt lying in the road, we removed our boot laces and wound them around the flywheels. A two-ply braid of two lengths tied together was long enough. We hoped this "jerry-built" fan belt might enable us to reach Gallina where we hoped we could find a replacement belt. It was a forlorn hope. The boot laces lasted just long enough for us to reach the top of the hill below which lay the little town and we proceeded to coast down the hill to a stop in front of the town's lone general store.

There was no gas station or garage in Gallina, but the general store stocked a variety of fan belts. Could we find one the right size was the question, and the answer proved to be "no." Frustrated, we decided to phone Tom Martin's store in El Rito. Surely, he would have the right size belt, and he could inform Carol of our plight and she could bring it to us in Gallina. Or, if he had no belt of the right size Carol could at least come and get us, and we could then drive next day to Espanola where we could surely get one, and we could come back, install it and then drive the truck [with our precious half-load of coal] home. We asked the Gallina storekeeper if we could use his phone. There were no telephones in Gallina, he informed us.

The nearest telephone was at the general store in the village of Regina, ten miles back, on the way we had just come! But how to get there? We lucked out when a customer in the store who had overheard our conversation with the owner, offered to drive us to Regina and back in his pickup if we would pay for the gas. We could do that.

Bob would go with him while I waited at the store which would not close for another couple hours. It was only about an hour before Bob returned. There were no fan belts at the general store in Regina, but he'd phoned Tom Martin, asking him to get word to Carol of our plight and ask her to drive our car to Gallina and bring us home. I was sure that she would oblige, and she did after stopping to let Carolyn know what was going on and to leave our children with her until Bob and I had been "rescued." Bob and I finally arrived back in El Rito well after dark.

There was a happy ending to this part of our rather weird adventure. Tom Martin <u>did</u> have a fan belt that matched our broken belt, which we had kept to insure we could replace it with one the correct size. I drove Bob back to Gallina the next day, and Bob installed the new belt and brought the truck in. Each family now had about a half-ton of coal which would help keep us warm through the fast approaching winter. It only partially met our expectations, however. We made the mistake of just piling the coal outside where it was exposed to the vagaries of winter weather. Towards the following spring the snow melt and rain had effectively ruined a good part of the soft coal. We did get a welcome benefit as long as it lasted, but not nearly what our high hopes had promised.

CHAPTER 25

A Bath, A Bath,
My Kingdom For A Bath!!

All in all, I really enjoyed life during those El Rito years. There was, however, one feeling of deep longing that kept insinuating itself into my consciousness with increasing frequency. I honestly could not remember the last time I'd taken a bath! I mean a <u>real</u> bath. Oh, I'd had showers, and I'd had "sponge" baths, but I was becoming obsessed with the desire for a REAL BATH, relaxed and mostly submerged in the wondrous luxury of hot water.

For our weekly ablutions, Carol and I had made do with an ordinary round galvanized metal wash tub. Here's how it was done. It was a two-person cooperative procedure. First move the kitchen table and chairs aside, then place the tub in the middle of the kitchen floor. Heat some water on the cookstove. The "bathee", would then strip, stand in the middle of the wash tub while the other poured water ranging from comfortably hot to lukewarm over the bathee. Said bathee, would then proceed to apply shampoo and soap until he or she felt reasonable clean. Then more warm water would be poured over the now somewhat cleaner bathee to rinse off the soap and shampoo.

It was a fairly effective way of removing some of the accumulated dirt and grime, but it made getting oneself clean a necessary evil, rather than a relaxing, enjoyable process. I was longing for a REAL bath, <u>sitting</u> and luxuriating in a tub of hot water and I was becoming resigned to the possibility of it being nothing more than a hopeless dream. Then, a ray of sunshine pierced the gloom.

Let me set the stage for the next act in this ongoing drama. Fireplaces in this part of New Mexico were still being constructed of adobe mud with, in this modern age, a little cement mixed in, and built into the corner of a room where two walls met. Bob Grant was building a fireplace, with Peter's permission, in the house the Grants were renting from him. Stopping by one late fall afternoon I found Bob in his yard mixing adobe mud and cement in a galvanized metal tub using an ordinary garden hoe to do the mixing. But this wasn't the usual round wash tub. This was an oblong tub perhaps 2 or 2 ½ feet wide by 4 feet in length. It was big enough to sit in with your legs stretched out!

Over the weeks, I observed Bob mixing his adobe mud several times. How I wished I had something like that tub! With it I could have a real bath! December had arrived and Bob had finished his little fireplace just in time for winter. Then one day he mentioned that he was going to be taking his family to spend Christmas with his parents in faraway New York. They would be gone for about 10 days. Hope sprang in my bosom, or wherever it is that hope springs from.

"Would you mind if I borrowed that galvanized tub you've been using to mix adobe, while you're gone?" *"No problemo,"* said Bob, "We're leaving tomorrow. I'll rinse it out good and you can pick it up whenever you want." They were hardly out of sight when I stopped by to pick it up. The following evening my fondest wish would be realized.

It was a cold and stormy day, and by evening there were several inches of snow on the ground. But, what the heck, I wasn't going to be denied my dearest dream by something as trivial as that. It was getting dark and we'd had supper and gotten the kids to bed. I moved the kitchen table and chairs back out of the way and brought the tub in from the porch, placing it in the middle of the kitchen floor, having first put two large kettles or pans of water on the kitchen stove to heat. Paradise awaited me.

But, to quote once again [I think this is the third time in this book!] as Robbie Burns, observed so prophetically: "The best laid plans o' mice and men, gang aft agley." Outside, the storm grew worse. We could ignore that. Or could we? Suddenly, the lights went off! A power line was down somewhere. Well, we could handle that! We had two or three kerosene lamps for emergencies. We lit those. While I undressed, Carol brought the two large pans of water that had been heating on the stove and poured them into the tub. I tested the water gingerly. OUCH! It was almost boiling! We'd have to add cold water before I could get in.

As mentioned earlier our home had cold water piped into the kitchen sink from our well, using an electric pump. The electric light in the kitchen had gone out, and suddenly the light in our minds had just gone on! With no electricity, there was no cold water available to cool my waiting bath enough for me to get in. My dream was turning into a nightmare!

Some premonition of disaster, I think, caused me to look down at the floor just then, to discover a growing sheet of water spreading out over the linoleum on the kitchen floor! My bathtub had sprung a leak!! [We discovered later that the bottom of the galvanized tub was full of tiny pinhole sized openings where Bob's hoe had worn through the metal bottom as he mixed his adobe mortar.] Still, this close to paradise, I was in no mood to give in.

Clad only in my birthday suit, I grabbed one of the now empty pans in which we'd heated the water, handed it to Carol, and told her to run outside, scoop up snow and bring it in to cool the water in the tub enough for me to get in before the leaks drained the tub. I grabbed up every spare towel and rag we owned to soak up what was rapidly becoming a flood. So, as I shivered in my nakedness, watching the ever increasing film of water spreading over the kitchen floor, Carol made two trips out into the storm to bring back snow to cool the water.

By the time I could get in the tub there was only an inch or so of water left. I hurriedly got most of my body wet while Carol grabbed a mop and began a one-woman effort of flood control. I quickly abandoned "Paradise Lost," wrapped a dry towel around my nether parts and dragged the now nearly empty tub outside, then went to Carol's aid mopping up the remains of Noah's flood. When everything was finally under control, we collapsed, exhausted. Fortunately, our senses of humor came to our rescue, and it wasn't long before we were both convulsed with laughter.

The whole exercise now strikes me as so ludicrous that I still regard it as one of the funniest and craziest experiences of my life. Since that eventful evening I've come to have a strong preference for a hot shower over a bath. I can't imagine why.

CHAPTER 26

A Change in Direction

Becoming a social worker represented a whole new phase in my peripatetic fiddlefooting through life. For the first time I felt like I had found my "calling" or my niche in what had until then been rather directionless perambulating. A "new" road through life lay ahead, though where it would lead was not yet fully apparent. Then at long last, a sign-post appeared. By the summer of 1962 I had begun to find that the long commute between El Rito and Espanola was becoming somewhat onerous. For our vacation, that year we drove back to California to visit our many friends around the Modesto area.

While there, I stopped at the Stanislaus County Welfare office and inquired about job opportunities. I found that my experience in New Mexico as a Child Welfare Worker made me eminently employable. For child welfare work in California, a Master's Degree in Social Work was needed, however for a position in public assistance only a Bachelor's Degree was required. The director, a youngish man named Don Quisenberry, and I "hit it off" well and, on the spur of the moment, I put in an application for a Public Assistance Casework position. Mr. Quisenberry said they would notify me the next time they had a casework opening.

Among various friends we visited in the area were, Sam and Carol Tyson, from the Saturday Night Group that Carol and I had been a part of when we lived at TCF. Sam and I had also joined in the protest against nuclear weapons testing in 1957. The Tysons lived on a farm about 12 miles east of Modesto and on their property was an old WWII-era prefabricated house that was standing empty, while slowly decomposing. I asked Sam about the possibility of our renting it.

It was extremely dilapidated, but with some work could be made livable. Sam said he could apply the needed "elbow grease" and they would charge only a nominal rent if we wanted to move in. It was really in pretty deplorable condition [I always referred to it as the "cardboard" house] but Carol and I were used to less than luxurious housing. I told Sam I didn't know when the job position would open up, but Carol and I agreed that when it did, we would move back, and set up house-keeping in their little house.

Things all seemed to come together in the fall. I hated to leave both our home in El Rito and our good friends the Grants and Langs. It was the first real home that we'd ever owned. We thought we would just have to leave it and Bob Grant would be on the lookout for a possible sale. Out of the blue, however, a buyer [an Anglo family] showed up and agreed to buy the house and move in later. I don't even remember how much we received in payment, but it was considerably more than the $1500 we'd paid. Almost simultaneously I received word of a casework job coming open at the Stanislaus County Welfare Department. We bid a sad "goodbye" to the Grants and the Langs. It was more difficult for me, as Bob and I had become very close friends, while Carol and Carolyn had not had quite as close a relationship.

I really loved our "adobe hacienda" and hated to leave it. A year or so later, we learned that the house had been totally destroyed by a fire. We never knew what the circumstances were, except that there had been no casualties, but the news was nevertheless very saddening. It was a beautiful little 1 acre "estate!"

CHAPTER 27

Back to the Future

In September of 1962 we moved into the Tyson's "cardboard house". As a place to live, it was nothing to write home about but in the generally mild climate of California's San Joaquin Valley, it would suffice. It was a quiet rural setting, with an irrigation ditch flowing close by which gave our three children space to roam and a refreshing place to cool off in hot weather. Here Talitha and Taavi enjoy a dip in the ditch. Most of the Tyson's farm was in orchards. Peaches and almonds took up most of the acreage, but along one of the irrigation ditches was a row of a dozen or so stately walnut trees.

We could help ourselves to fruit and nuts. Sam worked with crews of migrant farm workers to harvest the peaches and almonds in late summer and fall. The walnuts were allowed to drop to the ground when ripe, and then everyone helped gather them, including the older children. Sam and Carol had 5 children, all older than our three except for their youngest girl.

Speaking of children, our fourth was born June 18, 1963, while we were living on the Tyson's farm. Our doctor, a young man named Wilson, had an office in the little town of Waterford just 3 miles east of the farm, but the nearest hospital was in Modesto about 12 miles west and it was there that Kevin was born.

Both Carol and I were quite sure that this child would be another girl, giving us two children of each sex. We even had a name picked out. She would be named Kyra, thus fitting a pattern of two children whose names began with the letter "T" and two with the letter "K". Once again, however, Robbie Burns' prophetic observation would intervene and we had to scramble for a boy's name that we both liked and began with a "K". We settled quickly on Kevin.

Carol and I had stuck by our decision of trusting to nature when it came to family planning, but it was now obvious that some change was needed. We felt sure that 4 children were ample progeny and we should bring our procreation to a permanent end. I had Dr. Wilson perform a vasectomy, shortly after Kevin's birth. It was a decision for which neither Carol nor I ever experienced even a twinge of regret. We love our children, but four seemed like the maximum we could provide for.

Meanwhile, our lives proceeded apace. I enjoyed social work as a career. Public Assistance Caseworkers were grouped into units of 5 with a Unit Supervisor. I was lucky, perhaps, as I was in a unit with very congenial caseworkers and our supervisor, a lady of perhaps 50 named Margaret Barnes was, I would soon come to realize, the best supervisor in the entire office!

Mrs. Barnes was supportive, understanding and encouraging. It was not long before she began to urge me to consider going back to school to obtain a Master's Degree, which would be required for any future job promotion. A Master of Social Work degree required two years of study and at first such an undertaking seemed out of the question. The nearest School of Social Work was at the University of California in Berkeley. Neither Carol nor I were willing to consider moving to the extremely congested San Francisco Bay Area.

Those old Aztec Gods were still smiling upon us, it seemed, when we learned shortly after Kevin's birth that two new Schools of Social Work would be opening in September of 1964, the first such graduate schools in the California State College system. One would be at Sacramento State College, the other at Fresno State College. The first was some 80 miles north of Modesto and the latter about 80 miles south.

Both cities, Sacramento and Fresno were larger than Modesto, but neither was within a massive urban complex like the Bay Area. I visited both inland cities and had interviews with the individuals who would be in charge of the two programs. I found myself very impressed by the man who would be head of the Fresno State School of Social Work, Thomas [Tom] Brigham. To make a fairly short story even shorter, I applied for admission and was soon notified of my acceptance.

Carol was supportive of my opportunity. We located a reasonably priced rental home only a few blocks from the Fresno State campus. At that time the college was located on the extreme northern edge of the city. Since then, Fresno has grown far out beyond the College, which is now a full university, California State University [Fresno].

The Stanislaus County Welfare Department granted me a two-year leave of absence, during which time they would pay me a stipend for living and school expenses, on the condition that after graduation I would return to the Department's employ for a period of at least two years. It was too good an opportunity to pass up. We moved into our rental home on N. San Pablo Street in Fresno in time for me to start classes early in September of 1964.

CHAPTER 28

The Youngest Profession?

I found that I really enjoyed being back in a College atmosphere. On the whole the classes were interesting and the instructors were high quality people. I felt a bit intimidated when I found that I was assigned to an adult probation office for my first year practicum, or "field work." The apprehension soon passed, however, thanks in part to excellent supervision by the head of the agency. At the end of the first year, I was pleased to find myself with above average grades in all subjects.

One of my professors was a youngish man, Prof. Edward Bates. I remember an assignment in one of his classes where I was required to conduct a seminar on an assigned subject. I don't even remember the topic, but I must have done well. After class, Prof. Bates took me aside and complimented me on the job I'd done. He asked me if I'd ever considered becoming a social work professor? I said, "Not really," or something like that. Prof. Bates said he thought I had a talent for teaching and should seriously consider it after I finished graduate school. I never forgot that advice, and I think from that moment on, somewhere in the back of my mind, I had a goal of teaching social work courses at a college or university. I discovered that, once again, I truly enjoyed the educational atmosphere, and that feeling has never left me.

In addition to school course work, that spring of 1966 also provided two out-of-school experiences that left an indelible mark on me. One was the opportunity to attend a U.S. Congressional committee hearing that was being held in Fresno. It was chaired by Senator Robert Kennedy and was looking into unfair and demeaning practices in the use of migrant laborers by wealthy agriculturists in California. I was greatly impressed with "Bobby" Kennedy and his concern for those struggling to survive discriminating and arrogant practices of rich and powerful "growers."

The other non-school event was the March on Sacramento by the nascent United Farm Workers Union led by charismatic Cesar Chavez, demanding better working conditions and livable wages for migrant farm workers. The march followed U.S.

Highway 99 from Delano, the UFW headquarters, to the State Capital of Sacramento and I took the opportunity to join them for two days, as they passed by Fresno. It was inspiring and I considered myself fortunate to have had the opportunity to meet and observe two dedicated champions of ordinary Americans.

The second year was even better than the first. I graduated from Fresno State on June 8, 1966. It had been an interesting and rewarding experience. I'd not lost my enjoyment of college life. This photo shows me following the graduation ceremony, with Taavi, Kevin, Talitha and Kemet [L to R].

After my graduation we would move back to Modesto where I would return to the Stanislaus County Welfare Department for my two-year commitment in return for the stipend I received to obtain my Master of Social Work Degree. This time around, I would be the super-visor of a unit of six caseworkers. My good friend Margaret Barnes, had also received a promotion and would again be my immediate supervisor.

CHAPTER 29

Life Goes to the Dogs

Before moving back to Modesto, Felton Daniels, another student, had told me that his father-in-law, Harold Duncanson owned a rental house in Modesto, and Carol and I had arranged to rent it. This split-level, 3-bedroom, home located at 653 Lenore Drive was the finest living quarters we had ever enjoyed in 10 years of married life! Our kids were especially happy, I think. The elementary school was within walking distance, and Grandfather George, built and erected a play station in the fenced-in back yard, complete with ladder, swing, chinning-bar, climbing rope, etc. We still had Chipeta, who had earned her place as the best pet we ever owned.

With a large fenced in back yard, we thought the children would enjoy other pets in addition to Chipeta. We tried guinea pigs but I had a severe allergic reaction to them, so quickly gave up on that idea. Instead, we decided to add another dog to our household. It was **not** a wise decision! And it was all the fault of Charles Schultz! His "Peanuts" comic strip was all the rage and our kids were crazy about Snoopy, the comic's precocious Beagle. So, in a moment of insanity or just plain weakness, I bought a young Beagle. We named him Snoopy, of course.

It was a mistake. In the first place I paid money for him. The only pet we ever owned that cost us money to obtain. It didn't stop there. Snoopy, I'm convinced had been

160

born under a dark cloud. First he got distemper and shortly after recovering, from that, he got in a fight with another dog receiving numerous bites and cuts that required a dozen or more stitches. Both occasioned hefty veterinary bills. This dog was going to bankrupt us! His crowning offence and indignity, however, was that he refused to learn how to bark! Instead of barking he **bayed**! "AARRROOOOO!", "AARRROOOOOO!" It was enough to drive a sane person up a wall. After a few months [it seemed like years!] Snoopy went on a one-way trip to the Animal Shelter. Even our kids didn't complain.

Thankfully, we still had "Petey." She was a valued member of the family. The proof of just how valued she was is evident in an incident that took place not too long after the Snoopy debacle. It happened like this: Our vehicle at this time was a Volkswagen "window van" with windows all around. One day we were driving through Stockton and I made a fuel stop at a gas station. Those were the days when gas station attendants still came out to your car and filled the tank. Chipeta always rode in the back of the bus over the engine. As the attendant was filling the tank he looked in the rear window and spotted Chipeta. He became very animated and called to his co-worker inside the station, "Fred! Fred! Come here!! Come here!" Fred called back asking what was the problem? "Come here!" shouted our attendant, "This guy's got a Spanish Spaniel!"

Fred came to the vehicle and they both became very excited. Finally, one offered an explanation of their excitement: "Spanish Spaniels are the <u>best</u> hunting dogs in the world!! The very BEST! How much do you want for her?" I said, "She's not for sale." The attendant was insistent. "Name your price," he said. I said, "Look, she's my kid's pet! I can't sell my kid's pet!!" For several minutes they kept trying to get me to change my mind. Finally, I handed them the money for the gas, said "Sorry, fellows," and drove off. If I've ever been a hero to my children, I think it may have been that afternoon!

I'd never heard of a Spanish Spaniel, and I was curious. The first chance I got, I visited the Modesto Library, and after a search found an oversized illustrated book on different breeds of dogs. I turned to the Index, and to my utter amazement found a listing for "Spanish Spaniel." Excitedly, I turned to the listed page. There was no picture, and a simple two-line entry that read:

Spanish Spaniel
An extinct breed of dog.

I returned the book to its place on the shelf and left. In my mind, however, was the thought: "I may have the only Spanish Spaniel in the world! She could be worth a lot of money!!" But I didn't really believe it and, besides, Chipeta WAS my kids pet! [I've often wondered, however, if I missed my chance to be a millionaire!]

While I worked off my commitment to Stanislaus County Welfare Depart, I found myself heavily involved in working on committees and organizations involved in the "War On Poverty." I found it rewarding at first but after a couple years the momentum for the War on Poverty and Lyndon Johnson's Great Society began to lag and many of the groups began to close up shop.

I thought at one point that I was going to close up shop as well! At work, early one afternoon, I began to experience a distinct pain in my lower back. It steadily got worse and finally I decided to head for home early. Driving across town the pain was becoming unbearable. It so happened that at just that moment I was driving past the Modesto Hospital. On impulse, I pulled into the Hospital parking lot.

I went in to the front desk and told the receptionist that I was experiencing an agonizing pain and needed help. She told me that I could be admitted to the hospital only by a doctor. I didn't know Dr. Wilson's number so I decided to call Carol and ask her to call the doctor and get me admitted. I asked if I could use the telephone there at the reception desk. The answer was, "no", and I was told that I could use the pay phone outside! Fortunately I had a single dime in my pocket, so I staggered outside and called Carol.

She said she'd call Dr. Wilson, and she would come to the hospital as soon as she'd notified him which she did. Dr. Wilson phoned the hospital and I was finally admitted. The doctor arrived soon after, examined me and diagnosed the problem as a kidney stone. He gave me some pain-killing tablets and said that rather than performing surgery I should just go home and see if I could "pass" the stone, which he assured me was the usual procedure. With no medical insurance, it also seemed to us that it would be the best thing to do! In the meantime, the pain had eased up.

It took several days before I was able to pass the stone. During that time the pain would let up for a few hours, and then begin again as the stone moved. Never in my life, before or since, have I experienced such excruciating pain as when that stone moved through my urinary tract. Finally, it was over and I hope I never have to go through that kind of experience again. Knock on wood!

End of Part IV

PART V

Oh, CANADA!

INTERLUDE

"In Vino Veritas"

A brief digression. It was Olin Tillotson who taught me the pleasure of drinking wine. I had never had a single swallow of any kind of alcoholic beverage until the winter of my 36th year, 1966, while we were living in the Modesto area. Over the Christmas holidays, that year, some friends offered Olin and Betty Tillotson the use of a summer cabin in the Sierra foothills. [A summer cabin at Christmas time? Keep that thought in mind as we proceed.] The Tillotsons invited the Babcocks to join them for a few days and we happily accepted.

We drove up in tandem and all arrived late in the afternoon. Two couples and nine [count 'em!] children! We only had time to make sleeping arrangements in the icy cold cabin before dark. Olin and I were up early and got up with a single thought in mind: hot coffee!! When we went to make that much needed hot coffee we found that no water could be coaxed from the faucet in the kitchen sink. A modicum of investigation was all that was needed for us to realize that the problem was due to the fact that the water line was frozen!

Our examination of the course of the water line revealed that a section of some 10 or 15 feet of the water pipe was only shallowly buried and concluded that the cause of the problem lay before us. A rather brilliant solution to that problem then occurred to us. There was plenty of firewood handy, so if we built a fire on the ground in a long line immediately over the frozen pipe, perhaps it would melt the ice and we could then obtain the much needed water. "We'll thaw out the frozen pipe," we told the ladies who were now awake, "then, in return, we'd like some hot coffee!"

Olin and I proceeded with our plan but after an hour or so of tending the fire, there was still no water when we opened the faucet. In disgust and chilled to our bones, we sat down by the kitchen table. Olin went to tell the ladies, still huddling under piles of blankets, that we were still working on the problem. When he returned to the kitchen he brought with him a bottle of white wine, saying that in the absence of coffee, it might provide some much needed warmth.

I'd never had so much as a swallow of wine in my life, or any alcoholic beverage for that matter, but I was cold enough that I was willing to try anything. The wine was Chateau LaSalle, and it was absolutely delicious!! I'd never in my life tasted anything even a fraction so wonderful! It was pure ambrosia!!

Olin and I had just about finished the bottle when Betty and Carol, shivering with cold, came into the kitchen. They immediately began scolding us. "You're supposed to be outside trying to thaw the pipe! And here you are just sitting around inside, guzzling wine and doing nothing about the frozen pipe!" Olin and I were both wondering how could we escape the double-barreled salvo of wifely wrath? We were both speechless. We were not on 34th Street or anywhere near it, but the miracle happened before our eyes. At that very moment, water began to run from the tap we'd left open!!!

Olin and I recovered quickly. "What do you mean we're doing nothing? We've been busy sitting here all this time thawing the frozen pipe! We know what we're doing. We just discovered a better way to get the job done! There's your water, now where's that coffee you said you'd make?"

CHAPTER 30

The Road Runs North

Carol and I had known Olin and Betty Tillotson since we'd moved to the Modesto area after our marriage. They had been friends of the farm families at TCF and members of the Saturday Night Group which Carol and I attended during all of the times that we'd spent in the area. Olin and Betty had five children, Jane, Mark, Joel, Anne and Paul, and a close bond had formed between our families. Taavi and Joel, Talitha and Anne and Kemet and Paul were close in ages and they had become "best friends."

From a Babcock family perspective, we all missed our best friends when Olin accepted a position at the G.F. Strong Rehabilitation Centre in Vancouver, British Columbia, and the family moved to Canada in 1967. It was an easy decision for Carol and I and the children to use the kid's 1968 spring break to visit them in their new home in White Rock, a short distance south of Vancouver.

We found White Rock, a small coastal town just across the border from Blaine, Washington, to be a quiet attractive community. As I was just about to complete my two-year commitment to the Stanislaus County Welfare Department, I visited several Social Service agencies in Vancouver, as well as the School of Social Work at the University of British Columbia, putting in half a dozen job applications.

We had no firm intention or overwhelming desire to move to Canada, but liked the area, had close friends there and I was ready for a change in employment. I remembered Professor Bates encouraging me to think about a social work teaching career and was curious about what other job opportunities might exist. Olin and Betty were eager to have us make the move, and the children of both families were excited about an opportunity to continue their friendships. Meanwhile, we would return to Modesto and await possible developments, with no particular expectations.

Then a rapid series of events coalesced to change our thinking and bring about a rather sudden decision to move to Canada. We were shocked and pained by the assassinations of Martin Luther King, Jr. and then Bobby Kennedy, coming in rapid succession in April and May of 1968. Those tragic and terrible events coming as they did on top of the war in Viet Nam to which we were strongly opposed, made the prospect of living in Canada seem highly attractive. Then, as if the Three Fates were conspiring to determine our destiny, I received a letter from the director of the Family Service Agency in Vancouver offering me a job as a family counselor. We were not about to argue with the Three Fates!

I wrote to the Family Service Agency Director accepting the job, and turned in my resignation to the Stanislaus County Welfare Department. As soon as my termination with the latter was cleared, I headed for Canada to find living quarters and arrange for entrance to that country of myself and family seeking Landed Immigrant status. My introduction to Canada took me by surprise. I stopped at a small fast-food stand and asked for a hot dog. Handing it to me the man asked if I wanted ketchup. I said "No, but I'd like some mustard." The man gave me a blank look, hesitated a moment, then handed me a small glass bottle containing a clear liquid, and quickly turned away. I learned later that some Canadians were unfamiliar with mustard, but that vinegar was very popular as a condiment. Fortunately, this ignorance of mustard was far from universal, I learned later.

I stayed with the Tillotsons for the couple of days it took me to find and arrange the rental of a small house with an affordable rental price, in what is known as North Surrey, a fairly short commute from both Vancouver and from White Rock. It was vacant so I made a first-month's rental payment and headed back to California to corral and collect my family, rent a smallish U-Haul trailer to carry what limited furniture we had, and we were on our way to the Great White North.

Everything was happening at what seemed like the speed of light. I have no clear recollection of the details of entry into Canada of a family of six people and a "Spanish Spaniel," with a trailer load of furniture, but it seemed in those innocent years to be quite routine and uncomplicated.

The house was small with only one bed room, but had a large attic accessible by a pull-down ladder that retracted to the ceiling when not in use. The attic would become the bedroom where the three older kids could sleep. There was a hinged window at one end of the attic and I rigged up a ladder of two ropes with wooden rungs that could be dropped out of the window and serve as a fire escape if needed. [Fortunately, it never was, although the kids enjoyed frequent "test runs".] Kevin slept in the one bedroom with Carol and I.

Our living space was a bit congested, but it was to become even more so after a few weeks. The Viet Nam War was at its height, and more and more U.S. draft age opponents of the war were migrating to Canada to escape the military draft. The Vancouver area was a popular destination for many of these "draft dodgers." Carol and I had begun attending the Vancouver Meeting of the Society of Friends [Quakers] who were helping to coordinate and provide aid to the influx of young men from the U.S. We took in one such young man whose name I've forgotten. He stayed with us, sleeping on the couch in the living room for a month or so, until a more comfortable situation was found for him. We only stayed at the North Surrey house for 11 months. We were able to find another larger house for rent on 154th Street on the outskirts of White Rock and moved there in June of 1969, staying there until April of 1972.

By 1972 we had saved enough money for a modest down-payment for the purchase of a home. Through our involvement in the local amateur theater group, the White Rock Players, we'd met a lady real estate agent, who found a home that could be purchased with a low down-payment and a balance that could be retired in a relatively short period of time. We purchased the home and moved into it in April of 1972.

The house was on a hillside, and overlooked the beach of Semiahmoo Bay just two short blocks away. It was a two story building, with a lower, unfinished "basement". Upstairs was a kitchen, living room/dining room, two bedrooms, bathroom and a small room and deck that overlooked the beach. On the lower level were two small bedrooms, a workshop area, bathroom and an open, unfinished area. It was a tight fit but we were used to that and found our new "digs" quite satisfactory.

In the photo here our house is in the exact center inside the black circle with the lower story showing dark and the upper story, white.

The photo was taken from the beach looking north over the railway embankment [foreground]. There is another row of houses below us along Marine Drive but the view of them is blocked by the railroad embankment in the foreground.

The location, just two short blocks from the beach was a bonus. Semiahmoo Bay is very shallow and when the tide goes out a great expanse of sandy bottom is exposed to, and warmed by, the sun. Then, when the tide comes in the water is warmed by the heated sand, so that in summer the water is almost never too cold to make swimming uncomfortable, even for someone as "cold-blooded" as I am!

The photo shows the beach with the tide out and the White Rock, from which the city takes its name, about ¼ mile east of our home. An old legend has it that a giant living across the bay threw the rock at a rival, and it landed here. High School students whitewash the Rock every spring, to enhance the natural white color, in case you're wondering.

We enjoyed life in White Rock. We had good friends close by, in the Tillotsons, and some months after we moved to White Rock, we also renewed a previous friendship. I've mentioned Wilfred and Marcia Lang and their family that we'd known in El Rito. Through some convoluted set of circumstances, one of their sons, Stan, now married and a father, and his wife Rosa had found their way north to nearby Crescent Beach, along with a friend, Randy Rane, and his sister Michaela. So we did not lack for friends. Both Stan and Randy were avoiding the U.S. military draft.

When we first moved to Canada, however, the Tillotsons were virtually our only acquaintances and my job contacts were in Vancouver some 25 or 30 miles away, so we searched for some way to meet and become acquainted with a wider circle of people in White Rock. We found the solution through the local community theatre group, The White Rock Players. The group owned a small staged auditorium on Main Street and had a well-deserved reputation throughout British Columbia, [and Canada, for that matter] for high-quality amateur stage productions.

I'd done some acting on stage while at Milton College, so I found it easy to fit in. I discovered that I really enjoyed acting on stage and over a period of six years or so, I managed to appear in some 14 stage plays. I also directed one play and was assistant director of another and stage-manager of yet another. Carol became active in stage set design, which enabled her to exercise her artistic talents. We both developed a number of friendships through the Players Club and, after reaching High School Talitha also became very active in that organization.

White Rock Players were especially noted for their annual productions of British Pantomimes. These hilarious musical plays had been imported from Great Britain.

Wikipedia describes them as "incorporating song, dance, buffoonery, slapstick, cross-dressing, in-jokes, topical references, audience participation and mild sexual innuendo." Often referred to as "Christmas Pantomimes" because they have been traditionally performed during the Christmas Season, they are based on well-known children's stories and "fairy tales". I performed in "Snow White", "Sinbad the Sailor", "Red Riding Hood", "Robinson Crusoe", "Hansel and Gretel", "Puss In Boots", and "Jack and the Beanstalk."

There are a number of "conventions" that are usually included in these productions that enhance the humor. Some of these conventions include: the primary male [known as the "Principal Boy"] is played by a cross-dressed young woman, and his/her mother, known as "the Dame," is played by a man in drag. *Ad-libbing* is common and usually encouraged; music is supplied by a pianist, usually in the form of recognizable tunes with rewritten lyrics pertinent to the story line; there is often an "animal" character in appropriate costume and also a "Good Fairy" who often acts as a narrator to explain to the audience what's going on, and uses her "magic wand" to help good prevail over evil; an identifiable "villain" who must be overcome or frustrated; slapstick humor such as the villain shooting at the audience with a water pistol, or throwing a bucket of "water" [actually confetti] at the audience; and a "chorus" made up of "extras" on stage who perform a variety of songs and dances. These pantomimes are such great fun—both for the actors AND the audience—that I think it's a shame they're not standard and frequent fare for audiences everywhere!

My introduction to the White Rock Players got off to a somewhat rocky start. The first play I "read" for was the pantomime "Snow White." I read for the part of Snow's father, the King, and the director, Ed Carlin, chose me for the part. This drew the ire of a long term member of the Players Club, John Scott, who also read for the part. I told Ed that I'd be willing to accept a smaller role and was recast as the Town Crier, which smoothed things over to the satisfaction of all concerned.

I mentioned that *ad lib* lines were encouraged and I was especially proud of one such line I came up with two years later, that firmly cemented my acceptance by the long-term members of the club. The pantomime was "Robinson Crusoe" and I had a supporting role as "Mr. Morgan," the meek and "sissified" first mate of a pirate ship. In the first act, the ship docks at the island home of the Crusoe family. As I follow the pirate captain down the gangplank, a group of nubile young girls dressed in sarongs, rush onto the dock and greet the Captain and several of the crew members with hugs and by draping flower leis around their necks.

"Mr. Morgan" was not included in this welcome as he was following behind the Captain. On opening night, as this scene was playing, I had a sudden "brain storm". I stepped up beside the Captain and interjected the line that had just popped into my mind: "Captain! Why is it that every time we stop at this island, I'm the only one who doesn't get a lei?"

It brought down the house! I was told afterwards that James Barbour, the drama critic from the *Vancouver Sun* newspaper, sitting next to the aisle in the third row, laughed so hard that he fell out of his seat! The next day in his critique of the play that appeared in the *Sun*, Barbour even quoted my *ad lib*! From that time on, I was accepted as an "in" member of the Players Club, and never had to take a backseat to anyone in try-out readings for parts.

I grew to love acting on stage and later continued it after moving to Kamloops with the local amateur Kamloops Players, and was even able to perform in two plays with the professional Western Canada Theatre Company, and in two Gilbert & Sullivan operettas, with the Kamloops Operatic Society. [A complete list of my theatre activity is included in **Appendix A.**]

INTERLUDE

"I Went to the Animal Fair..."

The rental home on 154th Street was old, but much more spacious than the house in North Surrey, and we had enjoyed our stay there. It had seen us through a major population explosion of family animals two or three years after we moved in. Chipeta had died and gone to that great kennel in the sky, and we had quickly replaced her by obtaining a young female dog from the local Animal Shelter. She was a mixed breed and I named her Buffy. Chipeta had been named for a Native American woman and I wanted to continue that "tradition." The only Native American female I could think of off the top of my head was the folk singer, Buffy Sainte-Marie and the fact that our new family member sported a buff-colored fur coat, combined to make "Buffy" seem an appropriate name.

The "animal fair" referred to in the title occurred a couple years after we moved to the house on 154th Street. Somewhere along the line we'd acquired a female cat in addition to Buffy, and the cat, whose name I've repressed, chose that summer to present us with a litter of 5 kittens. Talitha had volunteered to provide a summer home for a pair of gerbils that her teacher had kept in his classroom, and within a few days of the arrival of the kittens, a litter of six baby gerbils appeared in their cage. Then, a few days later, Buffy did her part, giving birth to nine—count 'em, NINE—puppies! We were up to our ears in critters, and felt like we were caretakers of a regular Animal Fair.

Unfortunately, we knew nothing about the life habits of gerbils and before we knew it the adult male had attacked one of the baby gerbils and bitten off one of its hind legs. We were able to remove the adult male, confining him to a separate cage, before any further carnage could be inflicted. The injured babe survived, acquiring from Talitha the name "Hoppy," as he/she [we were never sure which] nimbly hopped around on three legs, and Talitha was able to return the family to the teacher at the end of the summer, minus only "Hoppy" who Tali insisted on keeping.

Thanks to Taavi and Talitha, and their friends, we managed to find homes for the kittens without too much trouble. But Buffy's progeny were another story. Talitha had become an avid fan [as had her father, who first read all three volumes to her, aloud!] of the Lord of the Rings books by J.R.R. Tolkien, and gave the puppies names like Frodo, Aragorn, Galadriel, etc. It took quite a while but we eventually managed to find homes for all nine without alienating <u>all</u> of our friends and acquaintances.

Buffy never quite won my heart as had Chipeta, but she made a good family pet. When we first got her she had one very annoying habit. Often when male visitors came to the house, Buffy would greet them with fierce barking. She did this with many men, but not all men, or with women. She never did anything more that bark, but the fierceness of it was sometimes quite frightening. This behavior was especially noticeable when the postman came into the yard on a daily basis to deliver our mail. He was obviously annoyed, if not somewhat frightened by our fierce-sounding dog, who grew to be much larger than "Petey." As time passed, Carol and I noted that Buffy did not bark like that at women <u>or to all men</u>. We watched closely and finally realized that her tantrums were directed only at men who happened to be wearing hats or caps!

I waited one day out on the street for the mailman, and stopped him, explaining my theory about Buffy's reactions. I suggested that he remove his mailman's cap before coming into the yard. He did so, and Buffy ignored him and did not bark! From then on, the mailman always took off his cap and hung it on the fence outside the yard before coming through the gate. Buffy never barked at him again!

Carol and I theorized that before we got her from the Shelter, Buffy must have had an owner, or frequent exposure to someone who beat her, and that someone was a man who always wore a hat or cap. We never knew for sure, be both Carol and I became convinced that Buffy had experienced something like that in her life. I told the mailman about our theory and he agreed that it was a likely explanation. Mostly, he was just relieved not to be greeted any more by a large and angry—appearing dog.

CHAPTER 31

Hi Ho, Hi Ho,
It's Back to Work I Go

I've forgotten the name of the director of the Family Service Centre in Vancouver, though I liked him and we got along very well. Professional Social Workers are usually divided into three categories; Case Workers, who work primarily with counseling individuals or families, Group Workers who lead groups organized around certain problem areas and Community Development Workers who work on a broader variety of community problems or concerns.

Although I maintained a small Caseload, I'd become especially interested in Community Development. A majority of my time came to be devoted to maintaining and staffing, along with a social worker from another social agency, a storefront office in a problem area of the city. My partner, Lynn Sigurgierson, and I christened it the "Action Centre" and handled, or tried to handle, a wide variety of local community problems and concerns.

Most of the Family Service Centre staff were older ladies, and I was the only male in the office other than the director. Most of my caseload involved marriage counseling. Some of the counseling involved only a single session, most covered a series of several sessions, and a few were fairly long term. One frustration of this work was that I often never knew how "successful" or "unsuccessful" the counseling was over the long run.

One client that I <u>was</u> able to help was a young mother of two small children who found herself in a very unhappy marriage. I worked with her for several months and my "success" was in helping her to overcome feelings of guilt and inadequacy for what she felt was a "failure" to make her marriage work.

I base my notion of counseling success on the fact that the lady, Barbara, valued my help enough to maintain contact with me up to the present day, some 45 years later! She's now remarried and proud of the fact that her daughter [who was just one year old at the time I worked with the family] is now a talented Hollywood actress, Carrie-Anne Moss!

Along with the social agencies I'd contacted on my visit to Canada while still living in Modesto, I'd also spoken with the Director of the School of Social Work at the University of British Columbia. I still remembered the encouragement from my professor at Fresno State to think about the possibility of becoming a college or university instructor, and that had become my ultimate goal. There was no vacancy at UBC when we moved to Canada, but I made it a practice to stop by the school at least once every month, just to let them know that I was interested in a faculty position!

In this instance persistence paid off. After about a year, I was contacted by the Director and offered a position as a Field Work Instructor. He said he'd been impressed by my frequent visits which gave evidence of a strong interest in joining the University faculty. It was what I'd been after from the beginning, so I gave notice at the Family Service Centre and went to work at UBC.

Master's Degree programs at Universities run for two years. In addition to classroom courses each student has to spend time doing "Field Work," working for a period of time at one of a variety of social agencies under close supervision by an employee of the agency [usually the Agency director, or his/her assistant] and also by a University Field Instructor. Each Field Instructor would be responsible for supervising 5 or 6 students each semester. One of the agency directors I worked with was a lawyer and politician of the NDP [New Democratic Party, in actuality a Socialist party] who later went on to serve as the Premier of British Columbia.

I was one of those Field Instructors and my job entailed lining up social agencies that were willing to accept a student trainee for a semester-long period of time, and then to supervise the student's progress. After my first year at UBC, I was also able to co-teach, with two other faculty members, a beginning level classroom course.

I enjoyed my teaching experience at UBC as much as I'd hoped, but it was not to last. The University had obtained a federal government financial grant with a "shelf life" of three years and that was the grant under which I'd been hired. When the three year period was up, the grant expired, and so did my job! To me, it was a major disappointment, but there was nothing I could do about it.

It was during that three year period that Carol's and my marriage underwent a period of extreme stress. I'm not proud to admit it, but it was my actions that I'm sure were the major contributing factor. I put our marriage in jeopardy by involving myself in an "affair" while I was teaching at UBC.

Her name was Anne, a tall, 5'10" blond lady in her late 20s, the wife of a graduate student in the chemistry department. Anne and I were both discovering that the "chemistry" in our marriages was becoming severely diluted. It started with meeting for drinks at the faculty lounge after classes once or twice a week and developed from there. It was a new and exciting experience for me.

As time went on I found myself thinking that my marriage to Carol was lacking in some vital, not clearly understood, aspects and that this new relationship held my only hope for a truly happy and fulfilling future. As a result I began trying to tighten my hold on the relationship with Anne. This had exactly the opposite effect that I hoped for.

After our "affair" had gone on for over a year, I noticed that Anne seemed to be pulling away from me and this sent me spinning into a deep state of depression and despair. I was telling myself that this relationship with Anne was my <u>only</u> hope for future happiness in life. I was losing Carol, I'd decided, and if this relationship with Anne ended also, I'd <u>never</u> find another! [I **was** in my 40's, after all, an "old" man!]

As a result of this delusive thinking, I found myself descending into a deep, deep depression. It lasted for months, until I realized that it was, in fact, my own delusional thought patterns that were causing the depression! After realizing the cause, I was able to very gradually overcome my self-destructive thinking. Life went on and Carol and I somehow weathered the storm, for a time at least, although things would never again be quite the same. Carol stuck with me through this very trying period. Why she did, I don't know, but she did!

CHAPTER 32

My Road Loops to Kamloops

My position on the UBC faculty was no longer existent and looking for a new teaching job was now priority *numero uno* in my mind. While at UBC I'd become acquainted with the man who was in charge of Staff Development for the Provincial Government's Public Welfare offices. I'd also learned that he had an opening in his department for a Staff Development Officer for the Fraser Valley District which stretched from Vancouver's suburbs [including White Rock] up the Fraser River to the city of Chilliwack. He indicated that he'd like to hire me but could not as Provincial Government jobs were open only to Canadian citizens, and my status in Canada was only that of a Landed Immigrant.

Then I had an idea. I'd just completed five years of residency as a Landed Immigrant which made me eligible to <u>apply</u> for Canadian citizenship! I wondered if he could hire me if I was in the <u>process</u> of obtaining Canadian citizenship? Somehow, he managed to arrange to hire me on that basis.

My new job consisted or arranging training programs, for all types of employees of the Public Welfare system in the Fraser Valley District—clerical staff, line workers, supervisory staff, administrators, etc. I would check with each of the directors of the eight local offices and find out what kind of training programs they needed or desired for all levels of their staff. Then my job was to design or arrange for the kinds of training that were requested. It was somewhat akin to being a teacher and I was happy to get the job, although it involved extensive travel.

In the meantime, I had applied for Canadian Citizenship. It was a relatively straight-forward process. I did a lot of reading on Canadian history and government, took the exam and passed it with no trouble. In becoming a "naturalized" U.S. citizen, a foreign-born applicant must renounce their previous citizenship. I asked if I would be required to take that step, but Canada's laws were more relaxed and I was told that I need not renounce my U.S. citizenship in order to become a legal Canadian Citizen.

Dual citizenship was an option which I chose to take. I had no trouble passing the tests and was granted Canadian citizenship. Since that day I'm a legal citizen of both the U.S. and Canada. Carol was content to just retain her U.S. citizenship. [I've heard recently that this option of dual citizenship no longer exists. If so, I regard it as unfortunate.]

I still had my mind set on getting back into teaching at a college or university, and during the approximately one year that I worked for the British Columbia Provincial Government, I applied for literally dozens of teaching positions in both Canada and western United States. I was getting discouraged, as I accumulated a large stack of "rejection letters." But diligence and persistence paid off in the long run. I was finally granted an interview with Alan Artebise, Chairman of the Social Science Department at Cariboo College, a 2 year "junior college" in Kamloops, British Columbia. Kamloops, a city of around 60,000 population at the time, was in the interior of the Province about 350 miles from Vancouver and White Rock.

We met, the interview went well and I was hired! Cariboo College offered a one year Social Service program and my job was to coordinate the program and teach some of the courses. The program's aim was to provide a work force of persons with a beginning level of social work skills and knowledge. The program had been operating for several years, but the incumbent coordinator/instructor was leaving.

Skipping ahead in my story, I took the job and moved to Kamloops. I retained some of the original program while adding some elements that I felt were lacking. Two or three of the courses I would teach myself, while using instructors from the College to teach courses in English and Psychology. I would also coordinate and supervise a field work program whereby students would work one day per week in a community social agency. These included the Provincial Government's Public Assistance program, and private agencies such as the Elizabeth Fry and John Howard Societies, a privately run Group Home for troubled teens called *Carpe Diem* [Seize the Day], a recovery home for individuals with alcohol or drug related problems and other similar non-governmental organizations.

The overwhelming number of students who signed up for the Social Service Worker Program were female single-parents with just a high school education, but in need of employment to support themselves. There were also a number of high school graduates with limited job skills looking for a way to upgrade their skills in order to find more remunerative employment. Here is a photo of my 1983 student group. Notice just one male student!

I enjoyed my work which involved teaching classes and working in close contact with the people operating and managing a variety of community social agencies. Altogether, I spent 11 years at this job which I think is an employment longevity record for me, leaving only after I reached the point where I could retire with a pension. The position gave me a lot of independence which I appreciated, and I enjoyed the friendships I made with other instructors at the college, one of whom, geography professor, Nelson Riis, went on to serve for many years as an NDP member of Canada's National Parliament in Ottawa, representing the Kamloops constituency.

Another Cariboo College Professor, Charles Mossop, I still consider my best friend. Charles taught courses in Anthropology, and was also a virtual virtuoso as a musician, playing mainly six and twelve string guitars and banjo. Every Friday afternoon after classes, Charles could be found in the faculty lounge playing and singing popular folk songs. A number of other faculty members were regular attenders and I was not slow to join them.

I owned a guitar myself, could play a few chords and loved to sing! It wasn't too long before Charles and I began getting together on our own as I tried to learn to

play and sing along with him. Over time, we discovered that we both had a special love for Irish and Scottish folk songs and began to concentrate solely on those, adding new songs whenever we found ones we particularly liked. In time we became good enough to play and sing at college events, and finally at Kamloops pubs and meetings of Irish and Scottish organizations such as the local Caledonian Society. We called ourselves "The Reivers" [say "reevers"] and enjoyed singing and playing together immensely! The photo shows Charles and I at one of our performances.

I still have several large note-books of Irish and Scottish songs complete with lyrics and guitar chords, which Charles was musician enough to arrange. I think the highlight for us was when we were invited to play at a large convention of the Canadian affiliate of the Women's Branch of the Orange Order of Canada, who were having their yearly National Convention in Kamloops that year. The word Orange was, of course, an indication that these ladies were affiliated with Northern Ireland's dominant protestant population. So we took care to avoid any and all songs that might be offensive to their sensitivities and the concert, lasting over half an hour, was a great success.

Afterward, as Charles and I were putting our instruments away the President of the group came into the little "dressing room" to thank us for what had been a very enjoyable evening for the approximately 60 or so "Orange Ladies." Then, as Charles was speaking with another lady, she asked me, where in Ireland were we from? Without thinking, I responded with the truth and said, "Actually, Charles is a Liverpudlian "[meaning from Liverpool in England] "and I'm a Yank." The lady looked at me in disbelief. Then, suddenly, she smiled, chuckled and said, "Ah! You're pullin' me leg!! I can tell you're both from Belfast!" I didn't argue, as I considered it the finest tribute we could have received.

Sadly, our musical gigs came to an end after I moved back Stateside, but I still consider Charles as my best friend, communicating regularly via email, and try to visit Charles and his wife Louise, and sing a few of the old songs, whenever we visit my son, Taavi, on Vancouver Island where the Mossops now reside. I really miss the enjoyment we experienced singing together and learning new songs. My love of Irish and Scottish music has not diminished, and I have a large collection of CDs, DVDs and cassette tapes, pleasant reminders of our time as "The Reivers".

An excellent musician, Charles is multi-talented. Legally blind since the age of 19, he remains a world traveler, and has served for twelve years as a member and officer of the Canadian National Institute for the Blind. He is also President of the North America-Caribbean Region of the World Blind Union, and a member of their Executive Committee. In his "spare" time since his retirement from teaching and from work in International education, training and development, he has turned to writing, becoming a published author of numerous short stories and two historical novels with a third nearing completion. A true "Renaissance Man", if there ever was one!

Changing the subject, I can't pass up a chance to insert a "plug" for the Canadian medical insurance program. It's what is referred to as a "single-payer" system. In other words, a not-for-profit, government health insurance. I had a number of occasions to observe its advantages over our private, for profit, medical insurance system here in the U.S. Systems like those in Canada are unfairly criticized by reactionary, right-wing, politicians and their simple-minded supporters here in the U.S. From my personal experience the Canadian system is far, far superior.

I'll give you an example of why I feel this way. One wintry Friday afternoon after classes, several of us faculty members were engaged in a basketball game in the college gym. As I ran to keep the ball in-bounds, I grabbed it and stopped suddenly to keep the ball in play. I planted my left foot to stop my momentum and suddenly felt something "give." There was no pain, but I knew something was wrong, and sat down on the playing floor. Ron Paulson a biology instructor came over and asked what was wrong? I said "My ankle." Ron felt my ankle that I was holding and said, "You've ruptured your Achilles Tendon." Ron and another colleague carried me to Ron's car and drove me to the Kamloops hospital. I was put on a stretcher, taken inside and examined by a doctor who confirmed Ron's diagnosis.

Within an hour, I was on the operating table and a surgeon was operating on my ankle. The tendon was re-attached, and I was placed in a toe-to-thigh cast. I was kept overnight and released the next morning. I had been making regular and very reasonable payments to the government for medical insurance, so the treatment I received did not cost me a penny!

I was living in a 2nd floor apartment, accessed only by a steep, open, outside stairway. A faculty colleague, Earl Bloor, and his wife who lived near my apartment took me in. They fixed up a bed for me in their living room, and I stayed there for several days until I learned how to get around on crutches, including going up and down stairs, and resume my teaching.

During my years in Canada, I had eye exams and new glasses, and a good bit of dental work, all of which cost me nothing out-of-pocket, thanks to the Canadian single-payer health insurance. Forty-some years later, I still have dentists tell me what a good job some dentist did on my many fillings. They were done by my Canadian dentist. After the Christmas break, I was able to resume teaching after being switched to a "walking cast", so everything worked out, with no extended, long-term, problems.

CHAPTER 33

The Family Wheels Come Off

There was an unfortunate side, however, to what I otherwise consider one of the happiest periods of my life. The physical separation Carol and I experienced with me in Kamloops and she in White Rock would eventually cost us our marriage.

Up until I received the job offer from Cariboo College, I'd not thought seriously of the prospect of moving my whole family once again. I hadn't really thought it through at all. Circumstances, at this time were different from any previous time. The kids were all in established schools and had made friendships in and around White Rock. We were living in a home that we owned. Moving the family now would involve a major "uprooting".

In my obsession with finding another post-secondary teaching position, I'd been thinking only of myself, and failed to take into consideration the desires of the rest of the family. The four children were adamantly against the prospect of pulling up the roots they had begun to put down. So, I discovered, was Carol.

Prior to our marriage, Carol had completed two years of college. Now, she had decided that she'd really like to enroll at the University of B.C. in Vancouver and get her BA degree and teaching credential with a major in Art. I neglected to mention it before, but Carol was skilled at both painting—oils, watercolors and pastels—and was particularly adept at making pottery. She had already made contact with UBC about enrolling in the fall.

I was happy with her decision to complete her degree, and after long and intense discussions we arrived at what seemed like the best plan for all of us. Carol and the children would remain in White Rock and Carol would enroll at UBC, commuting to classes. I would accept the teaching position at Cariboo College, rent an apartment in Kamloops, and return home to White Rock whenever possible.

We had become a two car family, but it was a three and a half hour drive between White Rock and Kamloops, so I quickly discovered that it wasn't feasible to make the round trip every weekend. As it turned out, I was only able to make the trip on long [holiday] weekends. It was not an ideal solution, except for the fact that Carol and I were both doing what we wanted to do with the non-family aspects of our lives. On the surface all seemed well, but inevitably, it created stresses in our relationship.

Those stresses were not diminished by my finding myself "footloose and fancy free" while away from Carol and my family. I'm reluctant to go into details, but honesty impels me to admit my "straying" into other relationships during the latter part of those eleven years that I was living in Kamloops. I have no excuses, am not proud of the facts of those relationships and find it difficult and unnecessary to go into details.

Although my memories of those liaisons do not now cause me regret or guilt, and I have only positive feelings toward the ladies involved, none were of such nature as to cause me to make a permanent break with Carol. The "affairs"—there were several—happened and they ended. None were of a nature that I envisioned as having any real possibility of permanence, and none involved students that I was teaching.

My job at Cariboo College included a two-month "free" period each summer when classes were not in session. Both Carol and I enjoyed travelling, and during the first summer of the new arrangement, I returned home and suggested a family trip to visit some of the National Parks in the U.S. southwest. Somewhat to my surprise both Taavi and Talitha declared their disinterest in such a trip! They had summer plans with friends from school and were old enough to look after themselves, so a compromise was reached. Taavi and Talitha would remain in White Rock and Carol and I with Kemet and Kevin would head south in our Volkswagen bus.

It was an enjoyable trip, highlighted by our "discovery" of Capitol Reef National Park in Utah. We found Capitol Reef every bit as attractive [perhaps more so] as Bryce Canyon and Zion, plus it was not as well-known and, hence, not nearly as crowded with visitors. From that time to the present, Capitol Reef has been my absolute favorite of all the wondrous vacation spots in North America.

That summer trip worked well, I thought, but by the next summer when I suggested another such trip, no one in the family, including Carol, wanted to accompany me. Carol and I had been, I realized, "drifting apart." I don't know how else to describe it. Nor am I sure of all the cause and effect aspects of what was happening, but I must have been a major contributor, due to my involvements that I described previously. For the next several years I would go alone to the southwestern U.S. on my summer vacations.

Well, to be honest, one summer I was joined by Diane P., a young lady I'd been seeing in Kamloops. This was the most serious of those "involvements" I mentioned above. Diane had been in a relationship with Arne S., the unmarried archaeology instructor at Cariboo, and they had recently returned from Egypt when we met. Diane was taking classes at Cariboo and over a period of time we became friends—well, more than "friends"—and she broke up with Arne, for a relationship with me. We took one summer trip together, camping out in a tent, and continued our relationship for some time after that. Eventually, however, she got an offer of a job at a museum in Toronto, and accepted that. We parted as good friends, and Diane later married someone she met in Toronto. I've never heard from her since. She was an attractive, intelligent and pleasant young lady and I think we sincerely cared for each other in spite of a rather large age difference.

Carol had obtained her Bachelor of Arts degree from UBC and managed to find work as a substitute teacher, but was never able to find a full time teaching position. Our marriage was essentially over, although we settled for a *de facto* separation. A divorce seemed unnecessary as neither of us was looking to remarry at the time. Later, as you'll note, we divorced and both Carol and I have since remarried, and both couples get along well as friends.

It was now 1985 and I discovered that I'd reached the magic early retirement age at Cariboo College, which was at age 55, if one had been employed there for 10 years or longer. I'd been there 11 years and had now reached the magic age. It was time to retire, but only from that particular job. Yes, it was time for yet another change in location and time for yet another new career.

End of Part V

PART VI

Back to the Future

CHAPTER 34

A Capitol Ship For a Desert Trip

Back to the U. S of A. And back to a **new** future! First, however, I need to explain how I arrived at these particular turning points.

I mentioned in the previous chapter that as a faculty member at Cariboo College I had two months of free time each summer. After the summer trips as a family had ended, I continued to head south without the family, tent camping, and enjoying the American Southwest that I'd learned to love. In my mind, and I believe in Carol's also, we both regarded, our marital situation, by that time, as a *de facto separation*.

On my summer trips, *sans* family, I found myself returning every summer to Capitol Reef. I'd bought a little Suzuki Jeep [left] and spent a good deal of time hiking the foot trails and driving the back roads of what had become my favorite National Park.

Dates are fuzzy in my mind, but on one of my visits to Capitol Reef, I discovered that the rustic Rimrock Inn motel, not far outside the Park was offering jeep tours in and around this little known scenic and geologic wonderland. I decided that such a tour might be interesting, so I signed up to take one. The decision marked another major turning point in my life.

The young man who owned the Rimrock Motel normally drove the jeep tours, but on this occasion he was ill and had found a rancher from outside the Park to be the driver/guide. For the excursion, I joined a middle-aged couple from Switzerland as passengers. I had been over much of the area and had thoroughly digested a couple of very detailed "guidebooks" to the back-road areas in and around the Park. As it turned out, I was more familiar with the roads we were travelling, and where and how to find places of interest, than was our driver/guide!

Our driver took me aside when we got back, thanked me for my help, and offered an insight into his problem: "I've been all over that country on horseback," he explained, "but I've never traveled those dirt roads before."

The next morning, as I was leaving for my next destination, I stopped to pick up some supplies at the Chuckwagon general store in the tiny town of Torrey. Eleven miles west of the National Park it was the nearest town. The wife of Rimrock's owner was also making a purchase at the store. She saw me and asked if I was I leaving? I said that was my plan and wondered why she asked.

She said that two ladies, staying at the Rimrock, wanted to take a jeep tour that afternoon. Her husband was still "under the weather," and the Swiss couple had been very complimentary about the job I'd done "guiding" their tour the day before! Was there any chance that I could stay over an extra day, and take these ladies for a jeep tour? She quoted a fee for my services. I had no hard-and-fast timetable. How could I resist the opportunity?

The tour went well, despite a flat tire during the trip, the two ladies were happy, and I was beginning to harbor thoughts of a new and very enjoyable type of work! That winter, back at Cariboo College in Kamloops, I wrote to the Rimrock indicating that I'd be interested in visiting again the following summer and, if I stayed for the entire summer, would they be open to hiring me to conduct their jeep tours?

A week or two later, I received a reply. The owners had sold the Rimrock, but the new owner, a man named Al Adamson, said that he'd spoken with the former owners about me, and he would be happy to have my services. He was totally new to the area, but thought that offering 4-wheel drive tours on back roads would be a fine thing. I'd traded in my jeep for a Honda Civic, but he owned a 4-wheel-drive SUV that could be used for the tours.

Rimrock was not just a motel. It had a restaurant and an adjacent campground. As a result, I spent my two "free" months the following summer, living in my tent pitched in the campground, and driving 4-Wheel-Drive Tours! I'd taken lots of photographs of the area which I'd made into slides, and offered to put together and narrate evening slide shows in the Rimrock's restaurant, which the new owner also welcomed. I'd enjoyed teaching on the college level, but this was even more satisfying, and there was even more to come, as Al was eager to have me back again the next summer.

I'd planned to tent camp again, but when I arrived, the following June, I discovered a small 2-room unpainted frame cabin in Torrey that was for sale. It was right next door to the Chuckwagon general store, and I bought it and moved in even though I had no furniture. That summer I slept on the floor with my sleeping bag and an air mattress.

This photo was taken a few years later, after I'd been living in the cabin for some time, furnished it and had a bedroom added to the original two rooms.

I was happy when the purchase of the cabin was completed, as the owner/builder had a troubling reputation. Ken Finkenbinder was a former Marine, who had never left his war experiences behind. Several locals warned me not to antagonize him as he had a "hair-trigger" temper. He was owner of a military "Duck",

one of those amphibious vehicles, a kind of water-going tank, which was parked behind the cabin. He also was the owner of a variety of weapons, including a "bazooka" and live ammunition!

Ken had been given a warning for firing his "bazooka" at the red rock cliffs for "target practice," and because of that had decided to sell the cabin and move away from Torrey. I was rather nervous while dealing with a man like that, but all went well and I was greatly relieved when the purchase was completed and Mr. Finkenbinder left town.

Everything went well that summer. Al Adamson was a product of Hollywood, where he directed low budget, low quality, sensational-type "B" movies, many starring Gina, his blond bombshell of a wife. Surprisingly enough, Al and I got along just fine. I only had to conceal what I thought of his really terrible films, all of which exhibited a plethora of sex and violence and little else. Thankfully, after seeing a couple of his films, I was able to avoid watching any more.

My son Kemet had come by with his then girlfriend, Shireen, to visit me and found that he liked the area almost as well as I. After finishing High School he moved to the area and worked for some time for Al, as a cook, restaurant manager and later as manager of the entire multi-faceted Rimrock Inn.

A few years later Al sold the Rimrock and returned to southern California. The Adamsons lived [and died] a life straight out of one of his "B" Movies. A few years after selling the Rimrock and leaving Torrey, Gina died of cancer and Al was murdered by a man working on his house near Palm Springs, who then entombed Al's body in concrete under a Jacuzzi he was building for Al. [See **Appendix B**, for more on Al Adamson.]

In Torrey, everything was going well for me, except for the fact that the demand for Jeep Tours dropped off towards the end of the summer, and I found myself with extra time on my hands. One day, I stopped by the Visitor Center in the Park and got to talking with George Davidson, the Chief Ranger. I asked him about the possibility of part-time work in the Park. Paid work, he explained, was not available on short notice, but George wondered if I'd be interested in doing some volunteer work. I said, "Sure!"

I began working at the information desk in the Park Visitor Center one or two days per week as a volunteer. I guess George was impressed with my knowledge of the Park,

the hiking trails and the history of what had been a small frontier Mormon community called Fruita. It was aptly named as the entire campground and area surrounding the Park Headquarters had been planted to family orchards many years before. Cherry, apricot, peach, pear and apple trees were still thriving, watered by the Fremont River which flowed through the area. The Mormon settlers had sold their holdings to the government and moved on, when the original National Monument became a National Park, but the orchards still flourished. One of the attractions of the Park was allowing visitors to pick fruit in season at a nominal cost. Some of the orchards are visible behind the barn in the photo.

The National Park incorporated a geological uplift some 60 miles in length that formed a barrier to travel. Early geologists called this uplift the Waterpocket Fold [left] due to the presence of many small basins eroded into the sandstone that filled with water after the infrequent rains.

Prospectors, many of whom were former sailors, referred to this rugged uplift as a "reef."

So that explains the "reef" in the name of the Park. But why "Capitol"? Where the Fremont River cuts through the "reef" is a large dome-shaped formation of whitish Navajo Sandstone which had reminded early settlers of the Capitol dome in Washington, D.C. Hence, that section of the fold began to be referred to as Capitol Reef.

Mormon pioneers had settled along the Fremont River west of the Reef, and during the 1920s and 1930s some of these settlers as well as infrequent visitors to the area began promoting its scenic beauty. As the area was located in Wayne County, it was then hyped as the "Wayne Wonderland." Their efforts culminated in 1937 when President Franklin D. Roosevelt designated the area around the little Mormon settlement of Fruita as Capitol Reef National Monument. In 1968 the Monument's area was expanded by President Lyndon Johnson to include the entire length of the Waterpocket Fold and in 1971 the Park's boundaries were again modified and the area was designated by Congress as Capitol Reef National Park.

I thoroughly enjoyed working at the Park's Visitor Center. At the end of the summer, George asked me if I planned to be back in the area the following summer? If so, he thought he could hire me through the Capitol Reef Natural History Association, a private entity, to which he was advisor and which operated and staffed the Visitor Center. I was delighted, and the next summer found me back in my little cabin, with a few pieces of basic furniture, and working at the information desk in the Park Visitor Center.

CAPITOL REEF

The Visitor Center at Capitol Reef is a marvel of design in my opinion. As you can see from the photo it blends in so well with the natural scenery that you can hardly tell there is a building there. [The photograph is one of several I took and had made into postcards.]

George had told me that to become a Park Ranger would require the submission of an application at least six months in advance. I'd taken care to meet that requirement, and by the next spring I found myself hired as an Interpretive [as opposed to Law Enforcement] Seasonal National Park Ranger! "Seasonal" meant for the busy summer season only. That new twist in my convoluted employment history coincided with my eligibility [age 55 or over and at least 10 years of employment at the college] to opt for an early retirement from the Cariboo College faculty. It all couldn't have worked out more perfectly.

I elected to take the early retirement, bid a rather sad farewell to my many friends in Kamloops and to my family in White Rock, rented a small truck, packed up my meager household belongings, moved back to the U.S. and into my rustic little cabin in Torrey. I'd really enjoyed living in Canada, but was glad to make a new home in a part of the U.S. I regarded as the nearest to heaven that I would ever get.

CHAPTER 35

A New Life and a New Wife
or
Stranger in a Strange Land

Looking back, I'm afraid that I was demonstrating a real lack of responsibility towards Carol and our children. I don't remember when I stopped sending them part of my salary. It must have been when I moved back to the States. By then I was convinced that our marriage was over. Carol was working as a Substitute High School Teacher, and the two older boys were both employed, as I remember. At the time, neither Carol nor I saw a reason to get a divorce as neither of us was thinking in terms

of remarriage just then. Later, Carol and the two younger children returned to make their homes in the U.S., while the two older children, Taavi and Talitha stayed in Canada, where they married and raised families of their own.

Carol and the four children seemed, at the time, [mid-1980s] to accept the end to our marriage also, and I was content with my new life. I visited the family when I could, even managing to attend Kemet's high school graduation in 1980, when Carol was not able to, and I always felt that I was on amicable terms with Carol and with our children.

Working as a Park Ranger was the most enjoyable employment I ever had, even more so than post-secondary teaching. I worked full time for six months of the year at Capitol Reef, and George managed to find two or three days work per week for me on a provisional basis during the winter months. It was a new life for me and I'd never been as happily employed before.

I'm very proud of the photograph of me as a National Park Ranger! Kemet, as I've mentioned, had visited me in Torrey and after graduating from high school he moved to Torrey and worked at the Rimrock, so I did have some contact with my family, or part of it, at least.

Still, I must have felt something was lacking, for when I happened across a publication called "American Friendship Club," I decided to "check it out." The Club's mission was to connect "third world" females with American men. Nearly all of the ladies listed in the "catalog" were from the Philippine Islands and during the winter months of 1986-1987 I began corresponding with a series of ladies from that country. Before long, I realized that I was looking for a serious and enduring relationship. A "new wife," in fact!

As soon as I realized "lady A" was not someone with whom I wanted a long term relationship, I would break off correspondence, and write to another. I was rather particular in terms of wanting to make the "right" choice. I had one "close call" when I began a correspondence with a young lady who had been orphaned and was living with an aunt. My correspondent seemed to be very sensible and mature, and we exchanged photos. I was beginning to think she might be "the one" when I received a letter from the aunt. The letter was an apology and confession. It was the aunt who had been writing to me all those weeks! Her niece had a boyfriend that the aunt disliked, and she was trying to break up that relationship by interesting the niece in me! But the niece and her boyfriend had run off together, and now the aunt was admitting her malfeasance!

That "close call" rather dampened my efforts at courtship by mail, a fact for which I was to be very grateful. After several months of fruitless letter writing I was discouraged. Then, out of the "blue", I received a letter from a young Filipina lady that I'd never written to. Her name was Zenaida Bolante.

It was a letter that immediately interested me, from someone I felt might be the kind of person I was looking for! It turned out that she had seen an advertisement in an English language newspaper about the "American Friendship Club." She thought it might be nice to have an American friend, so she sent in her name. In response she received a booklet with names and descriptions of American "professional" men interested in meeting Filipina ladies. One of those photos and one of those men happened to be me!

Zenaida had written to several American men, including me. Later she said that one reason she wrote to me was my description which included my height of 5' 4". She happened to be just 4' 10" and was interested in someone who would be somewhere near her height! So my lack of height, which plagued me on the basketball floor through High School and College, turned out to be a major dividend!

[Her name was Zenaida, but was called Zenith by her family. All Filipinos and Filipinas, it seems, **must** have a nickname! The obvious nickname for a girl named Zenaida would be Zennie, but this young lady had an Aunt named Zenaida who had prior claim to the nickname Zennie. So her parents, in order to avoid confusion, called her Zenith. I also called her Zenith at first, but we found that Americans had just as much trouble with the name Zenith as they had with Zenaida. As a result she learned, here in the States, to answer to either of those names, but also to Zennie and just Zen. [A little lady with many names!]

Everything was now moving at nearly light speed! A meeting, in person, was needed. So I arranged to fly over to the Philippines to meet Zenith and her family who lived in a small suburb of the capital city of Manila. My visit, lasting a week, went well, and it was decided that in the spring, Zenith would come to the U.S. and we would get married! Carol and I were still legally married, but she was agreeable to an uncontested divorce which was no problem since we had been separated for quite some time. So I filed for the divorce which was a simple matter and it was quickly finalized.

There had had been one little hurdle for me while visiting the Bolante family. Zenith had three brothers and two sisters. She was senior to one brother and one sister. She and her siblings were fortunate in having a very loving and hard working mother, Paciencia Capistrano Bolante. Their father, Mariano, however, had a long pattern of getting Zenith's mother pregnant, and then disappearing for weeks or months at a time. Then he would suddenly show up, resume his role as head of the household long enough to get his wife pregnant, and then vanish again.

During my correspondence with Zenith, her father had been gone and no one in the family had any idea where he was or when he might return. He must have had an information "pipeline" however, because he returned just a day or two before I arrived on my visit! His first order of business, as might be expected, was to sit me down and put me through a "third-degree" examination of my intentions regarding his daughter! He was going to play the role of a protective and concerned parent! I must have passed his examination, because he made no effort to obstruct our plans to marry. Here are Zen's parents at the time of my visit.

I spent a week in the Philippines, staying at the Manila Gardens Hotel, a large rather elegant hotel in the Makati district of Manila. I was dependent on taxis for transportation, and ate either at the hotel restaurants or with Zenith's family. I was able to meet her brothers, Jerry, Danny and Joey, and sisters Irene and Marie. Jerry, Joey and Irene were married and had their own homes, but were all curious to meet this strange American who was paying court to their sister. Irene and her husband, Rolly, also

helped show me around the city and made sure that Zenith and I were properly chaperoned at all times!

Zenith and I went to the U.S. Consulate and made the necessary arrangements for her to enter the U.S. which she would do, as an engaged bride-to-be. Everything was set. [This photo was taken, by Rolly in front of the U.S. Consulate in Manila.] I returned home, finalized the divorce from Carol, and a few weeks later met Zenith's flight in Salt Lake City. The year was 1988. I was 58 years old and Zenith was 28.

I was impressed that this young lady, who had never been on an airplane, or away from her home and family, had traveled halfway around the world, alone, to a country foreign to her, to join a man that she had met only briefly on a single occasion! It was quite an introduction to her new home that she experienced after arrival. First, the distance of almost 200 miles of arid desert country between Salt Lake City and my

home in Torrey, and, secondly, the extreme isolation of Torrey and the small size of both Torrey and my little cabin.

Fortunately, I had anticipated Zenith's arrival by employing a neighbor friend to add a third room, a bedroom, to my cabin, and had added a more efficient Ashley stove for heat. [The new bedroom is on the right in this photo, kitchen and bathroom on the left and living room in the middle.] The wood fence is the property line on that side. The property I'd purchased with the cabin, totaling two acres, is located behind and to either side of the cabin.

Zenith never complained, although she must have had some qualms about her decision to leave her home and family, to become a stranger in a strange land. Coming to the U.S. was quite an adventure for Zenith, but now that she was here the next order of business was to get married and that turned out to be something of an adventure as well.

Neither of us wanted a Church wedding. Torrey was a Mormon town and neither of us was Mormon. Most Filipinos are Catholic, but Zenith had been raised in a small protestant sect called Iglesia ni Cristo [Church of Christ] that was virtually unknown in the U.S. [It should not be confused with the American denomination of the same name.] The closest Friend's [Quaker] Meeting was in Salt Lake City. We decided that we preferred to have a civil, rather than a church wedding, anyway.

I made a trip to Loa, the County Seat, and asked the County Clerk, Sandra Rees, if there was a Justice of the Peace in the area who could marry Zenith and I. Sandra said that as County Clerk, she was licensed to perform marriages, so we made a date to drive to Loa the following week and be married there at the County Court House at 9 AM. We arrived at the specified time and date, only to discover that Sandra was not there! She'd forgotten her promise to marry us and was attending a workshop in Richfield, a neighboring County Seat, some 60 miles from Loa!

I explained our dilemma to Sandra's very embarrassed and apologetic secretary. She phoned the Richfield Court House and got Sandra on the phone. Sandra was even more apologetic and embarrassed for forgetting our appointment. Then she asked if we could drive to Richfield? She could marry us during her lunch break! *No problemo* ! We drove to Richfield where Sandra, on her lunch break, corralled two ladies from their workshop to act as witnesses, and by 1 PM Zenith and I were man and wife! Sandra took this wedding photo in front of  Richfield's Courthouse after the very simple ceremony.

Zen and I grabbed a bite to eat, then drove to Bryce Canyon National Park for what I think may have been the briefest Honeymoon on record, and then back home to Torrey. It was June 28, 1988.

CHAPTER 36

Welcoming the Warm

The summer passed and all seemed well. I had time to show Zenith around my favorite National Park. There were two or three female NPS Rangers or other Park personnel about Zenith's age and socially she was welcomed. Our best friends there were a Ranger couple, Glenn Sherrill and his wife, Ann Corson. We've kept in touch since then.

Here's Zenith in Pleasant Creek canyon, as lovely fall weather gave me a chance to show Zenith around Capitol Reef. When I was at work, however, days were lonely for Zen and she was eager to find a day job. Torrey had little to offer. She found some irregular work cleaning the two motel rooms at the Chuckwagon store and finally took a job as waitress at a little restaurant in Bicknell about 8 miles from Torrey, although that was mainly evening work, 7-11 PM. At least boredom was partially averted and I could drive her to and from work.

Winter, however, was another story. Although the Park headquarters is 1,500 feet lower, Torrey is close to 7,000 ft. above sea level. Winters there are **COLD**, especially for someone who had lived, until now, near sea level in a tropical climate. I was able to teach Zenith how to drive before the winter closed in, but it was quickly apparent to me that she was finding the cold temperatures and snow to be difficult to cope with. Although she never complained, I decided that relocation to a warmer climate might be both welcome and warranted.

I had a good thing going as a National Park Ranger and wanted to continue that kind of work. Well, there were National Parks in Arizona that were at lower elevations and farther south. Maybe I could get a job at one of those Parks. A transfer from one National Park area to another is not a common happenstance, but somehow it was arranged. I think George Davidson had a hand in it. [George and I had been on very good terms at first, but for some obscure reason, this had ended. It may have been that he was happy to have me move on? I'm not sure.] Zenith and I visited the Verde Valley area of Arizona and I met with Glen Henderson and Steve Sandell, the Superintendent and Chief Ranger, respectively, of the administratively combined National Monuments of Montezuma Castle and Tuzigoot. Zen and I contacted a real estate lady and she helped us locate a mobile home on a lot in Cottonwood that was affordable and we purchased it.

April of 1989 saw us moving to the home we still occupy today, and a new/old job as a National Park Ranger. The photo is what our home looked like after we had a 50'X14' addition built on several years later. We welcomed the move to a warmer climate, although I would miss Capitol Reef, which is still my favorite National Park.

For the next three years I remained a National Park Ranger, alternating time between the two small National Monuments,

both under a single administrator. Montezuma Castle was about 15 miles from Cottonwood, while Tuzigoot was only about two miles from our home. Both were sites of pre-Columbian villages of Native American inhabitants who'd been given the name Sinagua by archaeologists. The name in Spanish meant "without water" [*sin agua*]. For the inhabitants of the Verde Valley the name is a misnomer. Although the surrounding country is arid, these two villages were located close by fine perennial streams that provided plenty of water for irrigating the crops [mainly corn and beans] that these agricultural people relied on.

This picture is of the misnamed Montezuma Castle. Misnamed because it had no connection with the

Aztec ruler, Montezuma, who lived near present day Mexico City. Some early settlers in this part of the Verde Valley, sadly deficient in both history and archaeology, imagined that perhaps Montezuma had escaped the Spanish Conquistador, Cortez, and fled to this area where his followers built this imposing cliff dwelling for him. In life, Montezuma never came within 1500 miles of the cliff dwelling that mistakenly bears his name.

The structure, attributed by archaeologists to the Sinagua culture, was partially protected from the elements in its cave. It has been repaired a number of times, however. Built in the 1100s of limestone blocks set in mud mortar, the "Castle" consists of 20 rooms arranged in 5 stories, and was probably home to 45 or 50 people. Rooms are roofed by sycamore timbers overlaid with poles, sticks and mud and are arranged to conform to the arc of the cave. There are ruins of many additional structures within the area.

For years, visitors were allowed to enter the Castle by climbing a series of three long ladders, but the Park Service ended this practice in the 1950s out of safety concerns. All Park Rangers are allowed one tour inside, however, and it was worth the climb. The view over the canyon of Wet Beaver Creek is spectacular. [Wet Beaver is the branch of Beaver Creek that flows the year around!]

The excavated ruins of the Sinagua village of Tuzigoot, are near present Clarkdale, AZ, perched on a limestone ridge above the Verde River. This village probably dates to the mid-1200s, and is estimated to have had a population of about 225 people. The inhabitants practiced irrigation farming supplemented by hunting and gathering.

Here is a photo showing the ruins of Tuzigoot National Monument above the Verde River. Why the Sinagua people abandoned their villages in the Verde Valley remains a matter of speculation, although there are some interesting clues that I discuss in **_Appendix C_**.

In 1992 I reached my 62nd birthday and discovered that I was eligible to take an early retirement and begin drawing Social Security. My plan was to take the early retirement and still continue working in the two National Monuments on a part-time basis. Once again, Robbie Burns' words, [I seem to keep using this same quote over and over] "the best laid plans . . ." etc., applied to my situation, as a "hitch" in my plan developed. Steve Sandell, the Chief Ranger for the two Monuments, was unwilling to hire me on a part time basis. I could continue as a full time Ranger, but Steve said he wouldn't hire me on a part time basis, much to my great disappointment.

Steve finally revealed his reason. A few years before he'd agreed to keep another retiring Ranger on as a part time employee. It had, according to Steve, resulted in a major addition to his workload due to a "massive" [his word] increase in <u>required paper work</u>! He'd vowed that he would never venture down that road again. I tried my best to change his mind, but he was adamant. I'd already applied for Social Security benefits,

so I had no choice but to resign as a National Park Ranger.

My career as a park ranger, however, was not over. About 20 miles north of our home in Cottonwood, is the community of Sedona, situated in one of the most beautiful locations on earth. Flowing south from the high country of the Mogollon Rim is lovely Oak Creek. The creek has cut a deep twisting canyon and where it emerges from the Rim country has, with help from rain, wind and intermittent feeder streams, exposed a wonderland of weirdly eroded red rock formations. Where Oak Creek emerges from its canyon, surrounded by nature's splendid and imposing sculptures is Sedona, now a nationally known mecca for tourists.

A few miles south of Sedona, along both sides of Oak Creek, the State of Arizona in its sporadic wisdom gained title, in 1981, to 286 acres of land with the intention of creating a State Park. After a convoluted series of land sales and swaps the transactions were accomplished and in 1991 Red Rock State Park was opened to the public. With

a background that included employment as a National Park Ranger, I had no trouble in obtaining part-time work as an Arizona State Park Ranger. This photo shows a placid Oak Creek as it flows through Red Rock State Park.

Red Rock State Park is a day-use facility with a mandate to engage in environmental education. I spent three years there from 1992 to 1995, working the information desk in the visitor center, giving guided hikes, and leading environmental education activities for elementary and high school children. During my time at RRSP, John Schreiber, the Park Superintendent, let me take an 8 week "sabbatical" leave of absence to coordinate an Elderhostel program in Sedona on the geology and history of the area. I enjoyed being a State Park Ranger as much as I had enjoyed the same kind of work with the National Park Service. After three years, however, I decided that I deserved a break from eight hour work-days, plus a fairly lengthy commute, and resigned my position at Red Rock.

Zennie, from the beginning, was anxious to contribute financially to our marriage and worked at several jobs, beginning by cleaning rooms at a Sedona motel in 1989. The next year she moved on to being a sales person and cashier at a large chain drugstore, in Sedona, a job she held for close to four years. I disliked her having to drive to Sedona, on what at that time was a very busy 2 lane highway, five days a week. So, I was happy when she applied, in 1994, for a job opening in the Respiratory Department at Verde Valley Medical Center, a full service hospital here in Cottonwood. She didn't get the job, but when the person that was hired, quit after just a few weeks, Zennie was called back and hired for the job. She did well at it, being voted Employee of the Month for the entire Hospital in August, 1997. She worked in that position until 2001 when she transferred to the Health Information Management [HIM] department as a Medical Coder and has been working there ever since.

While working at the hospital Zennie took a number of college courses through Yavapai College in Cottonwood, plus a variety of workshops and courses related to the type of work that she was doing. An excellent student, Zennie has passed all challenges with flying colors. In 2006 she reached her goal, and received her certification as a Certified Medical Coder. She has continued her work as a medical coder up to the present, and will likely remain in that work until she retires.

The requirements are very stringent, and as this is being written, she's going through new batteries of tests as the hospital upgrades to a new set of International Classification of Diseases [ICD] set of codes. Every medical action or process carried out

by medical practitioners is assigned a specific code that must be recorded to determine costs and payment. So it's a job that involves a high degree of responsibility.

After leaving my job at Red Rock State Park, I continued to work at part time jobs. One was in the summers of 1991 to 1993 with the U.S. Forest Service, on the Prescott National Forest, in conjunction with another Natural History Association. I was officially designated as a "Forest Technician" and worked out of the Camp Verde Ranger Station during the summer season. My job was to drive a van loaded with books and maps to various campgrounds and other tourist points of interest in the Prescott National Forest and offer the books and maps for sale to campers or passersby. It was not particularly successful, as most campers were up early and away from the campground before I arrived. Not a good photo, but it got a story plus picture in the USFS Southwestern Regional News.

There was one notable success while working for the Forest Service the 2nd year, however, when I began going, not to a campground, but to a scenic overlook within the Coconino National Forest, at the head of Oak Creek Canyon. This was a place at which many travelers stopped, not just campers, or an occasional car as at the pull-off at the summit of Mingus Mountain in the above photo. It offered a spectacular view over the upper end of Oak Creek Canyon. Our information station there was so successful, that the Natural History Association purchased a small pre-fab cabin or shed, in which we constructed a counter and racks for displaying the books and maps. It has been a great success. I operated it for two years, and it has remained open continuously through the present, 2012. I was fortunate to have a very helpful and congenial volunteer assistant, Rod Moyer, while with the Forest Service. Rod and his wife Jo became our close friends, even after they moved from Cottonwood to the Phoenix area. Sadly, Rod passed away a few years ago.

CHAPTER 37

Out of Town on a Rail

I was to experience one more period of part-time employment before I reached full-time retirement. This would be working on the Verde Canyon Railroad, an excursion train that operates out of Clarkdale, Cottonwood's adjoining "suburb". A little background about the railroad itself seems warranted.

Clarkdale originated as a "company town" built in 1912 to house the employees of the copper smelter that was built there to process the copper from the mines in nearby Jerome. William Andrews Clark, the multi-millionaire owner of the United Verde Mine in Jerome, not only financed the building of the smelter, but also the building of the "company town" of Clarkdale as well as a 38 mile-long railroad to transport the copper from the smelter to an existing branch of the Atchison, Topeka and Santa Fe rail line at Drake, Arizona. Clark named his rail line, completed in 1912, the United Verde and Pacific Railroad. [An imposing name for an unimposing little short-line railroad!]

The copper mines in Jerome and the smelter closed down in 1959. After that the rail line operated as the Arizona Central Railroad which hauled coal and bauxite in to a large cement plant which had been built in Clarkdale to produce the concrete needed for the construction of the Glen Canyon Dam near the Arizona-Utah border.

In 1989 the entire 38-mile rail line was purchased by Dave Durbano, owner of several "short-line" railroads in the western United States. Durbano's renamed Arizona Central Railroad still hauls freight between Clarkdale and Drake, but it takes a "backseat" to a newer excursion train.

The first 20 miles of the rail line runs through the scenic Verde River Canyon to a nearly abandoned townsite called Perkinsville. On his first trip through the spectacular canyon, Dubano was struck by the possibilities of a passenger excursion trip. He set about obtaining needed rolling stock and engines, and Verde Canyon Railroad excursion trips began on Thanksgiving week-end, 1990. After taking a trip through the Verde Canyon, I too was struck by its beauty, and accepted a part-time position working for the Verde Canyon Railroad.

The excursion train included coach cars and open gondola cars and employed a man about my age, John Bell, to supply a running commentary over a Public Address system, to the entire train. John and I became good friends and it wasn't long before we were sharing the job of providing the commentary while riding on one of the open gondola cars. Sadly, John died of cancer a few years later. After that I continued as the narrator for the excursion trips. As early as the spring of 1993, I was "riding out of town on a rail." This photo of me appeared in the Cottonwood Journal of August of that year, speaking my narration into the microphone from one of the open gondola cars between the coaches.

I continued working part-time on the Verde Canyon Railroad excursion train off and on until 2009. Towards the end of that period I limited myself to three days a week during the three spring and three fall months. For the most part it was a job that I really enjoyed. Since 2009, I've considered myself as being fully retired as far as paid employment is concerned.

INTERLUDE

South of the Border, Down Guatemala Way [Plus Mom's death]

A good friend in California that I haven't mentioned was an older man, Russ Rosene. Russ' life had been as peripatetic as mine. He'd worked in Mexico and Guatemala, with the Peace Corps, had been a radio operator on an oil tanker, and had married Carol's sister Wilda, although the marriage did not last. During his Peace Corps days he had fallen in love with the country of Guatemala and had bought property there. By the time we knew him he was retired and living in California.

In April of 1997 Russ would be celebrating his 75th birthday. He planned to celebrate it in Guatemala, with his new lady friend, Darlene. I would have my 67th birthday about a week before Russ' 75th, so he urged Zenith and I to come and we'd celebrate together. It sounded like a great idea and my two younger sons, Kemet and Kevin also decided to come along and a friend of Kevin's named Steve also joined us. We all met in Miami and the five of us flew to Guatemala City, where

we joined Russ and Darlene, all of us staying at this large "hacienda" belonging to a friend of Russ' who was out of the country at the time. This photo does not show groups of rooms along the left side or in front, where they lie between this garden area and the street. Nor does a b&w photograph do justice to its riotously colorful landscaping. This patio is entirely enclosed.

Russ and I celebrated our birthdays, and all four of the Babcocks plus Steve enjoyed the sights in Guatemala City and the surrounding area. Guatemala's capital, Guatemala City is a large modern urban area, but the city also contains many ruined buildings, the results of past earthquakes. Some years before, Russ had purchased some land on the north shore of Lake Atitlan near Panajachel and took Darlene there on a private tryst, while at the same time urging Zennie, the 3 boys and I to come and visit them. We

had the use of a rental car and Kemet did the driving.

Getting to Russ' "hideaway" was a long roundabout trip by road. The best way to get there would be to drive to a little town on the east side of the lake, stay overnight there and in the morning take a "water taxi" to the dock near Panajachel where Russ and Darlene would meet us. The water taxi is an open motor-driven boat capable of holding ten or a dozen passengers. I've forgotten the name of the little town where we rented two upstairs rooms in the Hotel Primavera. It's the white building on the right, on the long main street, which featured many souvenir stands and shops. Zenith and I decided to go for a walk before turning in for the night. A pleasant walk turned into a kind of comic *opéra bouffe*.

We were nearly back to our hotel when a small girl, perhaps 8 years old stepped out of the shadows in front of us. She had a supply of necklaces, rings, bolo ties and other trinkets for sale. She spoke no English and neither of us knew more than a few words of Spanish. We never knew her name but it could have been "Persistence." She was <u>determined</u> to sell us something!

We kept telling her "No!" but she refused to listen. When we got to our hotel she quickly got between us and the door, chattering away like an auctioneer, and waving various items under our noses. I finally got to the door and Zenith and I dodged around her and started up the stairs. She followed us up the flight of stairs and as soon as I opened the door to our room, she ducked past us and quicker than lightning she had ten or a dozen items laid out on the bed! Finally, in desperation, Zenith handed her $2 and I scooped up her merchandise, thrust it into her hot little hands and hustled her out of the door, shutting and locking it in record time. As soon as she was gone the humor and jocosity of the whole episode hit us and we nearly collapsed in laughter.

After that, the brief visit with Russ and Darlene was something of an anticlimax, although the "water taxi" ride across Lake Atitlan was pleasant. I still wonder what ever became of that enterprising little girl. If she got into the selling business, she's perhaps head of a major corporation, or teaching salesmanship at a prestigious college or university by now!

The major highlight of the whole trip for Zenith and I and the boys was a three day journey to see the Mayan ruins at Tikal in northern Guatemala. We took a plane from Guatemala City to the town of Flores, and a bus from there to Tikal. The vast complex of hundreds of pyramids, temples, statues, monuments, ballcourts, stelae and causeways constructed many hundreds of years ago makes Tikal and other Mayan cities truly wonders of the world.

I took this picture [right] of the pyramid known as Temple II or Temple of the Masks, constructed about AD 700. It's just one of over 30 major ruins at Tikal. We stayed in a comfortable modern "motel", complete with swimming pool, and enjoyed walks on maintained trails through the jungle, inhabited by Howler Monkeys, heard far more then seen, but we did see a few.

After returning to Guatemala City, Zenith, the three boys and I, flew back to Miami, where Zenith and I rented a car and drove up the coast of Florida to Cape Canaveral. Kevin came with us. My cousin Patty, daughter of my dad's brother Edwin, and her husband, Jim Wharton were living then in nearby Rockledge. Jim had worked for many years at the Space Center, but had retired a number of years before our visit. Jim and Pat took us for an extensive personal tour of the entire Cape Canaveral facility. The next day we drove back to Miami and then Zenith and I flew back to Phoenix and Kevin to St. Louis. A fabulous trip, but we were glad to be home!

****

I have to end this **INTERLUDE** on a sad note. My mother's second husband, Paul, had died in 1968 and she sold our old home and moved to an apartment. My mother celebrated her 90th birthday in 1996 with a well-attended party we referred to as "Beulah's Birthday Bash." Her health appeared quite satisfactory at the time. A year and a half later, however, she suffered a stroke after which she was taken to Mercy Manor, a "transitional care" nursing home, in Janesville.

I drove to Milton and with wonderful support from a cousin, Herb Crouch, we were able to be with her on a daily basis for a week or so. Unfortunately she suffered another stroke and passed away on December 22, 1998. Zenith flew to St. Louis and then came on to Milton by car with Kevin. The three of us arranged for the funeral service held in the Milton SDB church on December 29, and Mom was buried in the Milton Cemetery beside my father.

My mother and I were never estranged, but we were not "close" over the later years. In both religion and politics we were at opposite "poles." Still, her death was a time of sorrow. Zen, Kevin and I disposed of her things, and a lot of her furniture and antiques we brought to Arizona and are still a cherished part of our home furnishings while other items were taken by each of her 4 grand-children. I wish we'd been closer in her later years but we had shared many good times.

R.I.P., Mom!

End Part VI

PART VII

Bitten By
the Travel Bug

CHAPTER 38

St. Patrick,
Here We Come!

So I'm really retired. Retirement can only mean one thing to a true Fiddlefoot, right? Keep moving! Even prior to my retirement from paid employment I'd been bitten by the travel bug. I'd always enjoyed travelling, as I think must be obvious from the foregoing narrative. I'm just a confirmed Fiddlefoot! My travels had, however, been confined to the western United States [including Hawaii], Canada [British Columbia and Alberta, only], Guatemala and the one visit to the Philippines [in the Manila area only] to meet Zenith. She apparently had been nipped by the same bug on her trip from her birth country to the U.S.

Since coming to the U.S., Zen has made three trips back to the Philippines to visit family and friends. Given her druthers, I know she'd like to make more trips back to her homeland, and I can't blame her. I'd like to go there, too, and see more of those Islands, but there are other places higher on **my** list. Zennie has been a good sport and indulged me, and I appreciate that with all my heart. My rationalization is that she'll live longer than me, and will still have years to go where **she** most desires. I don't know how much time I have left, so I push guilt feelings aside and indulge myself. I'm very grateful to Zennie for allowing me to do that, without complaints. Thanks, hon!

I've written about my love of Celtic music and seeing something of Ireland and Scotland, was at the top of my list of destinations. So, in 2001, Zen and I made plans to visit Ireland. To save money we'd decided on a self-drive tour, with a rental car and overnights at Ireland's popular Bed and Breakfast lodgings. That seemed to be the least expensive way to partake of overseas points of interest, while allowing us to exercise the option of visiting places I particularly wanted to see, rather than taking a fixed tour to places that someone else had chosen. So I created an itinerary and, using that as a guide, booked in advance reservations at B&B accommodations along our route. Given the fact that I'd never done anything like that before, it worked to near perfection.

We flew via Aer Lingus, Ireland's national airline, from Phoenix to Shannon airport in the west of Ireland. My two younger sons, both single and "footloose and fancy free" at the time had decided to join us and had arrived the day before. Kemet would drive our rental car and be with us for the entire trip. Kevin was working as a flight attendant for American Airlines and planned to stay for only three or four days, while Zenith, Kemet and I would spend 10 days on the Emerald Isle. [As an airlines employee, Kevin enjoyed free air fare!]

After an overnight flight Zen and I arrived in Ireland mid-morning of September 11. The boys met us and we picked up our car and checked into our first B&B called Dunaree, in the community of Bunratty, just a few miles from Shannon Airport. After lunch we looked over nearby Bunratty Castle and then visited the adjoining Bunratty Folk Park, both within easy walking distance. The Folk Park is a "living museum" recreating what life in 19th century rural Ireland would have been like. It contains a wide variety of homes of farmers, fishermen and townsmen, a church, and small village center, with docents dressed in period costumes to interpret what we were seeing. It was both interesting and informative.

At the final stop, we went into a home where the costumed lady docent explained how a poor farm family lived at that time including, during winter, keeping the family cow in one corner of the single room home! As she spoke, she kept interjecting comments that seemed completely out of place. Comments about a terrible "bombing" of New York City, thousands of people killed, etc. We had no idea what she was talking about. When we left the house we went over to the ticket office and told the lady there what the docent had been saying. The ticket lady then informed us of the attacks on the World Trade Center buildings in New York. That was how we first heard about the "9-11" terrorist attacks. But, for us, our vacation would proceed.

That evening we enjoyed a "Medieval Banquet" at Bunratty Castle. There was an introductory cup of mead, a delicious wine made from honey, followed by introductions of the costumed "Lord and Lady" of the castle and music and dancing from costumed performers. Then we were conducted to the dining room and seated at long tables. The only eating utensil was a knife for each person, and before the food was served everyone got a large bib! We each had a piece of chicken, a potato and a vegetable or two, soup to drink out of a bowl, and unlimited amounts of both red and white wine. [They served chicken instead of the usual beef because of a quarantine due to the "mad cow" disease that was attacking cattle in the British Isles and Ireland at that time.] The medieval banquet was great fun! The photo shows Kemet, Zenith and I with our lovely waitress just before we got our bibs and food.

After the banquet we went back to Dunaree and watched the television news broadcasts of the 9-11 attacks, until we finally went to bed well after midnight. Watching the news was especially hard for Kevin, an American Airlines flight attendant. As it turned out he knew some of the flight attendants on AA flights 11 and 77 which were two of the planes that crashed into the World Trade Center and the Pentagon respectively. Kevin had intended to return to the U.S. the next day, but all flights were canceled and he ended up staying with us the whole time until he was able to return just one day before the rest of us.

We would go ahead with our planned tour of Ireland. We did the "Ring of Kerry" drive which is a popular destination for most tour companies that operate in Ireland. Personally, I think it's a bit overrated. It's a nice drive, but nothing spectacular. One reason our enjoyment of this drive was muted, was that we stopped for lunch at the only place available, a Chinese Restaurant. The food didn't settle well on Zenith's stomach and shortly after we resumed our drive, she "lost" it. [I'll spare readers the details.] After that we proceeded to drive around the very beautiful Lakes of Killarney, which is a very lovely corner of green Ireland that I DO recommend highly as a "must see" area during a visit to the Emerald Isle.

Then it was on to the scenic Gap of Dunloe. I'd especially chosen a B&B there, called Holly Grove, because our guidebook said that traditional Irish music was featured at a Pub nearby. It turned out to be a bit of a disappointment. We made the short walk to the pub arriving early, about 7 PM. We supped on reasonably good "pub grub", but the 3 member band didn't show up until after 9 PM. Then they took a LONG time "tuning up". By this time we were wondering if they were ever going to provide some music. When they finally launched into their first song, I was ready to walk out! I'd expected traditional Irish music and the band opened with . . . are you ready for this? "She'll Be Comin' 'Round the Mountain!" . . . I was ready to head back to the B&B! I didn't, fortunately, and the band did improve after that totally lame beginning, so it wasn't a completely lost evening.

Next morning it was on to the lovely, picturesque seaport town of Kinsale. While there we explored the enormous old Charles Fort, a "star fort" dating to the 1670's as one of a line of forts built along the southwest coast of Ireland, in response to threats of invasions from France and Spain. Charles Fort overlooks the stunningly beautiful Kinsale harbor, pictured on the next page.

From Kinsale we drove to Cobh, [pronounced "Cove"], the harbor for the city of Cork. Cobh was the last stop of the liner Titanic, built at the Harland and Wolff shipyards in Belfast, Northern Ireland, as she left on her "maiden voyage" that ended so tragically on April 14-15, 1912, when the ship many had thought "unsinkable," hit an iceberg and sank with a great loss of life. It was also just offshore from Cobh that the passenger liner Lusitania was

torpedoed in May 1915 by a German submarine. She sank in just 18 minutes, 11 miles off the Head of Kinsale, killing 1,198 of the 1,959 people aboard, leaving just 761 survivors. The sinking of the Lusitania turned public opinion in many countries against Germany and contributed to the entry of the U.S. into World War I.

We spent some time going through the Cobh Heritage Centre with interesting exhibits depicting, among other things the conditions on board the "coffin ships" that

carried starving Irish emigrants to the U.S. during the Great Famine of the mid-1840s. From there we drove to Cahir, [pronounced "care"] and were able to explore the very well preserved Cahir Castle [shown here] and from there on to the Rock of Cashel and its extensive medieval ruins. Near the Rock was our next B&B called "Tir na Nog."

We learned that evening that the government of Ireland had declared the next day a National Day of Mourning to honor the victims of the terrorist attacks on the U.S. We were due in Dublin that day, and arrived at our B&B in a suburb of Ireland's capital by mid-afternoon. Because of the special Holiday most all businesses in the country were closed. Enroute to Dublin we had stopped and walked around the huge Kilkenny Castle, a Norman fortress in the city of that name. It was closed, of course, so we couldn't go in and we drove on to our B&B. [Fortunately, B&Bs, along with petrol (gas) stations, were not subject to the holiday closures.] Since it was just mid-afternoon, we decided that we might as well drive to downtown Dublin to see it even if nothing would be open.

We drove downtown and parked about two blocks off the "main drag", Grafton Street. There were quite a few people on the streets even though all stores and other businesses were closed. But, wouldn't you know it? We'd gone no more than half a block when Zenith was tugging at my sleeve. "I've got to go to the bathroom!" she whispered. "Good luck!" I thought. Not knowing what to do we kept on walking, hoping against hope for some inspiration of how to deal with this unlooked for emergency. Perhaps a dark alley? But there were none!

Just then we reached the corner where our side street joined Grafton Street, across from one corner of St. Stephen's Green, Dublin's big city park. As we rounded the corner, we were passing by the entrance to St. Stephen's Green Shopping Center, the largest in Ireland. This enormous, four-story, enclosed shopping center had a 4-door entrance built into the corner of the building. And the doors were wide open!

Our hopes for Zenith's relief soared and then immediately plummeted. In front of each door stood a uniformed armed guard! Well, an emergency is an emergency. I could do no less than try. With nothing to lose, I approached the nearest guard, explained my wife's predicament and politely asked if she could go inside just to use the "loo." The guard replied, "No, sir. I can't allow anyone inside the building" [my heart sank to my shoes] . . . "except Americans," he finished. My heart returned to its normal location, and I said, "Well, we're Americans!" "Oh!" he said, stepping aside. "Well, come right on in!!"

We wasted no time in getting directions to "the loo" [which as you might expect was on the topmost floor]. After Zenith returned, we looked around. The government of Ireland had designated this building as the centerpiece of their "day of mourning" honoring victims of the 9-11 attacks. There were U.S. flags flying, a series of speakers proclaiming Ireland's solidarity with the U.S., two pipe-bands playing in between speeches. Best of all, the cafeteria was open on an "all you can eat" basis, FREE food for Americans!

On the right is a photo of the entrance [*sans* the armed guards] taken on our 2007 visit to Dublin. Zennie, in the center is, I think, remembering the happy ending to what could have been a major embarrassment.

We enjoyed our lunch, then toured on foot Grafton Street and O'Connell Street [open to pedestrians only] and were able to see some of the notable sites including the GPO [General Post Office] the focal point of the failed "rising" of 1918 by the Irish Republican Army [IRA], and the statue of Irish hero, Daniel O'Connell, known as "the Great Liberator."

Also, along Grafton Street is the statue of a voluptuous Molly Malone, the fish-monger of song, pushing her cart from which she sells "cockles and mussels, alive, alive, O!" [Cynical Dubliners refer to this piece of art as "the tart with the cart."] Nearby is a sculpture of "Anna Livia," a personification of the River Liffy that flows through Dublin. This sculpture is of a [clothed] female figure stretched out in a sloping concave trough with water flowing over and around her to represent the River Liffy. Irreverent Dubliners have christened that piece of art as "the floozie in the jacuzzi", or "the hooer (whore) in the sewer. [I'm NOT making this up!]

From there we got a quick look by car at the Phoenix Park, the largest enclosed [fenced] park in Europe and Kilmainham Gaol, where 14 of the leaders of the 1918 "rising" were executed by firing squad. So our visit to Dublin wasn't a wasted day by any means.

The next day we drove north stopping for a tour of the large New Grange "passage grave", [right] built around 3200 BC. When excavated and restored by archaeologists in the 1960s, it was discovered that at dawn on the winter solstice [Dec. 21] the sun's rays shone through the entrance to light up the burial chamber. The New Grange passage grave is referred to as the world's oldest "solar observatory". Two other

passage graves are nearby, but New Grange is the largest and best known.

From the Passage Grave pictured here, we visited Oldbridge in the Boyne River valley, site of the historic "Battle of the Boyne" where in 1690 the protestant army of William of Orange decisively defeated King James the former Catholic king of England. James had been deposed as King, and William along with his wife, Mary [who was James' daughter] had ascended the throne as joint rulers of Great Britain and the Netherlands. James, in exile in France, had raised an army of French and Irish Catholics and his defeat here doomed his attempt to regain the throne.

We drove from there into Northern Ireland. Created as part of the partition of Ireland in 1921, the predominantly protestant six counties of Northern Ireland [Ulster] are a part of the United Kingdom along with England, Scotland and Wales and are not part of the Republic of Ireland. There was no evidence when we crossed into Northern Ireland of this political separation. We did not even know we had crossed the border until we noticed that the license plates on cars were different!

I'll try to briefly summarize the remainder of our tour of Ireland. [Get a map & follow our travels!] We drove north through Glenarif Forest Park and one of the famed "Green Glens of Antrim," to the coast at Cushendall. We then followed the northern coast of Ireland along Carnlough Bay where we could look across the North Channel of the Irish Sea and just make out Scotland's Mull of Kintyre.

Along the north coast, we stopped to see the Carrick-a-Rede Rope Bridge. This is a narrow bridge of cables and planks that hangs 80 feet above the sea and connects the Irish mainland with a small island on which is located a Salmon fishery. The bridge sways in the wind and looked scary enough that I didn't try to cross the 65 ft. span. Zenith wasn't in the least perturbed and she, with Kemet and Kevin, crossed it with ease. [Zen never lets me forget the fact that I "chickened out" but she did not!!]

A few miles further on, we stopped to visit the Giants Causeway, Ireland's only World Heritage Site. This unique formation, situated at the foot of craggy cliffs and headlands, consists of some 40,000 inter-locking basalt columns [I wonder who counted them?] resulting from a volcanic eruption some 50-60 million years ago. As the lava cooled, the accompanying contraction left the pillar-like, mostly hexagonal, columns. These basalt columns run from the coastal cliffs out into the sea. Yes, that's Zenith, Kevin and Kemet at the Causeway.

Similar basalt columns, from the same volcanic eruptions can be found on the lonely Isle of Staffa off the coast of Scotland, which gave rise to the fanciful story that the legendary Irish giant, Finn McCool, had built the causeway so that he could pay court to a lady he fancied across the sea in Scotland. Hence the name, Giant's Causeway. From the Giant's Causeway we went on to visit the ruins of Dunluce Castle, for long the fortress of Sorley MacDonnell who long ruled the north Antrim coast. We drove by, but didn't stop at Old Bushmills whiskey distillery, said to be the oldest distillery in the world.

The next day we spent the morning looking around the walled city of Londonderry. In 1613 the city of Derry, near the mouth of the River Foyle, was selected as a "plantation" for English Protestants organized by London guilds. The city was then re-named Londonderry, but most people in Ireland still call it Derry. Between 1613 and 1618 the city was completely enclosed by stone walls a mile in circumference, rising to an average height of 26 ft. and some 30 ft. across! This is a photo of Bishop's Gate, one of the four original gates in the city wall. Among the best preserved city fortifications in Europe, Derry's boast is that the walls were never breached, not even during a 105 day siege in 1689 when an estimated 4,000 to 7,000 residents, out of a population of 20,000, died of disease or starvation.

We were able to walk part way around the city on the walls, and saw the Ferryquay Gate where the siege of Derry began, when 13 "apprentice boys" rushed to close and bar the gate as the army of the deposed King James approached. When asked to capitulate, the answer was "No Surrender!" and the 15 week siege began. Today these events are celebrated annually, led by an organization called the Apprentice Boys Society. The fact of the city walls never having been breached, earned Derry the nickname of "the Maiden City," so that "No Surrender" remains an appropriate *sobriquet*!

Our next overnight stop was in Westport, County Mayo. While my companions went for a drive around the area, I enjoyed a pint of Guinness at Matt Malloy's Pub—Matt Malloy being the flautist with the world famous Irish band, "The Chieftains". Unfortunately, Matt wasn't there, but the pint of Guinness hit the spot!

We drove down the west coast of Ireland, through Connemara, past extensive peat bogs, stopping at imposing Kylemore

Abbey on the shores of Kylemore Lough at the foot of the mountains called the Twelve Benns. Originally built by a wealthy tycoon as a present for his wife, Kylemore became an abbey when Benedictine nuns, fleeing Ypres, Belgium, during World War I, sought refuge here. Today the nuns operate the Abbey as a select girl's boarding school so there is no admittance for tourists to the building but there's a fine large gift shop.

Then on to Aughnanure Castle, a six-story tower house built on a rocky island in the River Drimneen. Long a stronghold of the O'Flaherty clan, it became the home of

the famous female pirate captain Grace O'Malley in 1545 when she married Donal O'Flaherty.

From there it was on to County Clare, the location of several noteworthy features. One of which is a vast limestone plateau called The Burren, pictured here. This striking geologic feature was described in the 1640s by Oliver Cromwell's surveyor as, "a savage land, yielding neither water enough to drown a man, nor tree to hang him, nor soil enough to bury." Cheerful fellow, that, eh? Nearby are the breathtaking Cliffs of Moher rising as a sheer rock face some 650 feet out of the Atlantic and extending for about 5 miles along Ireland's west coast.

Not far from Ennis, the county seat, is Craggaunowen, billed as a "Living Past" site. It features a tower-house castle, but the most interesting part of the site is a

crannog, a man-made island, made by transporting rocks, logs and earth into a shallow lake, which is then connected to the shore by a narrow footbridge. On the crannog, enclosed within a wooden palisade are a number of "wattle and daub" and stone houses. The entire complex recreates a style of defensive villages or "ringforts" that date to the 1500s. If you travel to Ireland, I consider Craggaunowen a "must see" objective.

Another interesting exhibit at the Craggaunowen site is the leather-hulled boat built in the 1970s by the explorer Tim

CHAPTER 39

Driving Among the Great British

There is often confusion and disagreement regarding the terms England, Great Britain and the United Kingdom [U.K.]. Generally the term United Kingdom refers to England, Scotland, Wales and Northern Ireland, while Great Britain refers to England, Scotland and Wales. England is simply the largest of the above. Our next overseas adventure would not take place until 2005, and would be a tour of Great Britain.

Again, it would be a self-drive tour but this time the driving would rest on the ancient shoulders of yours truly! Car rentals in Great Britain and Ireland are normally restricted to drivers under 70 years of age. I didn't know this at the time, however. In 2005, I was 75, but no one asked my age and I was able to rent a car with no trouble. We flew into Heathrow airport in London, picked up our rental car, and off we went. We'd made reservations at a B&B within the city and we stayed there two nights, allowing us a full day to see London.

The day after our arrival, we toured London using the "hop on-hop off" double-decker city buses for transportation. There is a lot to see in London and we were only able to scratch the surface. Still, we managed to see quite a few of the usual tourist landmarks including Buckingham Palace, St. Paul's Cathedral, Westminster Abbey, the British Houses of Parliament, Big Ben, and the new London Bridge [the original bridge had been dismantled and reassembled at Lake Havasu on the Colorado River in Arizona in 1968-71. [We still haven't seen it!] We did take a cruise on the Thames River. The cruise took us past the original Queen Mary ocean liner, now permanently moored in the Thames, as is the WWII cruiser Belfast, now a museum ship. The cruise on the Thames also took us past the imposing Tower Bridge and by the infamous "Traitor's Gate" where prisoners condemned to die entered the Tower of London, plus many other interesting landmarks.

At one stop we "hopped off" and walked several blocks where we toured through Britain's Imperial War Museum. This is housed in the building that was originally London's large insane asylum, known popularly as "Old Bedlam!" After our cruise on the Thames, we also toured England's most famous landmark, the Tower of London, seen here, but as time was running out our visit there had to be aborted and we

weren't able to see as much of the Tower as we'd have liked. "Traitor's Gate" where prisoners condemned to die entered the Tower, is the low arch on the Thames River in the lower right of the photo.

The next day I drove south to Portsmouth, the big naval base on the English Channel. I found that driving on the "wrong" left side of the road or street to be not that difficult. I still managed to get lost in the streets of Portsmouth, trying to find our way to the naval base, but finally found it. I've never liked driving in large cities, not

even in my home country, and driving in cities in any foreign country was a good deal worse. I'll have more to say in that regard a little later in this story.

The main object for going to Portsmouth was that I wanted to see and board HMS Victory, Admiral Horatio Nelson's flagship at the famous battle of Trafalgar on October 21, 1805. That victory over the combined fleets of France and Spain was a resounding victory for the British navy but cost Nelson, one of Britain's greatest heroes,

his life. [His body was "pickled" in a cask of brandy and returned to England for burial!]

We were able to board and tour on our own through the Victory which lies in dry dock. Docents were present to answer questions and explain various "workings" of crewmen and equipment. We were able to wander at leisure through the three decks among some 100 large cannon. The cramped quarters on these old ships made for ingenious uses of limited space on board. A crew of about 800 men worked, ate and slept on board for weeks or even months at a time.

The crew was divided into "watches" that when off duty slept in hammocks, slung from beams, each hammock being allotted just 14 inches of space! Sharing their sleeping quarters were 30 cannon which fired 32 pound iron balls. During battles at sea the hammocks were rolled up in "splinter nets" and slung along the sides of the upper deck. Following our visit on board the Victory, we visited and toured the nearby Portsmouth Naval Museum.

Our next stop in England was at the city of Bath. There we were able to visit the old Roman Baths, built around the only natural hot springs in England by the Romans following their conquest of England in the 1st Century AD. The Great Bath, seen here, with the water at a constant temperature of 46° C is surrounded by smaller pools in separate rooms each with water of a different temperature. The whole complex was a religious shrine for the Romans, dedicated to their Goddess Minerva.

We'd planned to visit Stonehenge, but had been informed that visitors were no longer permitted inside a fenced off space surrounding the area and, as it was getting late, we passed it by. I wish now we'd gone to see it, regardless. At least we could have gotten some photographs.

The next morning, after getting lost in the large city of Bristol, we proceeded to the Severn River, and into Wales. I mentioned earlier that driving on the left side of the road didn't bother me that much. Driving the main highways was easy, however several things, did bother me! On all but the main highways the roads tended to be very narrow and had a low curb along the edge of the road with no "shoulder." The narrow roads made driving nerve-wracking as large trucks and busses approached, especially when rounding curves which were plentiful. The other problem, which accounted for frequently losing my way, was the system of signs that were in use everywhere except on the major "freeways." On other roads the roadsigns were small, and there was no rhyme or reason where to look for them. They might be found on telephone poles, sides of buildings, trees, fence posts, etc. You never knew where to look for them and they were small, posted at various heights off the ground, and often there would be as many as six or eight signs pointing in different directions.

To make finding one's way even more difficult, stopping to ask directions was virtually useless. I'm a "map person," and was trying to follow route numbers on maps. The local people at gas stations or on street corners knew nothing about the route numbers. If I asked how to get to M4, I'd get a blank look. "What's an M4?" If I then asked how to get to the road to Cardiff, I'd get directions such as, "Go ahead a mile or two, and turn left at the 2nd pub. At the next petrol station, turn right and then go straight until you've gone through 2 stop lights and a stop sign, then make a left turn at the second roundabout, and you should see a sign directing you to Cardiff from there." There was no way to write all that down and my memory is not sharp enough to remember directions like that! So we frequently wasted a lot of time trying to find our way to our next destination.

In this instance we finally found our way across the Severn River and into Wales. A highlight that day was a large outdoor "Museum of Welsh Life", similar to the Folk Park in Ireland that I described in Chapter 37. This museum, near a little town called St. Fagans, just west of Cardiff, is considered one of Europe's finest open air museums. We found no reason to disagree.

We drove on across southern Wales, then the next day turned north up the west coast through Aberystwyth and again inland to the north flowing Conwy River, stopping to tour the impressive and extensive Bodnant Gardens, left, covering some 80 acres, and then on to our next B&B in the walled city of Conwy on the north coast of Wales. The next day we toured the city walls and the ruined Conwy Castle, built by order of King Edward I, of England [colorfully known as "Longshanks], between 1283 and 1287.

Leaving Wales we turned east back into England, then north. Skirting the large urban areas of Liverpool and Manchester, we enjoyed a leisurely drive through England's scenic and peaceful Lake District, stopping for the night in Carlisle. After touring impressive Carlisle Castle, we spent the next day visiting several sites along Hadrian's Wall. Built by the Romans, beginning in 120 AD, by order of the Emperor Hadrian, this great wall stretched 73 miles across the narrow "waist" of England from the North Sea to the Solway Firth. Built to halt frequent invasions by warlike Scottish tribes, it marked the farthest expansion of Roman Britain. Like other walls or fences built to keep peoples either out or in, from the Great Wall of China to the Berlin Wall, it was far from a complete success. Sections of a much lower wall have been rebuilt following the original course. Also exposed in a number of places are the foundations of old Roman barracks.

We then headed north into Scotland. Our first stop in Scotland was at the coastal town of Largs on the broad Firth [estuary] of Clyde. Just offshore was the site where an important sea battle took place in 1263 in which the Scots defeated a fleet of Viking ships which effectively ended Viking raids which had plagued Scotland and Ireland for years. After visiting an interesting museum called Vikingar in Largs, we bypassed Glasgow and headed north toward the Scottish Highlands.

After driving along the length of fabled Loch Lomond we took the "high road" over Rannoch Moor down into Glencoe, site of the cruel massacre of the Glencoe MacDonald clan by order of Britain's King William in the winter of 1692. A small but very informative Visitor Center helped interpret that sad, tragic story. We then travelled north alongside Loch Linnhe, spending a night at a B&B overlooking the long, narrow loch, to Fort William at the foot of Ben Nevis, Scotland's highest mountain (pictured here). We walked through the "down town" section of Fort William, before resuming our trip headed for the Isle of Skye.

Driving west we stopped at the Glenfinnan monument marking where "Bonnie Prince Charlie" [Charles Edward Stuart], known to his enemies as "the Young Pretender"

to the English throne, landed to begin the 1745 Jacobite "rising" aimed at restoring his father's Stuart line of Kings to the thrones of Scotland and England. Resulting in one of the more famous and tragic episodes of Scottish history it ended at Culloden Moor which we would visit a bit later.

That's a statue of Prince Charles on top of the column, looking south over Glen Shiel. Zen looks north across the road at the long 21 arch West Highland Railroad viaduct which was seen on film in three of the "Harry Potter" films.

Next we would board a ferry at Mallaig which took us across the Sound of Sleat to the Isle of Skye, the largest of the Hebrides Islands off the west coast of Scotland.

We visited the Clan Donald Center with its lovely gardens, near the ferry landing at Armadale, then drove up island to Dunvegan Castle, the stronghold of Clan McLeod for over 800 years. We toured the castle, still the home of the 29th McLeod Chief, staying that night nearby at a local B&B.

The next day we crossed the Isle of Skye and returned to the mainland via the long modern bridge connecting the Isle of Skye with the Scottish mainland spanning the narrow Kyle of Localsh. A few miles took us to the restored Clan MacRae castle of Eilean Donan on a small island at the juncture of 3 sea lochs, Loch Alsh, Loch Long and Loch Duich. A short causeway now connects the little islet to the mainland.

The castle was shelled by 3 English frigates and totally destroyed in 1719 and lay in ruins for some 200 years. In 1920 the original ground and floor plans were found and between 1920 and 1932 the castle was rebuilt to exact specification, a project financed entirely by two men of Clan MacRae.

Eilean Donan Castle has been the setting for a number of Hollywood movies and bears the distinction of being the most photograph-ed castle in Scotland. Cameras were not allowed inside, but we took several photographs of the exterior. Unfortunately, the day we were there was dark and rainy which resulted in poor quality photos. Eilean Donan deserves a better showing so here's a photo that I copied from Wikipedia. Beautiful, eh?

Our course then took us up Glen Shiel past the Five Sisters mountains and then

down Glen Morriston to what is probably Scotland's best known feature, Loch Ness. We drove down the west side of this 23 mile long, narrow fresh water loch, stopping for a look at the ruins of Urquart Castle and on into the city of Inverness. And, no, we did not encounter, or see, "Nessie" the mythical "Loch Ness Monster."

After a quick look at Inverness, we stopped at a B&B a few miles east of the city. We spent a good part of the next day at the nearby Culloden Battlefield. This was the site of the last major military engagement in Great Britain. A number of Highland Clans had rallied to the call of 23 year old "Bonnie Prince

Charlie", in a vain attempt to restore to the throne his father the exiled King James VI [of Scotland] and James I [of England].

The "Bonnie Prince" had landed with 7 men at Glenfinnan, and proceeded to raise an army of Highland Clansmen who won a decisive victory over a much larger English army at Preston Pans near Edinburgh. Flushed with victory, Prince Charles' troops then invaded England, taking the city and castle of Carlisle, and then pressing south through England until they reached Derby in central England. Against the wishes of Prince Charles, advice from his officers and rumors of English armies gathering stopped the advance and the Highlanders turned back.

The retreat did not end until the badly depleted force found itself back in Scotland, on Culloden Moor east of Inverness. There on April 16, 1746, the exhausted, half-starved Highlanders, hampered by boggy ground, lack of artillery and poor command decisions were routed by a larger English army under the Duke of Cumberland. The victory by Cumberland was followed by an orgy of killing that earned the Duke the well-deserved *sobriquet* of "Butcher" Cumberland.

Prince Charles escaped and aided by sympathizers eventually returned to France where he lived to be a dissipated and dissolute old man. Zenith and I explored the battlefield and excellent Visitor Center on a bitter cold, windy day, much like that on the day of the battle of Culloden Moor. We then resumed our trip, turning south to visit and tour Blair Castle, at Blair Atholl, home of the Dukes and Earls of Atholl, and the Atholl Highlanders, the only legal, private army in Europe.

From there we stopped near Perth [pronounced, in Scotland, as "Pairth"] to visit Scone Palace, where the monarchs of Scotland were traditionally crowned seated on the Stone of Scone, until Edward I of England had it removed to Westminster Abby

in London! We were able to tour both Blair Castle and Scone Palace which were filled with beautiful furnishings, antiques and historic memorabilia. Both were surrounded by lovely gardens, and Scone palace had an old cemetery with ancient gravestones. Again no photos were allowed inside either one as they are occupied as homes by present-day families.

Our final destination on this trip was Edinburgh, the capital of Scotland. We explored the vast complex of buildings that consti-tute Edinburgh Castle, which dominates the city, high atop a volcanic crag. (pictured at the bottom of p. 229)

After a tour of the castle, we enjoyed strolling down "The Royal Mile" past a number of historic churches interspersed with a variety of stores shops, and restaurants, between the Castle and Holyrood House. This royal "palace" was built between 1501 and 1505 and became the official residence of Scots royalty after the marriage of James IV and Margaret Tudor. After the Union of Scotland and England in 1707, Holyrood House lost its primary functions, however Queen Elizabeth II spends one week in residence at the palace at the beginning of each summer, where she carries out a range of official engagements and ceremonies.

The following day we caught our flight for home, but decided that we hadn't seen enough of Scotland and began making plans to visit both Scotland and Ireland again.

CHAPTER 40

Bus-man's Holiday

We wanted to visit both Ireland and Scotland again, but I'd had my fill of trying to drive those narrow roads, and I was unlikely to be able to rent a car anyway due to my age. Our next trip we planned for 2007 and, this time, we would try a regular bus tour. I checked out several companies that ran bus tours and found a company called C.I.E. Tours that offered a trip that included a tour of Scotland, a ferry trip across the Irish Sea and then a tour of the Irish Republic.

Overnights would be at hotels, the same bus would be used but there would be different Driver/Tour Guides for the two countries. For this trip we flew into Glasgow, Scotland, and were met by our Scottish driver/guide Jim Alexander. He took us to Jury's Inn overlooking the River Clyde. We had time that afternoon to wander around the area near the hotel, where we strolled across the Ha'penny Bridge, a footbridge over the River Clyde, free now but during its early life a half-penny toll was charged to cross.

The next morning we boarded the bus, making our first stop at in interesting Transport Museum which featured a wide variety of transportation methods found in Scotland, from trains to cars of all varieties, to bicycles and Gypsy wagons. Small

cars are the rule in all parts of the British Isles, though not all as small as the one behind Zen! Having tried my luck driving on the many very narrow roads, I heartily approve.

That afternoon we headed north through country we had seen on our previous trip to Scotland, along the shore of Loch Lomond across Rannoch Moor and down into Glencoe. We didn't mind seeing some of the places for a second time because Jim imparted a lot of information that we hadn't been fully aware of when we were on our own. For example we stopped at the tiny village of Inveruglas, near the upper end of Loch Lomond. Jim pointed out a small island offshore where Inveruglas Castle, the stronghold of Clan MacFarland, stood until Oliver Cromwell's army razed it to the ground. I was interested because my father's maternal grandmother was a MacFarland, so this had a special meaning for me.

We crossed the beautiful, wild country of Rannoch Moor. It was chilly in this high country where a sparkling stream, Allt Coire, coming down the mountainside behind Zen would soon join two other streams at "the Meeting of Three Waters" and begin its journey as the River Coe, down through the glen of that name, to Loch Leven and Loch Linnhe. In the last chapter I'd mentioned Glencoe which also had a special meaning for me. A Scottish song that had been a favorite of The Reivers when Charles Mossop and I were singing in Kamloops, had been "The Massacre of Glencoe," so I was interested to learn more about that tragic event from Jim and from the exhibits in the small but very informative visitor center in the glen.

From Glencoe we traveled north to Fort William and then up The Great Glen to Fort Augustus at the southern end of Loch Ness. From there we embarked on a small excursion boat for a cruise part way up this storied Loch and learned more about the Loch and the Great Glen. [We were not surprised that we failed once again to see anything of Nessie.]

After the cruise we drove on up the Great Glen to Inverness, and on to the Culloden battlefield. Again, this was a repeat visit for us, but Jim provided information of various kinds that we'd not been aware of.

A few miles further brought us to the village of Nairn, where we stayed in the absolutely lovely old Newton Hotel that had been built originally as a private residence.

From the hotel we could walk to the bluff overlooking the great Moray Firth, or estuary, and out to sea. That's our CIE tour bus in front of the hotel.

In the morning we headed south down the Strath Spey, in other words the valley of the River Spey. Jim stopped a couple of times just to let us get out of the bus and stretch our legs, while he interpreted what we were viewing, identifying flowering plants like foxglove. Much of the area is treeless except along rivers and one can see for miles, mostly empty country except for scattered crofts or farms, a few grazing cattle and an occasional small loch.

We stopped at Blair Atholl and toured Blair Castle, with its many beautiful furnishings, paintings and historic memorabilia as well as an extensive garden area. The castle, located in Glen Garry was long the home of the Murray's, Dukes of Atholl, and the last castle in the United Kingdom to undergo a prolonged siege. Like Dunvegan Castle and Scone Palace, Blair Castle is another fully restored building that currently serves as a family residence so no photographs were allowed inside and parts of the castle were off-limits to visitors. These castles are all so large that the areas open to the public are still quite extensive.

In the nearby village of Blair Atholl we were given an interesting tour of the whisky distillery. In Scotland, we learned, the beverage is Scotch <u>whisky</u>, without the letter "e". Other brands of the beverage such as rye, bourbon and even Irish, are spelled whiskey. I don't believe Zennie has ever let her lips touch any kind of alcoholic beverage, but from the expression on her face, I think that just inhaling the fumes inside the building got to her a bit!

From here we went on to Edinburgh for a two night stay. The first evening we attended a Scottish Caberet show. The singers, dancers and house comedian made this a totally enjoyable evening.

We even got to try Scotland's "national dish," haggis, after the main dinner. It was spicy, and somewhat to my surprise, tasted really quite good—even if cooked in a sheep's stomach! [I was careful not to inquire as to what constituted the edible portion of the haggis.] On the right is a photo of the Master of Ceremonies, Bill, and our gem of a tour guide, Jim Alexander, who added immeasurably to our enjoyment during this visit to his native Scotland. I think Jim is blushing at something Bill said, but I don't know if it was a compliment or an off-color joke!

The next day was a full day of sightseeing in and around Edinburgh. The old city is built on a massive basalt "plug" formed by a now extinct volcano rising some 400 ft. above the surrounding country. The new city has spread out over the lower land bordering the Firth of Forth [the estuary of the River Forth]. Dominating the old city is Edinburgh Castle, which is a whole complex of massive stone buildings perched, as it were, on the highest part of the volcanic outcrop. We also had an opportunity to stroll up and down the Royal Mile, the narrow street that leads from the Castle to Holyrood House.

The climax to this part of our tour came that evening as we attended the famous Edinburgh Military Tattoo, held on the floodlit esplanade of Edinburgh Castle. The Tatoo has been held annually since 1950 and features performers from all over the world. The performance opened with a "march through" of all performers present, including the massed pipes and drums of the Royal Scots Dragoon Guards, seen here, the Royal Signal Corps, The Black Watch, Royal Regiment of Scotland, Royal Gurkha Rifles, Auckland Police of New Zealand, the Royal Caledonian Society of South Australia and the Royal Army of Oman. Our admission was free, one of the "perks" provided as part of the CIE tour.

The "march through" of all the performers was just the opening event! Performing separately were the Taipei Girls High School Honor Guard and Drum Corps, whose precision marching was outstanding, the Mounted Band of the Blues and Royals performing on horseback, the Massed Commonwealth Highland Dancers from Canada, Australia, New Zealand, and South Africa., and from the U.S., the Middlesex County Volunteer Fifes and Drums, and many others including the IMPS Motorcycle Display Team composed of 38 boys aged 5 to 16 performing intricate maneuvers on motorcycles of varying sizes.

The very moving Tattoo Finale featured all of the performing groups marching in sequence to the strains of "Scotland the Brave". It was a fantastic performance and I'm delighted to say that we have it all on a DVD, and can enjoy watching the entire show again whenever we feel like it!

The next day Jim drove us across the country from Edinburgh to Troon on the Firth of Clyde where our bus was taken by ferry across the North Channel to Larne, Ireland.

Jim drove us south to the Burlington Hotel in Dublin where he bid us goodbye and turned us over to John Broughill who would be our driver/guide for the Ireland part of our trip.

The Hotel was just a few blocks from the beautiful St. Stephen's Green a 22 acre park and one of the largest "greens" in Europe. Laid out in 1880 thanks to a grant of money from the Guinness family it features a lake, flower beds, fountains and many memorials. Zen and I enjoyed a leisurely exploration of the Green.

One of the memorials is this one commemorating the Irish humanitarian and patriot, Countess Constance Markievicz. [In case you're wondering about the title and name, it came about when Ireland-born Constance Gore-Booth married a Polish Count, Casimir Markievicz.]

During the "Easter Rising" of 1916, the "Rebel Countess" was second in command of the Irish Citizen Army detachment that held St. Stephen's Green for six days. Most of the leaders of the Easter Rising were executed by British firing squad. The Countess was given the same sentence, but it was commuted at the last minute. When notified of this, Markievicz' statement to the court was, "I do wish your lot had the decency to shoot me." After a year in prison, she and others were freed when the British government declared a general amnesty.

In 1918 Markievicz became the first woman elected to the British House of Commons but refused to take her seat. She was in jail again for anti-conscription activities the following year, when she was elected to the Dail E'ireann the first government of the new Irish Republic. After her release she served in the Dail until 1922, and became the first female Cabinet Minister. She died in 1927 at the age of 59. Irish writer Sean O'Casey wrote of her, "One thing she had in abundance—physical courage; with that she was clothed as of a garment."

The next morning John bussed us on a tour of Dublin city, including a stop to tour Dublin Castle. This complex of buildings served as the residence of the Lord Lieutenants, the representatives of the British Crown from 1250 until the birth of the Irish Free State in 1922. We spent two nights at the Burlington Hotel. The second evening we were treated to a performance of Doyle's Irish Caberet, held in the hotel. It featured a fine 4-course meal followed by an evening of singing and dancing and a delightful performance by "Ireland's Greatest Comedian," Noel V. Ginnity. I had the good fortune to purchase a DVD of a Ginnity performance so, like the Tattoo, we can enjoy Noel V. Ginnity's humor whenever we want.

From Dublin, John bussed us to the Rock of Cashel [left] and the imposing ruins of the former religious center. The very impressive ruins tell of a sad end to a tragic story. Our visit to the "Rock" was followed by a stop at the Dualla family farm where we enjoyed a light brunch of tea and scones prepared by the wife and several daughters. That was followed by a demonstration by the husband/ father of how dogs are used to herd sheep. Just as this demonstration ended an Irish mist turned into a rather hard rain and we passengers ran to re-board the bus, which we managed to do even without help from the sheepdogs.

Our next stop was at Blarney Castle. Neither Zen nor I was interested in kissing the well-known Blarney Stone. [Zennie says that she's exposed to all the Blarney she can handle from her husband, and is in need of no more!] We did enjoy going through the Blarney Woolen Mills store, admiring the beautiful, but rather expensive merchandise while demonstrating great forbearance in resisting temptation to make purchases. While some in our party were smooching a stone wall, Zen and I visited Christie's Pub and enjoyed some tasty "pub grub" along with a pint of Guinness for me.

Then it was on to Killarney, where we would spend two nights at the Killarney Towers Hotel. The hotel included a pub featuring a pub band that played Irish music in the evening, much to my delight!

The next day we were treated to a ride in an "Irish Jaunting Car." Also known as "pony and trap" rides, the drivers are known as "Jarvies" whose families have done this

for generations. We rode in a "jaunting car," a small 2-wheeled or 4-wheeled cart drawn by a single horse, to nearby Ross Castle, built about 1420, on the shore of one of Killarney's lovely lakes. The weatherman was trying to rain on our little parade so my photos were poor, but here's how our "jaunt" would've looked like on a sunny day.

We then took the obligatory "Ring of Kerry" drive, around the Iveragh Peninsula. I've toured the "Ring of

Kerry" more than once as it seems like every tour that goes near the southwest corner of Ireland includes it. It's a pretty drive, but not really anything spectacular in my opinion. Next time I'm in Ireland, I want to visit the Dingle Peninsula instead!

On this trip around the Ring of Kerry, we stopped at a roadside pull-off, where an enterprising but somewhat bored looking gentleman and his equally bored looking "family," were "busy" earning a living. Tourists who stopped would leave coins in the kettle slung under the tripod, as a "tip" for the privilege of taking a photograph. We obliged, as it appeared to be perhaps the only source of income for an unemployed husband and father. [Note the donkey's patient canine passenger.]

I thought the most interesting part of our tour of the Ring of Kerry on this occasion, was a visit to Valentia Island, connected to the mainland by a long causeway. On the island we enjoyed an audio-visual program, "The Skellig Experience," a history of the small monastic settlement on one of the two rocky pinnacles known as the Skellig Islands that rise from the sea a few miles off the coast. It requires a monumental stretching of the imagination, I believe, to think of these two mountain peaks rising from the sea, as "islands." It's even more of a stretch, I think, to imagine how the settlement on the largest "island", called Skellig Michael, existed there from the 6th to the 12th centuries!

After the Ring of Kerry, we headed back to Killarney. The area around the three Lakes of Killarney is, I think, the prettiest in Ireland. Any visitor should try to include this on their itinerary. Don't miss "Ladies View" so called from the delight it gave to the Ladies-in-Waiting of Queen Victoria when they visited Ireland in 1861.

[Fortunately, men can enjoy the view as well as ladies!] The lake in this photo is just called "Upper Lake."

We continued from Killarney north to the Shannon River Estuary, crossing it by Ferry into County Clare. The Cliffs of Moher were, of course, on the itinerary. [The pronunciation is mo-HER—or mo-HAIR, if you're from Belfast!] These sheer cliffs rise abruptly from the Atlantic Ocean on the west coast of County Clare. Rising 650 to 700 feet above the water, they extend for approximately five miles. On the point of land in the photo rises O'Brien's Tower, a relatively modern structure built for tourists who enjoy views of endless, usually empty, ocean waters.

There are miles of paved walking trails near the cliff edge that provide a variety of scenic views. The enjoyment of walking these trails is enhanced by the usual presence of several individual or paired musicians singing or playing along-side the walkways. There is an interesting new Visitor Center, built partially underground, which is well worth visiting. The exhibits are excellent, and I like the way it's built as it minimizes detraction from the scenic beauty of the

area. Now, I ask you: Isn't this a major improvement over a large, modern building rearing its walls above the green hills and against the blue [sometimes] sky?

Our trip ended with another visit to the Bunratty Folk Park and another Medieval Banquet at Bunratty Castle. Even in two visits, it's hardly possible to do justice to the Folk Park. On each visit there are new things to see and differences in the experiences. And each medieval banquet is also unique and enjoyable.

The next morning Zen and I had time to visit a famous "watering spot," Durty Nelly's Pub [established here in 1620] which we'd missed on our first visit to Bunratty. I enjoyed a farewell pint of Guinness, while Zennie contented herself with soaking up the ambiance. Then we bid goodbye to John, our driver/guide, who drove us to nearby Shannon Airport for our flight home via Aer Lingus, Ireland's customer friendly national airline.

CHAPTER 41

Crusin' Down the Rivers
[Part 1]

We decided that we'd seen enough of Ireland and Scotland for a while. We still want to make at least one more trip to Ireland to see some of things we've missed, like the Aran Islands off the west coast and the Dingle Peninsula, so hope to take one more trip to the Emerald Isle at least. But in the meantime a new species of Travel Bug had sunk its teeth into us. We'd been receiving catalogs from various travel companies, and we were intrigued by the advantages of River Cruises.

We've taken two of these and will take a third in 2013. If you're looking for a relaxed, non-stressful way to travel and learn about the people, scenic locales, history and customs of the areas you visit, River Cruises are the way to go in our opinion. I wrote the following account after we returned from our 2010 cruise. I'm going to just include here it in full, rather than re-writing it.

CASTLES ALONG THE RHINE AND DANUBE
Bryce and Zenaida Babcock's river cruise, June 28-July 15, 2010

THE TOUR COMPANY—VANTAGE DELUXWORLD TRAVEL

VANTAGE
DELUXE WORLD TRAVEL
Castles along the Rhine and Danube
**BRYCE BABCOCK
ARIZONA**

VANTAGE
DELUXE WORLD TRAVEL
Castles along the Rhine and Danube
**ZENAIDA BABCOCK
ARIZONA**

This summer we decided on a river cruise as a change from self-drive or bus tours, both of which we've done in past years. The major reason was that it would be a new experience and also because it promised to be less stressful. It would be like taking a room at a nice hotel and then take the hotel on a trip! Several things appealed to us including not having to pack and unpack every day or two of a two-week-long trip. We hoped this kind of cruise would be minimally stressful.

We checked out several tour companies and decided on using VANTAGE DELUX WORLD TRAVEL. Of the wide variety of places that could be visited, the tour called Castles Along the Rhine and Danube seemed to offer what we were looking for. We contacted several tour companies that offered river cruises and after perusing numerous catalogs and brochures sent to us by the companies, we chose Vantage. We don't regret that choice.

I chose the period just after the summer solstice for our trip as it would offer the maximum daylight hours for enjoying the scenery. In addition to River Cruises in many parts of the globe, Vantage also offers escorted land tours by motor coach and train, "Small Ship Cruises" and traditional Ocean Cruises. They really offer "something for everybody."

THE SHIP—*MS RIVER ODYSSEY*

The ships used on these European river cruises are similar to each other. Ours was called *MS River Odyssey*. They are long and narrow, because they're navigating rivers,

and have 3 decks inside plus an open "sundeck" forward with individual chairs where passengers can relax and enjoy the scenery, take photos or visit with other passengers. Just aft of the open forward deck is the "wheelhouse" from where the Captain or another officer operates and steers the ship

The roof of the wheelhouse and the radar antennae fore and aft can be dropped down where necessary to pass under a low bridge. When this happens the Captain, or whoever is piloting the ship is sitting in his usual place, but with his head poking up through an open hatch. Here's Captain Michael in a rare off-duty appearance.

Behind the wheelhouse is an enclosed area with tables and chairs where people can eat, drink, play cards, visit, etc. There are windows all around so one can still enjoy looking at scenery even if it is cold or raining. [We experienced no rain or uncomfortably cold weather during our trip.] The stern area "up top" is open and has a walking track for exercise and lounging-type chairs for sunbathing, with some awnings for shade available except when going through an area with low bridges to pass under. Then the awnings are taken down.

The upper, largely open deck can be accessed from the main interior deck by stairs on either side. There is also a "lift" alongside the stairs upon which a person can ride up or down if climbing the stairs is a problem.

The main deck is just below this upper, mostly open deck. The forward part of the main deck is the large "Latitude 52 Degree Lounge," with comfortable chairs and tables, a bar and also a piano and electronic keyboard for music in the evenings. Tea, coffee, hot chocolate, etc. are available free of charge in the lounge at most all times, and the pay-for-service bar, serving wines, beer and mixed drinks is also available except in the "wee hours." Large windows frame three sides of the lounge.

Here I am in an unusually empty Lounge. Lectures and musical entertainment take place in the Lounge at scheduled times, and there is a large screen for slide shows that can be put in place when needed. The center area can be used as a dance floor. I have to admit that I spent most of my on-board time either in the lounge or the open air upper deck described earlier.

Just aft of the lounge is an open central "lobby" containing the reception desk, the doors on either side for boarding or leaving the boat, racks with postcards, souvenir items, etc., for sale. There is a corner area where at least one of the four "Program Managers" is usually available to answer questions about the day's activities including scheduled shore excursions.

Aft of the reception area this deck has two levels. On the upper level is a small but well stocked library and two computers for use by passengers, along with the largest most luxurious [and most expensive!] passenger cabins on each side of a center hallway that leads to the large "Compass Rose Restaurant" at the rear of the ship. This restaurant is on two levels and is where all meals on board are served.

On the lower level behind the reception area are the next best passenger cabins which also extend forward under the lounge and under the cabins above as far back as the restaurant level. There is also a fully equipped exercise room. Under the upper level of the restaurant, is the kitchen area which is off limits to passengers. There is still another deck below this with the engines forward, and the least expensive passenger cabins [I call it "steerage"] and the quarters for the crew. I chose one of these cabins for our trip as I figured that we would spend little time in our cabin. It would have been nice to have a little more comfortable and spacious cabin, but we basically used it only for sleeping.

I should mention that the dress code on board the ship is strictly casual. The only times that passengers are encouraged to "dress up" were the Captain's Welcome Dinner on the evening of the first day, and the Captain's Farewell Dinner at the end of the cruise. Even on those occasions, I noticed that a majority of passengers were still dressed fairly casually.

Here are some of the technical facts about the *River Odyssey*:

Year of construction:	2002
Length:	410 feet
Width:	38 feet
Draft:	5 feet
Height above waterline:	25 feet with extended wheelhouse
	19.7 feet with retracted wheelhouse
Speed:	9.70 mph upstream
	13.40 mph downstream
Passengers:	168 maximum
Crew:	45
Usage:	about 55 gallons of diesel oil per hour
Route:	From Amsterdam thru the Holland-Amsterdam-Rhine Canal
	Up the Rhine River to Mainz
	Up the Main River to Bamberg
	Through the Main-Danube Canal to Kelheim
	Down the Danube River to Budapest

STAFF AND CREW

The 45 staff and crew members came from a wide variety of countries. The crew members that we had the most contact with were Ladislav, who had the title Hotel Manager, and his assistant, a very pretty dark haired girl named Cristina from Romania. Zen took my photo with Cristina, my favorite crew member! [For the Captain's Farewell Dinner I had even worn a tie!] Ladislav and Cristina worked the Front Desk and we saw and dealt with them several times every day.

The head bartender was a very pleasant young lady with a ponytail named Daniella who filled my frequent orders for glasses of Chardonnay or Pinot Grigio throughout the trip. I got this photo of Daniella and her boyfriend, who was a crew member. I never saw Cristina or Daniella without a smile!

Detlef, the Executive Chef, was in charge of the kitchen and was very businesslike and helpful, while we especially appreciated one of the *sous* [assistant] *chefs*, Radu, who made mouth-watering breakfast omelets to whatever specifications you wanted. Zenith was an especial favorite of Radu who, although a native of Romania had worked with Filipino chefs and spoke Tagalog, Zenith's native language.

Most of the ship's crew we hardly saw while many of the staff we knew by sight but most of the contact was in regard to their jobs as waiters, food servers and maids. The head of housekeeping was Mariana, a very pleasant young lady whose ready smile and cheerful greeting always seemed to light up the entire ship! Our maid was a very shy quiet girl named Nara, making her first river cruise. She and Febry, a young man working as a waiter in the restaurant, were from Indonesia. Without exception **all** of the staff that we had contact with, were unfailingly friendly and polite. They all did their jobs efficiently and courteously.

The staff with whom passengers had the most involvement were the four Program Managers: two Dutch ladies, Tineke van den Berge and Erna Hoek and two men, Werner Kren from Germany and Marc Sullivan from Great Britain. These four were in charge of all the daily excursions off the ship and had, perhaps, the most difficult but enjoyable jobs of anyone aboard. The passengers were divided, roughly equally, into four groups and each group was assigned to one of the Program Managers with a color-coded designation.

The Program Managers all seemed very capable, but Zen and I were grateful that we were in Marc's "Blue" group. He, more than anyone else on board, made our whole experience a special treat. Extremely knowledgeable, unfailingly cheerful and helpful, always with time to answer any kind of question and with the patience of Job! Zen and I both thought that Marc was the individual who contributed the most to our enjoyment of the trip. Marc was SUPER!! The photo on page 244 shows Mark and Erna.

GOING AND COMING

I won't say much about the flights over and back, but a few words may be appropriate. Vantage booked our flights. We just gave them the departure and arrival points. We were booked on United Airlines from Phoenix, AZ, to Dulles Airport in Washington, D.C., and then from there to Amsterdam. The first leg of the flight was not too bad, but the flight from Dulles to Amsterdam was the most uncomfortable flight I've ever experienced. The Economy Class seats had virtually no leg room, and—even for people as short as Zen and I—were extremely uncomfortable. I don't think either of us got any sleep on the night flight and were stiff and sore [and sleepy!] when we arrived.

The contrast with the return flight on Lufthansa was remarkable. I don't think I've ever had better flights than the ones from Budapest to Munich and, especially, the LONG flight from Munich to Charlotte, N.C. Roomy seating, free movies to choose from with free earphones, free drinks [wine and beer included!], tasty free meals, and attentive flight attendants made the flight quite enjoyable. Our advice: whenever possible, if you are going to fly, fly Lufthansa! The only LONG flight we've ever had that came close to comparing with Lufthansa, was the non-stop flight we made in 2001 from Los Angeles to Dublin on Aer Lingus. U.S. airlines have much room for improvement!

THE CRUISE—CASTLES ALONG THE RHINE AND DANUBE

DAY # 1, June 29—Amsterdam, Netherlands

We arrived at the Amsterdam airport shortly before noon [local time] and were met upon arrival by Marc Sullivan, one of Vantage's Program Managers for this cruise. A bus chartered by Vantage took us to a downtown hotel where Vantage had booked a meeting place. Several cruise passengers had arrived on the same flight and we all joined a number of others who had arrived earlier and still more continued to arrive through the afternoon. Marc, who had to meet other flights, turned us over to another of the Program Managers, Erna Hoek. A lunch catered by the Hotel was served as it would be several hours before we could board the *River Odyssey*.

Zen and I found ourselves at a table with two other couples who would be frequent companions on the cruise. Steve and Shirley Townsend, from Rochester, NY, had been on Vantage cruises before. Shirley has difficulty walking and uses a cane, which limited her from participating in some of the land excursions, but said she still enjoyed going on the cruises. The other couple who shared our table was Larry and Nora King from

North Carolina. Some years younger than the Townsends, they were also veterans of several cruises.

Erna had told the group of several things we could do on our own during the afternoon while we waited to board the ship. Zen and I had talked about visiting the Anne Frank Museum while in Amsterdam, if that were possible. The museum is the building where the teenaged Anne Frank, with her family and several other Jewish acquaintances were hidden during the Nazi occupation. If you haven't read "The Diary of Anne Frank" written by this remarkable girl, you should. Erna had mentioned the museum being within walking distance, so I asked for and received directions for finding it, and Steve decided to join Zennie and I in visiting it.

Erna also gave us advice regarding being pedestrians in Amsterdam! The main point being, "Watch out for bicyclists!" It was needed advice! I've never seen so many bicycles in my life. They have the right of way over pedestrians, and side-walks virtually belong to them! The riders—men, women, boys, girls, young and old—all seem to careen along at their top speed. So walking the 12 or 15 blocks to our destination was a bit harrowing until we got used to the two-wheeled traffic.

"Parked" bikes crowded all available space along every street! Of course, the streets themselves belonged to automobiles, so a sharp lookout had to be maintained when crossing streets. The streets and even the bridges are lined with racks full of bicycles as you can see from the photo.

Amsterdam has almost as many canals as it has streets, over 100 km of canals and some, 1,500 bridges! Steve and Zennie and I groped our way in the direction of our destination and finally reached it: a tall building jammed in the middle of a block of other similar tall buildings. We recognized it by a long line of people stretching along the block and around the corner, squeezed tightly against the buildings to leave room for the bicycle traffic!

From across the street we could make out a small sign identifying the Anne Frank Museum. We watched for some time and realized that the line wasn't moving! Finally, after several minutes, 4 or 5 people emerged from the building and 4 or 5 of those at the head of the line entered. The line moved up a few feet and stopped again. It was

obvious that we would have a LONG, LONG wait to get in and we didn't have all day. Stopping only to view a small bronze statue of Anne Frank nearby, We decided that we would take a pass on visiting the museum.

As we walked back—it was a fairly hot, sunny day—dodging bicycles as before, I noticed many boats making their slow and quiet way up and down the canals and remembered that another option Erna had mentioned was to take a ride up and down some of the canals. As it turned out, it would have been a much better choice. Unless you are a real glutton for punishment, my advice to anyone going on this tour would be unhesitating: take the canal boat ride!

Upon our return to the hotel, I told Erna, that we'd found the Museum but hadn't gone through it because of the glacial slowness of the long lineup. "Oh", she said," it's always like that!" I couldn't help thinking, "Really!! Why didn't you tell me that in the first place?" She was, I'm sure, somewhat embarrassed, but was "rescued" by another member of our group who intervened, at that moment. I decided that I'd made my point and didn't pursue the matter. I thought it was not a very auspicious start to our holiday, but it turned out to be one of the very few negative moments of the entire experience. The *River Odyssey* left the dock at 9 PM, made its' way through the Holland-Amsterdam-Rhine Canal and into the Rhine River and began its journey up that large stream. Zen and I were tired from our long rather fruitless walk on a fairly hot afternoon, so I treated myself to a glass of wine in the lounge, and then went to bed. We wanted to be fresh and ready for the next day.

Day #2, June 30—Up the Lower Rhine River

There is very heavy ship traffic on the lower Rhine, going in both directions. Mostly long narrow craft with a small cabin near the rear and a cargo area covering about 75-80 percent of the vessel. Some smaller ships and pleasure vessels were in evidence as well. This was a quiet peaceful full day of sailing upstream on the broad and busy Rhine River.

The country at first was fairly flat and featured pastoral scenes of farms with fields of grazing cattle and sheep. We sailed under many bridges which featured a wide variety of design and structure. I never dreamed that there were so many different ways to build bridges. Many of the newer bridge designs are imaginative and artistic—some a treat to look at, others look ready to collapse.

The pattern of meals on board held up through the entire trip. An "early riser" breakfast consisting of a variety of breads and sweet rolls was available in the forward Lounge between 6:30 and 7:30 AM. Two dispensing machines were available from which coffee, tea, hot chocolate and other "breakfast drinks" could be obtained. There were usually anywhere from 10 to 20 passengers that could be found in the lounge during that hour. Then the regular breakfast was served in the Restaurant between 7:30 and 9:30. This was a buffet style meal, and just about any kind of breakfast could be had. A variety of rolls and breads, a toaster where you laid a slice of bread on a rack and it went through the machine in less than a minute, coming out perfectly toasted, a variety of cold and hot cereals, eggs [cooked in a variety of ways], bacon, sausages, a variety of fruits and fruit juices—just about anything most Americans would think of for a breakfast meal. A highlight, I thought, was Radu, one of the cooks who would fix an omelet to your specifications while you waited [it took him only a minute or two per omelet!] which were invariably delicious!

On this first day of the cruise, the Captain and the Program Managers spoke to all passengers at a 10 AM meeting in the Lounge about the choices and optional excursions that would be available on subsequent days. Various crew members and staff were introduced and spoke briefly. At 11 AM Werner Kren, one of the Program Managers presented a lesson on the German language since two thirds or more of the cruise would be in German-speaking areas. He gave everyone a handout of common German words

and phrases and spoke about some rules of pronunciation which we found to be both interesting and helpful.

Lunch was served daily at noon in the Restaurant and, like breakfast, was a buffet style meal. Being a notoriously fussy eater, I was appreciative of this as I could always find things to eat that were pleasing to my "picky palate."

The afternoon of this first day's cruise was free and Zen and I spent time exploring the ship and its facilities. We even did a few laps—Zennie a few more than I—walking around the open rear deck "walking track." I spent several hours sitting on the open foredeck just enjoying the scenery and taking pictures. Zen played with one of the computers a bit and found a couple of books in the library that looked interesting.

Three o'clock was "tea time" in the lounge, and everyone gathered there at 6 PM for the "Captain's Welcome Drink", which was followed by the first of a daily "Port Talk". This was usually given each evening by one of the Program Managers in rotation. The purpose of the Port Talks was to inform the passengers what to expect the next day: Where we would be, what activities—both on board and ashore—would be available. Details of the town, city or region where we would be spending the day would be discussed, the procedures to be followed on the next days' land excursions, the choices available to passengers, restroom availability, and any cautionary matters such as how much walking or stair climbing would be involved, etc. Our stop on Day 3 would be in the city of Cologne, Germany, and we were given a brief description of that city and its' history. We found that these daily "Port Talk" briefings on the next day's activities were VERY helpful and interesting.

The "Captain's Welcome Dinner" followed at 7 PM in the restaurant. It was one of the two occasions [the "Captain's Farewell Dinner" was the other] that were at least semi-formal in nature. We arrived in Cologne at about 8 PM.

I should also note that each passenger cabin had a television and two or three movies, which differed each evening, would be available to choose from. In addition a semi-documentary film on a topic related to the area we were traveling through would also be available. Tonight was a 55 min. Film on "The Rhine" river. There was also a channel showing live a view looking ahead which was interesting when approaching a canal lock just barely wide enough to accommodate our ship!

DAY 3, July 1—COLOGNE

Every morning of the cruise we would find, slipped under our cabin door, a 3 or 4 page mimeographed "newspaper" with summaries of latest U.S. and world news, sports, stock reports, etc. Also a Daily Program sheet was available each morning. This was extremely helpful as it gave passengers the day's schedule of events, a weather report and lunch and dinner menus. I won't repeat every day the schedule of meals, the afternoon cocktail hour and Port Talk, etc. which were daily occurrences.

Incidentally, daytime temperatures were in the low 80s F, most days. Today's scheduled off-ship excursion was a walk to the large Roman-Germanic Museum, located on one side of the Cologne square and next to the beautiful and imposing Cologne Cathedral pictured below. For most on shore excursions there was a fairly set procedure.

As I said earlier, we passengers were divided into four roughly equal groups each designated by a color: blue, green, yellow and orange. Zenith and I were in the Blue group. Each group was assigned to the same Program Manager for the entire trip. We "lucked out" as our Blue group was assigned to Marc! The schedule called for a staggered start for the 4 groups at 15 minute intervals. This helped to avoid congestion both on board as we prepared to leave and at our destination for the day. The order of the start was rotated every day. Today we, the Blue group, were first.

[A slight digression for something I forgot to mention earlier: Upon boarding, we had turned over a credit card to the front desk attendant, either Cristina or Ladislav. This was used to cover costs of drinks at the bar, souvenirs, postcards, stamps and various incidental expenses that we might incur. We were also given—for use during the trip—a set of earphones that we kept in our possession for the duration. Before we left the ship on a planned land excursion we would leave the key to our cabin at the desk—each person had a key—and we would be given a small transmitter. We

would plug our earphones into the transmitter and would then be able to hear directions and commentary from our Program Manager or local guide. Upon returning to the ship we would turn in the transmitter at the front desk and our room key would be returned. This arrangement was VERY helpful, as we could always hear our guide no matter how far away or how many people were between he/she and group stragglers.]

Back now to our first off-ship excursion: At their appointed time each group would gather near the front desk, turn in our keys and receive a transmitter. Then, led by our intrepid Program Manager we would disembark and receive instructions as to what channel to set the transmitter and receive final instructions while making sure that everyone could hear the Program Manager. Oh, yes, the Program manager would also have a large wooden "paddle" painted to match the group's color code—remember, we were blue! He/she would from time to time hold the paddle high overhead so everyone in the group could see where he/she was and see if a corner was being turned, or if he had stopped to explain something or describe what was going to happen next. It sounds rather complicated, but actually worked very well.

We would then proceed, led by our Program Manager, to our objective if it was a walking tour,

or to a bus if we were to be driven first to a destination. On this day we followed Marc as we walked to the city square, with the beautiful Cologne Cathedral on one side and the large Roman-Germanic Museum on the other. We were then told where to meet Marc after our tour of the museum, and were turned over to a local guide, [in this case a Museum employee]. Also equipped with a microphone and transmitter he conducted us through the museum.

Cologne had been a large Roman city during the glory years of the Roman Empire and the museum was devoted to artifacts from those days that had been found or excavated. It was a very extensive display housed in a huge modern building. During the excavating, a large mosaic floor was uncovered and as it was too big to move, the museum was simply built over and around it!]

After the museum tour, we had a couple hours free time to explore the city. [Marc had given us explicit directions for finding our way back to the ship.] Zennie and I explored around a bit and I bought a new wrist watch at a shop we found as my old watch had died the day before. Zen bought several T-shirts as gifts for friends.

We found our way back to the ship OK, and enjoyed the usual cocktail hour, Port Talk, and dinner. Later there was music in the lounge provided by Richard the ship's resident musician, on piano and keyboard. The *River Odyssey* departed Cologne at 11:30 PM.

Day 4, July 2—THE RHINE VALLEY & RüDESHEIM

The Rhine Valley is beautiful, with the hills along both banks crowned with 20 or more castles such as Marksburg Castle seen here near the town of Braübach. Some in ruins, and some restored, modernized and occupied. I spent most of the morning on the sundeck taking pictures. From here on I won't bother to repeat all the daily Procedures, but will only describe the experiences unique to the particular day. This morning consisted of a relaxed cruise up the Rhine River Valley. A commentary by the Captain, speaking from the ship's bridge and broadcast only to the forward sundeck and lounge, described the Rhine and the area we were going through, between Koblenz at the mouth of the Moselle River to Rüdesheim.

About halfway along this stretch of the Rhine, the river flows through a narrow gap dominated on the east by the famed crag known as the Lorelei. Old legends told of a beautiful maiden who, disappointed in love, threw herself from the crag to her death in the river. Her spirit haunts the area as a siren called Lorelei, whose unearthly beauty and enchanting songs bewitched sailors, distracting their minds from the dangerous rapids and whirlpool at the foot of the crag, often causing them to be wrecked and drown. Poems and songs have made the Lorelei Rock world famous. At the foot of the cliff is a sculptor's depiction of the Lorelei. The statue is better viewed from the road than from the river. If accurate, one look is all it takes to understand how the sailors, boatmen and passengers could be bewitched just by listening and looking for her and neglect to watch for the hazardous rocks, rapids and whirlpool!

The Captain also described the onshore options that passengers would have during the afternoon after we arrived and docked at the town of Rüdesheim. We could choose from two options. One option was to board a "mini-train" at 1:45 PM which would take passengers to Siegfried's Musical Instrument Museum in the town, which we were told was pronounced *"Rudess-heim"* not *"Rudeh-sheim"* which most of us were saying. [Thanks, Werner!]. This small museum features a collection of mechanical self-playing musical instruments covering three centuries. For the benefit of those passengers who were not up to a fairly long walk back to the ship, they could look around the picturesque little town at their leisure and the mini-train would pick them up at 4:15 PM and return them to the ship.

The other option was to stay on the "mini-train" to a station in town where we could ride in cable gondola cars to an enormous monument high on the mountainside

above the town. It's known as the Niederwald Monument, built to commemorate German unification in 1871. Zenith and I chose that option. We rode up in small cable cars, 2 persons to a car, to this huge monument. From that point about 225 meters above the town there were lovely views over the town and river. Extensive vineyards covered many of the surrounding slopes.

The Monument itself, on the edge of the forest, is mammoth in size, standing 38 meters in height. It is topped by a bronze female figure representing "Germania" who is holding aloft a replica of the German Emperor's crown and holding in her other hand the Imperial Sword. Germania, alone, weighs 32 tons! Below this hefty lady is a huge, finely detailed bronze relief showing some 200 life-size figures. These include the Emperor Wilhelm I on horseback, surrounded by German princes, statesmen, generals and soldiers from all branches of the armed forces. On either side of the monument are two more large statues representing "angels" of war and of peace. [I got only their wingtips in the photo!] Erected between 1877 and 1883, the entire monument cost 1.2 million gold marks, more than one million coming from donations from German citizens.

After riding the cable cars back down to the station Zen and I took the rather long walk, with many of the other passengers, back to the ship. It was a hot, humid afternoon and we were tired, so after the evening meal we skipped a performance in the lounge by two local musicians. We sailed from Rüdesheim at 11 PM. A 48 min. film on our next destination, Heidelberg Castle, pictured on the following page, was available on the cabin TVs this evening.

DAY 5—July 3 FRANKFURT/HEIDELBERG CASTLE

Heidelberg Castle, is enormous! It sits on the side of a mountain just outside the modern city of the same name. Part of the castle is in ruins, but part has been restored. The ship arrived and docked in Frankfurt about 6 AM. Frankfurt is on the Main River [pronounced "Mine"] just above its junction with the Rhine. [pronounced Rhine!] Two optional "land tours" were available again on this day. One was described as a two and a half hour motor coach tour of Frankfurt that included a walk through the historical part of the city in the morning. The other was a full day excursion by motor coach to the nearby city of Heidelberg that included a walking tour of Heidelberg Castle with

lunch at a local restaurant. We chose that one! [Zen and I agree. We're sure that it was the right choice!]

The bus, after a restroom stop in the city, took us to the castle entrance where we were turned over to a local guide. His name was Peter, born in Montreal, Canada, and now living in Heidelberg. Peter was a fantastic guide, extremely knowledgeable and with a great sense of humor! We felt we were both educated and entertained on our tour of the castle, and I rate it as perhaps the best of our land tours.

There's an interesting story behind the statue pictured on the previous page that Peter explained to us. Take a close look at the statue. Notice the middle finger of the warrior's right hand. This rather ostentatious gesture is **not** an obscenity, but it **is** a deliberate warning message to all who might encounter him. Here's the explanation: During the period of the 100 Years War [1337-1453] the English longbow had become by far the most lethal weapon of war. It had far greater range <u>and</u> accuracy, plus it offered a much more rapid process of "reloading" than the clumsy crossbows of other nations during that era.

Soldiers captured in battle were often "exchanged" during lulls in the almost constant warfare and when longbow soldiers were captured it had become an established practice for their captors to amputate the middle finger of their right hand before an exchange took place. Why? Without that digit a man could not effectively draw the longbow, so by cutting off that finger you made certain that he would no longer be a feared warrior.

By being "disfingered" the soldier would be effectively disarmed! The man portrayed in the statue is signaling to any potential enemy that he's still an effective longbow warrior! The deliberately displayed digit is not meant as an insult, it's a boast and a warning to actual or potential enemies! "Don't mess with me, Dude! I can still pull a mean longbow!" Information like this was one of the things that made Peter's presentation a special treat.

There was an unfortunate accident during our tour of Heidelberg Castle, when an elderly lady in our group missed her footing and fell while descending a stone stairway. She suffered two cuts to her scalp. Two young girls, leaders of another tour group, witnessed the accident and immediately gave assistance. Betty, the injured lady, was taken to a hospital, received seven stitches and rejoined our group before we returned to our ship! That kind of service is why I so strongly favor "single-payer," government medical insurance! [Unpaid commercial!]

After leaving the Castle we enjoyed a fine catered lunch at the Ritter Hotel, followed by a stroll around town including a large "open-air" market in the city square. After that we were bussed back into Frankfurt, where our ship was docked. We all re-boarded the *River Odyssey* about 5 PM, in time for dinner on board and the ship got underway at 10 PM bound for our next port of call, Wertheim. It had been a <u>very</u> enjoyable day.

DAY 6—July 4 WERTHEIM [VAIRT-heim]

Being the U.S. Independence Day holiday, and given the fact that almost all of the passengers were from the U.S., we found when we went for breakfast that the *River Odyssey was* festooned with red, white and blue banners and other patriotic symbols.

At 10 o'clock in the morning we were treated to one of the most enjoyable and interesting onboard events, a glass-blowing demonstration by a Wertheim resident and a highly skilled practitioner of that craft, Mr. Karl Ittig. He demonstrated the basics of glass-blowing with deft skill and an unexpected droll sense of humor. He had many objects of his craft for sale and did a brisk business.

We bought a "Galileo Thermometer," with the different colored floating glass balls inside a glass tube, such as the one standing just in front of Mr. Ittig's right hand in the photo. Later, during our afternoon walking tour through Wertheim, we were able to visit Mr. Ittig's family operated shop and store in which hundreds of their products are crafted and may be seen and/or purchased. The walk gave us a good sense of the atmosphere of a German town, with typical narrow cobblestone streets lined with shops of all kinds.

That walking tour began at 2 PM. We took it instead of making a visit to a local family which was an option available but required an extra fee. Besides seeing Mr. Ittig's place of business, it was a pleasure to take a leisurely stroll along the cobble-stone streets and "window shop." The *River Odyssey* left Wertheim at 7 O'clock that evening while passengers enjoyed a "4th of July dinner" followed by music in the lounge by our onboard pianist, Richard.

DAY 7—JULY 5 WÜRTZBURG / ROTHENBURG

The *River Odyssey* arrived at Würtzburg at about 8 AM. The first event of the day was an informative hour long lecture on "The European Union" in the Lounge at 8:30. Passengers had a choice of two on-shore excursions. One was a motor coach trip to visit the "Würtzburg Residenz." This vast gilded baroque palace, on the edge of town, was built between 1720 and 1744, as the residence of a series of ruling Prince-Bishops. The visit concluded with a wine tasting session of Franconian wines in the cellar. Würtzburg was almost totally destroyed by allied bombing raids during WWII, but has been meticulously rebuilt, mainly by women, known as *trümmerfrauen ["rubble women"]* as the men of the town were mostly dead or in prison.

Zenith and I chose the other option, an excursion by motor coach to visit the quaint medieval walled town of Rothenburg [say ROE-ten-berg] ob der Tauber. The town lies on a bluff overlooking the Tauber River, a tributary of the Main. After a pleasant drive which gave us a good picture of the prosperous looking countryside, with fields growing a variety of crops, we received an introduction to Rothenburg from Werner who acted as our Program Manager on this trip. Most of the visit we were on our own to wander at leisure exploring this very interesting town.

The photo gives a view of the town square, the open space a real contrast with the narrow crowded streets. We were each given 15 Euros by Werner to buy our lunch at a place of our choice [there were many eating establishments] and Zen and I ended up at a restaurant right on the town square. By the time we finished lunch the square was packed with people, as a visiting high school band from Michigan [!] arrived to give an outdoor concert. We got to listen to a part of it.

After another half-hour drive in the motor coach through the peaceful countryside, we were back on the *River Odyssey* by about 4:30 and the ship sailed at 5 o'clock for our next stop at Bamberg. The four Program Managers entertained passengers in the Lounge after dinner, with a "Liar's Club" game which we missed as Zenith had a headache and I was just plain tired.

DAY 8—JULY 6 BAMBERG

The morning was spent cruising leisurely as we continued up the Main River. Bamberg is where the cruise leaves the Main River and enters the Main-Danube canal for the next leg of our trip. It was hardly recognizable as a canal. It looked much like the rivers except that there were a number of locks spaced along the way between Bamberg and Kelheim, where we would enter the Danube River. We arrived in

Bamberg at noon and a motor coach took us into the city center where we met our local Bamberg guide. He took us on a rather lengthy walking tour that led through the city square and its' open air market along and over the little river Regnitz that flows through town, then uphill to the magnificent cathedral, several beautiful rose gardens, along with other historic buildings.

After this enjoyable but somewhat tiring walking tour, we stopped for a bite to eat at a little outdoor restaurant. I had a pint of Bamberg's "Smoked Beer" and pizza! Then it was back to the *River Odyssey,* arriving about 5 PM. After dinner a local musical group the Günzenheimer Trio entertained in the lounge. The movie tonight was "Judgement at Nuremberg," that city being our next port of call.

Day 9—July 7 Nürnberg [Nuremberg]

After an 8:30 lecture on "The Development of Nürnberg" [the German spelling] we left the ship by bus at 10 AM for the drive to and through the city. Nürnberg was a major center for Nazi Party activities, rallies, etc., during Hitler's regime. The focus of our visit was an enormous building called the Documentation Center. This huge Nazi edifice has been converted into a history museum which presents a chronicle of the dark days of the rise to power of Hitler and the Nazi Party, their subsequent atrocities and final fall during World War II. Visitors make their way along a seemingly endless series of exhibits, in and out of a maze of rooms and hallways. Each exhibit has a printed description of the various events and a longer commentary that you can hear using a handheld transmitter and earphones which we picked up at the Information Desk.

It is an impressive and, as far as I could tell honest examination of the rise and fall of that "evil empire." If, as I believe to be true, we can learn valuable lessons from history, this was a fantastic opportunity. However, our visit here was the most disappointing and frustrating of all the Vantage arranged excursions. The reason being, that there was not nearly time enough to listen to the audio commentary or even to read the printed panels by each exhibit. I thought our visit was a total waste of time. Here was a rich historic mine of information, but no time to dig into it. We hardly had enough time to even scratch the surface. I found the experience extremely frus-trating!

A walk through Nürnberg, public square and lunch at a café with a group of university students before returning to our ship was much more rewarding, and the day was "saved" by a very interesting and enjoyable hour-long lecture, back on the *River Odyssey, on* the subject of Bavarian Beer! Being able to sample four different kinds of local beer was a treat that helped wash away the day's frustration. Nevertheless, I was not sorry when we headed up the canal at about 7 o'clock that evening

Day 10—July 8 Kelheim/Regensburg

We arrived at the town of Kelheim where the canal meets the Danube River at about 8 AM. Here, those passengers who had signed on for an Optional Tour to the Weltenburg Monastery, left the ship. Zenith and I had not signed on for this as we were not particularly interested in monasteries, but also because it was not covered by the base fee for the cruise and would have cost the two of us an additional $178! We stayed on board and the *River Odyssey* proceeded to Regensburg, arriving there at about 1 PM after another morning of leisurely scenic cruising now going down-stream on the Danube River.

That afternoon we took an interesting walking tour of Regensburg [*Ray-gens-burg*] with a local guide. Originally a Roman military outpost, Regensburg features one of only two complete Roman arches in Germany, along with a lovely old stone bridge over the Danube River, built between 1135 and 1146! For hundreds of years this was the only bridge over the Danube River. It was also the jump-off point for both the 2nd and 3rd Crusades.

Despite being the site of a Messerschmitt aircraft factory and an oil refinery, Regensburg was targeted only twice by Allied bombing raids during World War II, and escaped major damage. Today it is regarded as one of the best preserved medieval cities in Europe and is listed as a UNESCO World Heritage Site.

We enjoyed an informative tour of the city with our pretty Bavarian guide. Here she is telling us about the beautifully ornate St. Peter's Dom [Cathedral], just behind her. The Cathedral was completed in 1634 and houses a museum of medieval and renaissance church art. We were disappointed that time limits prevented us from going inside and viewing the contents of the museum.

Our visit to this interesting old town had to be cut a bit short due to another scheduled program. After returning from our walking tour, we were treated, back on board the *River Odyssey*, to a very interesting lecture by a local man, Daniel Gürtler, on the Main-Danube Canal.

Stretching 106 miles from Bamberg on the Main to Kelheim on the Danube the Main-Danube Canal utilizes 53 locks, averaging one every 2 miles, rising to a summit of 1,332 feet above sea level on the European continental divide. Such a canal project was first undertaken in 793 AD by Charlemagne. Another attempt by Napoleon also failed with his defeat at Waterloo in 1815, and successful completion had to wait until 1992. After an enjoyable and informative day in Regensburg we departed for Passau about 7 PM.

Day 11—July 9 PASSAU

Often called the "Venice of Bavaria" or "City of Three Rivers," Passau is located at the confluence of the Danube, the Inn and the Ilz rivers at the western edge of Bavaria near the Austrian border. Like Regensburg it is one of Germany's oldest and most picturesque cities. We arrived there at about 7 AM, and after breakfast left the ship at 10 AM for a walking tour of the city guided by Marc, our Blue group leader.

This enjoyable tour was topped off by attending an impressive half-hour-long organ concert at St. Stephen's, the Dom [Cathedral] of Passau. The organ, seen here, [left] is notable as the largest pipe organ in Europe with more than 17,000 pipes and 233 stops.

After a "Bavarian lunch" buffet back on the *River Odyssey*, Zenith enjoyed a tour of the ship's small, compact galley conducted by Detlef, the ship's Executive Chef. She was introduced to the small galley crew who labor from sunup to sundown to provide the 168 passengers with the great meals served three times a day. Bryce contented himself with a couple margaritas in the lounge as part of a special "Mexican Happy Hour" before dinner.

We sailed at 6 PM, but this very enjoyable day was not over! At 9 PM the lounge was the site of the hilarious "one and only Crew Show", a conglomeration of original skits, plus songs, dancing, and joking—a general clowning around by about 15 members of our fine crew, clad in an assortment of costumes. Great job, guys and gals!!

DAY 12—July 10 WACHAU VALLEY / VIENNA I

The next morning we sailed through the scenic Wachau Valley of Austria. Along the way we passed the small tourist town of Dürnstein. Above the town stands the ruined Dürnstein Castle. Known for having been the place where the King of England, Richard I [known to history as Richard the Lionhearted], was held captive by Duke Leopold V of Austria after being taken prisoner as he was returning to England from the 3rd Crusade, thus giving birth to the legends of Robin Hood and Ivanhoe!

An interesting sidelight: In 1753 a group of Moravian Church members settled in Forsyth Co., North Carolina. Their leader, Bishop Spangenberg, called the 100,000 acre colony "Die Wachau" because the area reminded him of the ancestral home of the sect's patron, Count von Zinzendorf. Now the name Wachovia, the Latin form of the name, is used.

We arrived in Vienna, the Capital of Austria about noon on Saturday, July 10. We would spend this afternoon and all of tomorrow in Vienna. This afternoon one group of passengers took the option of a "Musical Vienna" motor coach tour of the city, which included visits to the State Opera House and to the composer Mozart's Memorial House.

Zenith and I opted to tour

the vast Schönbrunn Palace, now one of the most important and beautiful cultural monuments in Austria, & a UNESCO World Heritage Site. For many years it was an imperial residence for a succession of Habsburg monarchs.

Designed and begun in 1692 under Leopold I whose ambition was for it to surpass in beauty the palace of Versailles in Paris. It was completed by Empress Maria Theresa in the 1740s. Both the Palace itself and the extensive gardens behind it which cover 197 acres, illustrate the tastes, interests and aspirations of Austrian royalty.

Altogether the Schönbrunn has 1,441 rooms, including 139 kitchens! The residence of such rulers as Empress Maria Theresa and the birthplace of Emperor Franz Joseph I, it was the site in 1918 of the abdication of the last Austrian Emperor, Karl I. The furnishings of the rooms and hallways inside the Schönbrunn are beyond my ability to describe. The two photo-graphs on the left will have to suffice.

DAY 13—JULY 11 VIENNA II

Today was our 2nd day in Vienna. It began, after breakfast, with a lecture on board the *River Odyssey* by Prof. Edward Kudlak, a fine musician in his own right, entitled "Musical Vienna." A native of Montreal now residing in Vienna, he "illustrated" his very informative talk with recorded excerpts from different Viennese composers and their different types of music. At 9:30 it was back on a motor coach for a "panoramic city tour" of Vienna. We observed a great many interesting sights, buildings and places too numerous to list or show here.

The morning tour ended with a bus ride to, and a walk through, the Austrian National Library. Again, words can only provide a very inadequate portrait of this truly indescribable and wondrous place. It was yet another unexpected highlight of a marvelous trip! An incredibly ornate series of rooms featuring, among large globes, statuary, and magnificent frescos, wall to ceiling shelves [on two levels, accessed by roller-mounted moveable ladders] containing some 2.2 million books and manuscripts of all kinds and types. As a lover of, and collector of books, I felt like I'd gone to heaven! The photo, at the bottom of the previous page, gives an idea of what I'm trying to describe, but it shows only a very small part of this wondrous place.

After returning to the *River Odyssey* for lunch we enjoyed an afternoon at leisure exploring "Albertina," the downtown area of Venice, the highlight being a visit to the magnificent complex of buildings known collectively as the Hoffburg Palace. Then, in the evening, another treat! We were bussed over to the Kursalon for a very enjoyable concert by Vienna's Salon Orchestra. The program consisted of 8 numbers played by the small 8-10 piece [I neglected to count!] orchestra plus 2 numbers by a pair of singers—soprano and baritone—and 2 more numbers by a pair of graceful, energetic male and female dancers, all accompanied by the orchestra. [Sadly, no photographs were allowed inside.] A very memorable evening to conclude a truly memorable day!

DAY 14—July 12 BUDAPEST I

The *River Odyssey* traveled through the night headed for our final destination on the *Castles Along the Rhine and Danube* cruise: Budapest, the capital of Hungary. We

had another morning of relaxed cruising, reaching Budapest about noon. Budapest is an especially beautiful and interesting city in my opinion. In part this is due to its setting on both banks of the Danube. Originally two separate cities, Buda and Pest [pronounced *"Pesht"*]. On the west bank where high hills rise rather abruptly is the older city of Buda, while the newer and larger city of Pest lies on

a mostly flat plain on the east bank. Buda, the seat of the royal castle became the capital of Hungary in 1361. Then in 1872 Buda and Pest were officially united to become Budapest which has served as the country's capital since then.

High on a hill overlooking the city known as "The Pearl of the Danube", on the Buda side is "Lady Liberty", officially the Statue of Liberation, a 14 meter-tall b r o n z e female figure holding aloft a palm branch, erected in 1947 to commemorate the liberation of the city from Nazi rule by Russian troops.

There are six bridges connecting the two parts of the city. This one is called the Chain Bridge and was the 1st permanent bridge to join Buda and Pest. Begun in 1832, it was not completed until 1849. It is 380 meters long, the supporting chains are laced through the arch-shaped piers and the ends are secured in under-ground chambers on the two river banks. This view is towards the Buda side of the river.

On our first afternoon in Budapest we enjoyed a bus tour of the Pest portion of the city visiting Hero's Square, dominated by the Millennium Monument [right] laid out in 1896 to celebrate the 1,000[th] year of the

Magyar conquest and the founding of Hungary. The statue crowning the pillar is a depiction of the archangel Gabriel, a traditional symbol of triumph. The work of Gyorgy Zala, the bronze sculpture won 1st prize at

the 1900 World's Fair in Paris. At the base of the pedestal are the mounted figures of the seven conquering Magyar chiefs.

This photo shows me on the Buda side at a favorite tourist site, the Fishermen's Bastion. Named from a defense by men of the Fishermen's Guild during a battle, the edifice was actually designed for decorative rather than defensive purposes. The site on Castle Hill commands magnificent views over both Buda and Pest, the Danube River and its six bridges. We returned to the ship about 5 PM, enjoyed the Captain's Farewell Cocktail in the Lounge and the Captain's Farewell Dinner. Then it was time for our final night on board ship.

Day 15—July 13 BUDAPEST II

Zenith and I had signed on for an optional 2 day extension in Budapest, primarily because her older sister, Irene, has been living and working in Budapest for about 10 years, and it was a perfect oppor-tunity for them to spend some time together. Forty one of the *River Odyssey* passengers had also signed up for this 2 day extension and after a final breakfast on board ship we bid goodbye to the other passengers and were bussed by Vantage to the big Corinthia Hotel in the Pest portion of the city, under the guidance of Marc our Program Manager.

After checking in and finding our room, Zen and I walked around town for a while and were able to find an ATM where we exchanged some Euros for Hungarian currency. [Unlike the rest of our trip where Euros were the monetary unit, Hungary continues to use its own currency called Forints.] Feeling a bit homesick, I guess, we had lunch at a Pizza Hut across the street from our hotel! Zenith's sister, Irene, showed up at our hotel room in the afternoon. We had a good visit and the two sisters made plans to spend most of the next day together, with Irene showing Zenith some of the sights of Budapest.

There were still more activities that were included in Vantage's itinerary for the Budapest extension. After Irene returned home for the night, Zen and I boarded the bus with the rest of our diminished tour group and traveled through the city to a hall called the Festival Theatre of the Palace of Arts. There we were treated to a lively and exciting ninety-minute exhibition of boot-slapping dances and folk music by the Hungarian State Folk Ensemble. There must have been 40 or more men and women participating in the dances, dressed in a variety of colorful folk costumes, performing to music provided by a group of 5 musicians playing violins, flute and a bass fiddle. It was a **great** show, and I rate it among the top 2 or 3 attractions of the entire cruise.

Unfortunately, we were not allowed to take photographs during the performance. I was able to buy a DVD of another performance of the group, but it isn't as good as the show we saw!

Day 16—July 14 Budapest III

After breakfast in the Corinthia Hotel's Brasserie restaurant, I left on the final excursion of Vantage's 2 day extension, while Zenith stayed behind to spend the day with Irene. Escorted by Marc, I joined the other "extension passengers" on a bus trip through the city, past some old excavated Roman ruins to a stop at a place called Caprice that deals in precious stones, especially diamonds. We were shown through the exhibit hall to their show-rooms full of all kinds of **very** expensive merchandise featuring diamonds and other jewels.

The cost of even the least expensive items was way out of my range, but I think there were some of our group that actually made purchases! I was told by Marc, afterward, that the reason for this stop was that this establishment funds some of Vantage's costs on this cruise, and in return Vantage includes this stop where some cruise participants may make purchases. "You scratch my back and I'll scratch yours."

After this stop we proceeded to a fascinating, quaint little artist's village called Szentendre. With a village square and a small museum the town featured narrow, crooked, cobblestone streets and wall-to-wall shops selling all kinds of clothing, crafts, and other items, plus a variety of places where one could buy food and/or drinks. It was an entertaining and fun stop in a picturesque little village! A bit of a "tourist trap" I suppose, but I thought the prices were reasonable—perhaps because every shop is competing with a number of similar shops—and I enjoyed the visit to Szentendre. Inspired, I think, by the costumes of the Folk Dance group the previous evening, I bought an embroidered vest and then joined some of our group for a refreshing pint of beer in a shaded patio out of the hot sun.

We joined Marc and the rest of our diminished group from the cruise for a "Farewell Dinner" at the Brasserie after a full day. The next morning we all checked out of the Corinthia Hotel and were bussed to the Budapest Ferihegy Airport where we bid Marc and others goodbye and boarded the first of our Lufthansa flights home. Thanks again, Marc!! All in all, *Castles Along the Rhine and Danube* was an expensive, but **very** enjoyable and worthwhile experience! **We recommend it most highly!**

CHAPTER 42

Crusin' Down the Rivers
[Part 2]

In 2012 we took a second European River Cruise, in order to complete the voyage down the Danube River. Unexpectedly, the cruise ship was the same one we'd sailed on in 2010, *MS River Odyssey.* Not only that but two crew members from the previous cruise were aboard, pretty Cristina, and Febry a young Indonesian waiter in the ship's restaurant. This cruise was called **"Eastern Europe and the Black Sea,"** and the write-up will be much shorter than that of our 2010

river cruise! This trip began where we left off in 2010, in Budapest, Hungary, and took us to Constanta, Romania's port on the Black Sea.

We had a second look at some of the sights in Budapest, such as Fisherman's Bastion, and Heroes Square, plus some new ones. I find Budapest to be a fascinating city—one of my favorites! This photo of Zenith, taken from Fisherman's Bastion, shows the enormous and magnificent Hungarian Parliament Building across the river.

We saw more of Hungary on this trip as we continued on down the Danube to the southern part of the country. We stopped in the town of Kalocsa, [Kal-**oh**'-sha] the "paprika center of the world" with a tour of the town including a paprika museum! A few miles out of town we enjoyed a visit to the Bakodpuszta Equestrian Center, with a demonstration of equestrian skills by a group of "ciscos", Hungary's "cowboys." In the photo, a cisco straddles two of an eight-horse team at a full gallop!

We stopped next for tours of St Peter's Basilica and the Necropolis, a buried Roman ruin undergoing excavation, in Pecs [say "Pesh"], Hungary. This was followed by a visit to Vukovar and Osijek in the nation of Croatia. Vukovar, on the Danube, had been the scene of a bloody and vicious 87 day siege during the terrible 1991-1995 "civil war" between Croats and Serbs. It was anything but "civil" with several bloody massacres. Many damaged buildings still stand as mute evidence of the fighting. A tall water tower shot full of holes has been preserved as a kind of memorial.

We went inland, by bus, to Osijek where we visited an elementary school on the last day of the school year. A group of mixed boys and girls performed group dances for us. Then we went outside into the school

yard while other children demonstrated several group games under the supervision of their teachers. We were then bussed to enjoy an appetizing lunch [actually a full dinner!] at a Croatian farm, each of our four busses going to a different home. Ours was at a prosperous-looking farm, hosted by a wife and her daughter. [If there was a husband/father he never appeared!]

On the return bus ride returning to our ship we had a surprise treat when we spotted this famous European symbol: a pair of storks with their nest atop a house chimney. Our bus driver, obligingly, stopped so we could get a picture.

Then on to Serbia, like Croatia, part of the former Yugoslavia. In Belgrade, the capital of Serbia, we toured the interesting and imposing Kalemegdan Fortress surrounded now by a remarkably beautiful and spacious park at the junction of the

Danube and Sava Rivers. The skyscraper horizon line of Belgrade can just be made out over Zenith's head and the forested river bank. Lots of grass and shade trees were welcome on a very warm day.

In Belgrade we also had a ride on "Tito's Blue Train", which had been the private train of Josip Broz, "Tito," the leader of Yugoslavia's "Partisans" who fought the Nazis during World War II and then served as Yugoslavia's President from 1953 to 1980.

At the end of the train ride we were entertained by a children's folk dance group. Later we visited "downtown" Belgrade, where we stopped for a cool drink and also watched more colorfully dressed street folk dancers perform.

Nearly every evening of this trip we were also treated on board ship to folk singing and dancing by local groups. Sometimes these groups were adults, some-times children, and sometimes mixed groups, always dressed in colorful costumes and

performing with great enthusiasm and skill. This evening was no exception, as a fine mixed group of adults, called Talija, danced up a storm in the River Odyssey's lounge.

Continuing on down the Danube, after leaving Belgrade, we cruised through the scenic "Iron Gates" of the Danube River, a series of four successive gorges where the river cuts through the mountains. This most scenic stretch of the Danube River forms part of the boundary between Serbia and Romania.

The highlight of the cruise through the Iron Gates is this sculpture of the Dacian King Decebalus, carved by 12 sculptors over a ten-year period, 1994-2004. It is the tallest sculpture in Europe and is that continent's version of Mt. Rush-more. Just why

Decebalus was singled out to deserve the honor of this imposing monument is beyond me. King Decebalus was defeated in battle by the Roman Emperor Trajan in 101 AD. Trajan generously allowed Decebalus to remain as king of the Dacians, only to have him lead a second rebellion and be defeated again. This time Decebalus committed suicide!

After the Iron Gates, the Danube flows almost due east through rather flat plains on its way to the Black Sea

and becomes the boundary between Romania and Bulgaria. Our next stop was at Rusé, Bulgaria's main port on the Danube River. We had a walking tour of Rusé, and then

were bussed to two spectacularly beautiful towns deep in the interior of Bulgaria.

Veliki Tornovo was Bulgaria's ancient capital. The "old town" clings precariously to the steep banks of the meandering Yantra River and to two hills, Tsarevets and Trapezista. This photo will give you an idea of the setting of the homes along the Yantra. Not a place you'd want to live if you were subject to sleep-walking! We had lunch in a modern Veliki Tornovo hotel with a group of local students, followed by a walking tour of the winding cobble-stone streets of the older part of town, as well as a new street featuring wall-to-wall souvenir shops!

We were then bussed to the neighboring town of Arbanasi. Like Veliki Tornovo, it is a contrast of an "old town" and a new modern town. The old-town houses were built with solid stone walls with living quarters on the 2nd floor. They were actually built like small fortresses as a protection against bandits that infested the area. We visited one of those homes that is now open to the public as a small museum and also visited an ancient church where we were treated to a "concert" by

an un-accompanied men's quartet of clerics, featuring exquisite harmony! [No pictures were allowed to be taken inside the church, however.]

These two small cities, Veliki Tornovo and Arbanasi, were among the most interesting highlights of the entire trip. I would like to have had more time to explore them. The round-trip bus ride was also enjoyable. Mostly it was through farm lands,

including acres and acres of sunflowers which are grown commercially. The timing was perfect as we caught the sunflowers during their blooming season.

After the bus trip back to Rusé, we re-boarded our ship, and were entertained that evening by the rousing songs and dances of the Bulgarian Children's Folklore dance group. All of the folk groups, some of adults and some of children, that performed for us during the cruise were very good and very entertaining. This group, I'd say was perhaps the best and most spirited of them all!

That night we sailed to Oltenita, Romania, where, after bidding good-bye to our great crew aboard the *River Odyssey* in the morning, we boarded a bus that took us to Constanta, the country's chief port, on the Black Sea. After stops at the Romanian Historical and Archaeology Museum and the city square, we were taken to a suburb called Mamaia, located on a narrow spit of land between the Black Sea and a lagoon. We had lunch at the Iaki Restaurant, and then enjoyed visiting a "free" beach behind the restaurant. Zennie picked up some interesting shells which covered the sandy beach while I rolled up my pants legs and waded in the Black sea.

Leaving Constanta, we were then bussed to Romania's capital and largest city of Bucharest. Arriving in Bucharest, we did a bus tour of some of the city which is Romania's largest with a population of over 1 ½ million. After bussing around the city we stopped for a walking tour of the "People's Palace", Romania's Parliament building. It has the distinction of being the 2nd largest building in the world, the largest being the Pentagon in Washington, DC.

The People's Palace has 1,000 rooms including 400 offices, 30 conference rooms, 4 restaurants, 3 libraries and a concert hall. Some areas are said to still be "under construction."

We had an early dinner at what I would consider the most preeminent restaurant I've ever had the good fortune to visit. Called Pescarus Restaurant, it's situated on the shore of Herăstrău Lake which was visible

from our table through a window framed with bright red geraniums. The enormous dining room offered patrons superb ambiance, delicious food, attentive and gracious waitresses and waiters. On top of that was a high-spirited seven-man orchestra and a group of brightly costumed, highly energetic male and female dancers, all performing on a raised stage a few feet from our tables!! A multi-course meal of delicious and plentiful food included red and white wine. <u>A 5 star rating in my book</u>!

After the Pescarus Restaurant, we were bussed over to the Intercontinental Hotel, where we would spend the night. The next morning we would be bussed to the Bucharest airport and begin the flight home via Amsterdam and Atlanta.

FINI

[Well . . . almost!]

COUP
[An instance of successfully achieving something difficult]

We're back home in Cottonwood now, and I'm going to end this account of the tribulations, trials and travels of this Fiddlefoot. I'm 82 1/2 now and expect to be around for a while longer, but I want to bring this little book to a close while my feet can still "fiddle".

Zennie and I have booked another Vantage River Cruise for September of 2013. It will be on a brand new ship, as the *River Odyssey* is being sold to a competitor. The cruise, called "Switzerland and the Heart of the Rhine and Moselle", will start in Amsterdam [we'll actually get to cruise the canals this time] and we'll travel up the Rhine to the Moselle, then turn up that river stopping in tiny Luxemburg, and the French province of Lorraine. Then back down the Moselle and enter the Rhine again, following it all the way to Berne, Switzerland. Then we've opted for an extension to Lucerne with a boat ride on lovely Lake Lucerne and a tram ride to the top of Mount Pilatus. Then home.

I mentioned earlier, that I still want to do another trip to Ireland with special destinations to include the Aran Islands and the Dingle Peninsula both on [or off] the west coast. I'd like to make that a Chauffeur-driven tour, if the money holds out! Perhaps, by that time, the Travel Bug venom will have pretty well worn off. But, I make no promises!

Having reached the end of this story, I suddenly realized that I've included considerable detail regarding the overseas trips I've taken, while saying little about the **many** vacation trips I've taken within my native countries, the U.S and Canada. I don't plan to undertake what would entail a major revision that might well double the length of this tome. Let me just mention that I, along with both Carol and Zenith, and in many instances with some or all of my four children, have visited a great many beautiful and interesting sites in the U.S. and Canada. Many of them are every bit as worthy of a visit [or two, or three!] as the places that I've described here. Also, Zen deserves another visit to the Philippines and I'd like to accompany her.

My hope is that readers will enjoy traveling as much as I have. Take to heart this observation, *"Traveling is like falling in love; the world is made new."* Readers who have followed this Fiddlefoot from the beginning may doubt my conjecture that I no longer carry a trace of the Travel Bug venom in my veins. But I think it has been diluted enough to at least partly diminish the wanderlust in me. I've settled down here in Cottonwood since 1989, and I don't expect to move again. So, it's just possible that the "go and return" journeys will come to an end as well as the household moves. The bow for my fiddle is down to a few worn strings I'm afraid, and I don't see a new or restrung bow in my future. It's been an interesting life and I have few regrets. [Some, but not many.] I'll just close this little book with a couple more quotes that I like. ***"The moment may be temporary, but the memory is forever."***—*unknown*

Or, as a lady named Isabella Eberhardt observed, ***"A nomad I will remain for life, in love with distant and uncharted places."***

—Bryce

The End
[except for the Appendix!]

APPENDIX

Definition [1]: *{a} A vestigial blind-ended, tube-like body organ connected to the cecum. {b} Evolutionary baggage.*

Definition [2]: *Any addition to a document such as a book, contract, journal or chronicle.*

[Note: For purposes of this document, please use definition # 2.]

****

A—Bryce Theatre involvement

B—Al Adamson newspaper story

C—Early Native Americans of the Verde Valley

D—The "Two Ronnies"

APPENDIX A

Bryce Babcock—Theater Involvement

Name of Play	Author	Role	Year
Milton Union High School—Milton, WI			
Spring Green	author?	Dr. Blodgett	1947
The Dear Departed	Stanley Houghton	Ben Jordan	1947
Milton College—Milton, WI			
The Merchant of Venice	Wm. Shakespeare	Stephano	1950
Out of the Frying Pan	Francis Swann	1st Cop (Mac)	1951
The Taming of the Shrew	Wm. Shakespeare	Grumio	1951
Much Ado About Nothing	Wm. Shakespeare	Borachio	1952
Twelfth Night	Wm. Shakespeare	Fabian	1953
White Rock Players—White Rock, B.C., Canada			
* Snow White	Ed Carlin	Town Crier	1969
##A Clear View of an Irish Mist	Ray Bradbury	Casey	1970
* Sinbad the Sailor	Sharon Romero	Caliph Ornia	1971
* Red Riding Hood	Ed Carlin	Chorus	1971
The Man Who Came to Dinner	Moss Hart and George S. Kaufman	Dr. Bradley	1972
*Robinson Crusoe	Charlotte Johnson	Mr. Morgan	1972
##Rumplestiltskin	improvisation	The Miller	1973
# Enter a Free Man	Tom Stoppard	Brown	1973
* Hansel and Gretel	Gary Holt	Willie Weinerschnitzel	1973
The Effect of Gamma Rays on Man-in-the-moon Marigolds	Paul Zindel	*(Stage Manager/ Asst. Director)*	1973

# Spreading the News	Lady Gregory	(Director)	1974
The Drunkard	Raymond Hull	Stickler	1974
*Puss In Boots	Franklin Johnson	Chorus	1974
The Matchmaker	Thornton Wilder	Joe Scanlan	1974
*Jack and the Beanstalk	Charlotte Johnson	Colonel Catastrophe	1975

Kamloops Players—Kamloops, B.C., Canada

# Bell, Book and Candle	John van Druten	Sidney Redlich	1975
A Marriage Proposal	Anton Chekov	(Asst. Stage Mgr.)	1975
Sweet Charity	book by Neil Simon music: Cy Coleman lyrics: Dorothy Fields	Cop, Waiter & Chorus	1977
The Curious Savage	John Patrick	Samuel Savage	1979
Move Over Mrs. Markham	Ray Cooney and John Chapman	Walter Pangbourne	1980
My Fair Lady	Jay Lerner and Frederick Loewe	Jamie and Lord Boxington	1981
Bedroom Farce	Alan Ackbourne	Ernest	1981
Lock Up Your Daughters	Henry Fielding, (Adapted by Bernard Miles), Music: Laurie Johnson, Lyrics by Lionel Bart	Faithful	1982
# Rattle of a Simple Man	Charles Dyer	(Director)	1983
Don't Drink the Water	Woody Allen	Father Drobney	1985

Kamloops Operatic Society—Kamloops, B.C., Canada

Trial by Jury	Gilbert & Sullivan	The Judge	1980
The Mikado	Gilbert & Sullivan	The Mikado	1981

Western Canada (Professional) Theater Company—Kamloops, B.C. Canada

Oliver!	Charles Dickens, Arr. by Lionel Bart	Mr. Sowerberry, and Chorus	1978
Desire Under the Elms	Eugene O'Neill	Simeon Cabot	1979

* English Christmas Pantomimes
# British Columbia Drama Assn. Zone Festival
##British Columbia Drama Assn. Zone Festival and Finals

APPENDIX B

This article and photo appeared in a local Wayne County, Utah, newspaper, Bicknell City Weekly, July 20, 2000. I've edited the newspaper story to delete information specific to the Bicknell Film Festival. Gina, Al Adamson's wife shown with Al in the photograph, played the lead female role in many of his movies. Both Kemet and I knew Al Adamson well, as an employer, and—as difficult as it is to imagine—a friend.

—Bryce

"B" Bad, Very Bad

The Bicknell International Film Festival beckons all who dare sit through intentionally bad movies.

—by Mary Dickson

"We never, ever went out to make a bad film. I don't think anybody goes out to make a bad film."

—Al Adamson

Bad films or B films? You can be the judge when the Bicknell International Film Festival presents "King B, The Fine Films of Al Adamson," a retrospective of the director's work . . . This year's theme is Al Adamson . . . Why Al Adamson this year? There is a local connection to Adamson. He owned the Rim Rock Inn in Torrey, just down the road from Bicknell . . . "There's a great deal of local interest in this year's theme as Al was kind of "unique" around here. Almost everyone has a story about him," said program organizer Galen Rosenthal.

Adamson was known as the Ed Wood of the 1960s and '70s. "By virtually any standard the 32 films of Al Adamson embrace badness," said James Anderson, another festival organizer. "Some contain a surprising number of saving graces, intentional or otherwise, and remain entertaining, watchable and occasion-ally inspired. A few shock and disturb. Others are merely foul cinematic miscarriages, deserving only anonymity. Adamson's films-designed for a once-thriving drive-in market—are blatant products, if seldom more. Even a casual viewing of any of his movies reveals that art was not only unintended, it was likely impossible."

That said, Anderson also believes Adamson's work is undervalued. Critics have dismissed virtually every Adamson effort, regularly dubbing him as heir to the "Worst Director of All Time" award . . . "Genre mavens," if they acknowledge Adamson at all, do so with a distancing stance, while most film websites denounce his work with indulgent glee," Anderson says.

"Attempts at honoring the filmmaker—most notably, David Konow's recent *Schlock-o-Rama: The Films of Al Adamson*—routinely rely on personal reminiscence or the self-promoting blather of Adamson's partner/producer Sam Sherman, at the expense of critical interrogation. Can Adamson be so without merit as a filmmaker that he deserves such critical spite . . . Can the small but vocal fan base his paltry movies boast [a group to which I confess membership] be so utterly, laughably deluded? Perhaps."

Adamson and his work will undoubtedly always annoy, even enrage, Anderson says. But they will continue to entertain anyone willing to look hard [or look at all] for some sign that he did the best he could with what he had, despite what he may have lacked.

Life imitating his art, Adamson died badly, murdered in 1995 by a contractor [sic] living in his home while remodeling it. Grotesquely, he was entombed by the perpetrator in the structure supporting a new Jacuzzi where his body went undiscovered for many weeks.

"Unfortunately," Anderson says, "this remains [his] most wide-reaching claim to mass recognition. Worse, it begs the kind of loony karmic hypothesizing that fuels fundamentalist views: he got what he deserved; he made violent, mostly amoral movies for venues aimed squarely at young people, and he died violently at the hands of a monster devoid of conscience. Irony!"

Hell on earth: Al Adamson in *Halfway to Hell*.

APPENDIX C

My work as a National Park Ranger dealt with interpretation: Helping visitors to better understand what the Park Service was trying to protect and preserve. At Montezuma Castle and Tuzigoot [and to a certain extent as an employee of the Verde Canyon Railroad] that interpretation dealt in large part with understanding the people who built and lived in the pre-Columbian village ruins that I was helping to protect and preserve.

This essay deals with the pre-European peoples of the Verde Valley of Arizona and covers the peoples that archaeologists have called Hohokam, Hakataya and Sinagua. Most of the area's archaeological ruins that are protected by the National Park Service belong to the Sinagua peoples. I'm including this essay here as it was written about these peoples as part of my effort to help visitors better understand what they were observing.

—Bryce Babcock

Native Americans of the Verde Valley: The Hohokam and Sinagua

By Bryce Babcock

HOHOKAM AND HAKATAYA

There is little or no evidence of humans in the area of the upper and middle Verde River (upstream from the lower end of the Verde Valley) prior to what archaeologists call the Archaic Period (8000 B.C. To 1 A.D.). A few sites in the Perkinsville area are sometimes assigned to that period, but the evidence is scant and most probably represents temporary or seasonal camps of semi-nomadic Yavapai peoples only, rather than permanent living sites.

Even in the Phase 1 (A.D. 1 to 800) period the evidence of permanent occupation is slight. It is only during the Phase 2 (A.D. 800 to 1000) period that settlement by newcomers to the area is evident from pottery fragments and pit-house sites. The cultural evidence indicates that these people were from the Hohokam (**Ho-ho KAHM**) culture that occupied the Gila and lower Salt River areas around what is now Phoenix during this period.

The presence of established villages, some fairly sizeable, dating from this period have been noted and excavated, and irrigation canals are evident. That these people were agricultural and not simply hunters and gatherers, can be inferred from these canals and from the presence of various artifacts. The Hohokam life style was first and foremost an irrigation-based agricultural technology, with corn, beans and squash as the main crops. (These three plants have been referred to as "the trinity of early native American agriculture.") Hohokam agriculture was undoubtedly supplemented, however, by hunting and gathering of wild foods and animals.

The creosote bush has been called "the drugstore of the desert" due to the many medicinal uses of this common desert plant by Native Americans. If the creosote bush was the drugstore of the desert, the ubiquitous mesquite tree was a virtual shopping mall. The "fruits" of that tree, mesquite beans, were a highly nutritious staple food. The tree's wood supplied fuel, building materials, tools and weapons and various parts of the tree were also used medicinally.

Among animals hunted were mule deer, pronghorn, desert bighorn sheep, both jack and cottontail rabbits, rock squirrels, woodrats, beaver, porcupine and various birds, fish and other animals. Most archaeologists surmise that Hohokam people moved up the Verde River from the south to settle in the area of the Verde Valley. Some believe that the presence of salt, argillite and copper which could be used in trade may have been one reason for this movement.

Albert Schroeder, a prominent archaeologist of the 1950s and 1960s, postulated that these Hohokam peoples encountered an indigenous culture that he called the Hakataya, **(hah-kah-TY-ah)** who had entered the Verde Basin area prior to AD 700 or 800. He believed that the Hakataya, were semi-nomadic hunters and gatherers who lived primarily in the uplands where they could best employ their natural resource-based existence. Other archaeologists believe that the Hakataya were actually either Yavapai or Sinagua from the San Francisco Peaks area who were beginning to move south.

The Hohokam farmers congregated in villages along the river. As the Hohokam prospered, some Hakataya (or Sinagua) families joined them, suggests Peter Pilles a Flagstaff based archaeologist with the U.S. Forest Service. The Hohokam gradually influenced the Hatakaya to adopt the more "advanced" Hohokam styles and technologies and gradually the two cultures merged with the Hohokam dominant. The alternative theory is that, if the hunters and gatherers were actually Sinagua, [**see-NAH-wah**]they began to learn and adopt the technology of irrigation farming and as more and more of them moved south, the Hohokam gradually began to withdraw southward along the Verde River.

During the following Phase 3 period, (AD 1000 to 1125), the Hohokam presence in the <u>upper</u> Verde River area seems to gradually fade out. Only scattered small dispersed villages seem to have survived for a time as larger villages in that area disappear. In the <u>middle</u> Verde River area, however, the Hohokam presence seems to have been maintained into the post 1125 period. There is evidence of shifting cultural boundaries along this part of the river, but all of the evidence for Phase 2 and 3 remains scanty so that interpretation is difficult.

THE COMING OF THE SINAGUA

It is only during the Phase 4 period (A.D. 1125 to 1300) that evidence becomes more solid and certain. It shows a slow decline of Hohokam-type archaeological evidence and the appearance of evidence that closely resembles that of the Sinagua culture of the Flagstaff area.

The foremost archaeologist who had studied that area was Harold Colton. Up until the time that Colton began his work in the Flagstaff area, archaeologists believed that the people who had lived there belonged to the same culture that had earlier been identified by the name Anasazi (**ah-nah-SAH-zee**).

It was Colton who turned up convincing evidence that "his" people represented a culture that was distinct from the Anasazi and he was able to persuade other archaeologists of this fact. So a new name had to be found for the pre-historic peoples of the Flagstaff area, and the archaeologist who "discovered" the fact of a difference was conceded the privilege of supplying the new name. And so it was that Harold Colton "invented" the name Sinagua for these people. In the Flagstaff area the number of permanent streams and springs are few and far between, so Colton thought the name Sinagua (from the Spanish words *sin* meaning without and *agua* meaning water) was appropriate.

The retention of the name Sinagua for the people of that culture who came to the Verde Valley, where there has never been a shortage of water, is grossly incongruous, but Colton was "stuck" with the name he himself had coined! He settled for making an idiomatic distinction between the Northern Sinagua (Flagstaff area) and Southern Sinagua (Verde Valley).

There IS evidence that the Southern Sinagua learned the techniques of irrigation farming from the Hohokam peoples and that the two groups were able to live fairly harmoniously with each other. Gradually, the Hohokam in the Verde area seem to disappear. Did they all finally move back to the Valley of the Sun where they had come from? Or were they gradually absorbed by the more numerous Sinagua culture until the distinction between the two was no longer recognizable? No one has satisfactorily answered that question as yet, and perhaps never will.

The Southern Sinagua (to use Colton's linguistic distinction) lived for a time in pit houses as had the Hohokam, but gradually abandoned that practice and built above-ground homes out of stone. These dwellings were sometimes single homes, but more often several families lived in close proximity and over time they began to construct large villages such as we see at Tuzigoot and Montezuma Castle. In these villages rooms often had common walls and family dwellings were grouped together.

Incidentally, it's interesting to know that the ruin that is seen today, early in the Verde Canyon Railroad excursion train trip, is only a remnant of the original structure. Visit the VCRR Museum and check out the photo of this ruin and you will notice that as recently as 1950 there were a series of rooms along the ledge, an indication that this was home not to a single family, but to several, very possibly extended or related families. That cliff dwelling ruin, high on the cliff early in the trip usually provokes a number of questions from passengers. Hopefully the following information will be helpful in providing answers to some of these questions.

A frequent asked question is why did they build homes in places so difficult to access? It's a fact that many Sinagua dwellings were in high caves, such as the one we point out from the train or like Montezuma Castle which many visitors to this area will have seen. Other sites such as Tuzigoot are built on top of ridges or hills. Why not down by the river? There are actually a number of good reasons.

The usual guess at an answer is probably not the right answer. Most people will assume that building in difficult places of access was primarily for reasons of defense from attacks by other humans. This was probably not the major reason however. For one thing, there is very little archaeological evidence of warfare among the Sinagua, or of battles between the various villages which were built at fairly close intervals up and down the Verde River. Well, if not primarily for defense, why choose such difficult locations?

First off, building in caves had some advantages. In a cave you already had a roof and some walls, and a structure built in a cave would last longer and provide more protection against weather and "varmints."

It's well demonstrated that, like the Anasazi, the Sinagua preferred caves that were south facing. That provided the maximum light and warmth from the low winter sun and were shaded and so cooled in summer. Still, when push comes to shove, if you were going to build in a cave you had to take it where you found it! There is no evidence that major human excavation occurred. The Sinagua, we know from archaeological evidence, knew how to make ladders and often used them to help with access. Montezuma Castle required 3 long ladders. The Sinagua used 2 types of ladders: Sometimes just a single fairly straight pole (usually a tree trunk) with notches cut in it to form steps. But they also made ladders similar to those that we're familiar with, two parallel poles with cross pieces lashed in place to form rungs.

But even when not building a home in a cave, the Sinagua almost invariably chose the tops of hills or ridges such as Tuzigoot, sometimes fairly steep to climb, instead of building their villages along the river bank close to water for drinking or for irrigation. There were several good reasons for building on high points that did not involve reasons of defense, at least not against human enemies.

Reason #1. Flash floods are very common in this country and can be extremely dangerous as well as bothersome. It was only common sense to have your home located where you didn't have to worry about the danger of flash floods. That's a lesson that many people today seem not to have learned, or have forgotten.

Reason #2. It's cooler in the summer if you're on a hill, a bluff or cave that is located fairly high up, because you get more of a breeze. Conversely, it's also warmer in winter because, as you'll remember, cold air sinks and warm air rises. Winters are colder down by the river. If you don't have central heating or air conditioning even a few degrees can make an important difference.

Reason #3. These were farmers. Land around here that can be farmed needs to be irrigated. (O.K. The Hopi learned how to grow crops through dry-farming practices. But that's hard to do and irrigation is both easier and more productive.) So, you don't want to build houses down near the river or in low-lying areas that you might be able to irrigate and use to raise food. Build them where you can't grow crops.

Reason #4. This is probably the most important. An illustration may help here. When the U.S. Army came into this area they built a military post near the present town of Camp Verde. They built it down close by the river. It didn't take long for many of the troops to come down with malaria! After a year or so they moved the Fort up on top of the bluff and the incidence of malaria was greatly reduced. My guess is that the Native Americans had learned that lesson—perhaps the hard way, from experience—several hundred years before.

A similar question to that of locating homes in hard to reach areas can be raised in terms of why—when they built homes of stone on open ground and not in caves—did they enter through a hole in the roof instead of having a door at ground level? It's more difficult to climb up a ladder to the roof and then down another ladder to the floor than to simply make a door at ground level. The answer is actually rather obvious.

The Sinagua did not have close fitting doors with hinges. A door, for them was an animal hide hung over the opening. This country has a lot of "varmints" that can be rather unpleasant houseguests: rattle-snakes, scorpions, centipedes, skunks, even a mountain lion or bobcat for example. A hide hung over the doorway will not be very effective in keeping any of them away from a family's food supply or from sleeping people. But not too many of those varmints will bother to climb up and down two ladders to find what they're looking for!

A side benefit of having the entrance through the roof that's often overlooked is that the flat roof made a usable work and living space. Something to keep in mind is that the rooms they lived in were dark, stuffy and poorly ventilated. Archaeologists agree that these people spent as little time as possible <u>inside</u> their dwellings. They used the room or rooms (seldom more than one) almost exclusively for sleeping and as shelter in bad weather.

Beyond that they spent as much time outside as possible. The hole in the roof for entry and exit also provided an exit for smoke from cooking or heating fires when they were necessary to have inside and admitted a little light as well. Most cooking and most daily work such as weaving, grinding corn or skinning animals and drying meat was preferably done outside and often on the roof.

WHERE DID THEY GO?

Archaeological evidence indicates that in the early 1400s the Sinagua population along the Verde River had begun to decline and that by about 1425 the abandonment of the area was pretty complete. What happened to the Sinagua people has baffled archaeologists and others and no definitive explanation has been agreed upon. Often it is said that like the Anasazi to the north, the Sinagua "disappeared" by about 1425.

One thing is certain. They did not "disappear" into thin air. They left the area, but <u>where</u> they went and <u>why</u> they left are the unanswered questions. We'll look at some possibilities involving "where" first and then examine the "why" question. First of all, it's unlikely that a plague of some sort or sudden warfare broke out killing off large numbers. There is just no evidence of mass graves or burials that would support such a theory. Nor were they carried off by "spacemen" as credulous individuals such as Erich von Daniken have argued.

What evidence there is suggests instead that the Sinagua abandoned the area and moved out. But, if that was the case, where did they go? And why did they go? It's possible that some migrated south to the old Hohokam homeland. This answer seems unlikely, however, as the Hohokam civilization was also undergoing a slow dissolution at about the same time. There is more evidence for a move north by the Southern Sinagua to join the Hopi people who were already established near Chavez Pass and at Homolovi (**ho-MOLE-oh-vee**) near present Winslow, AZ. The inhabitants of those villages were almost certainly ancestors of some present-day Hopis. This theory is supported by Hopi accounts that the ancestors of several of their clans came from "a warm, well-watered region to the south," and were accepted into Hopi society.

The Hopi name for this region to the south is Palatkwapi (**pah-LOT-kwa-pee**) meaning "place of the red rocks." The Hopi account even names the specific clans involved in this move: Raincloud, Water, Young Corn, Frog, Tobacco, Parrot and several others. These clans claimed that their gods, through their priests, had told them to move north before settling down permanently.

The Verde Valley was so hospitable that when they reached it they were reluctant to leave, and life was so good that they became a pleasure-oriented society. Finally a series of natural disasters persuaded the people to heed their priests and resume their interrupted move on to the northeast. The chief of the Water Clan, so the story goes, was able to convince the Hopis that he had the power to bring rain and so the Hopis agreed to accept the newcomers into their villages, especially at Walpi. (**WAHL-pee**)The Palatkwapi people then returned to their old, temperate, disciplined and responsible ways.

The highly regarded archaeologist Jesse Walter Fewkes of the Smithsonian Institution lent his support to the acceptance of the Verde Valley as the legendary Palatkwapi. He presented considerable evidence that a well-used trail linked the Verde River area with the Hopi villages, via Chaves Pass, Stoneman Lake, Rattlesnake Canyon, Homolovi and Sunset Crossing of the Little Colorado River. This trail, about 145 miles in length, was long known as the Chavez Trail but was renamed the Palatkwapi Trail in the 1980s by NAU professor James W. Byrkit. (It was probably this trail over which the Hopis guided Spanish conquistadors to the mines where Jerome is now located in 1583.)

This explanation of where the Sinagua went when they left the Verde Valley is the best explanation that I've found. But, it leaves the question of why they left only partially answered. The legend that a northward migration, ordained by their priests, was interrupted by a stay in the "promised land" of the Verde Valley, and then renewed after natural disasters prompted their priests to recall them to their true path, is likely part of the story it seems fair to say. But, there is another element to the answer, I believe.

The Sinagua people lived in the relative paradise of the Verde River valley from about 1125 to 1425. That's 300 years. Over that period of time the abundant natural resources of the area would most cert-mainly have been negatively impacted. The cutting of nearby timber for fuel and building purposes would have undoubtedly combined with soil depletion, and growing scarcity of animal and plant resources to have negatively affected both the agricultural and the hunting-gathering aspects of the Sinagua economy. The evidence also shows that this coincided with a growth in population as represented by the increase in the number and size of villages.

The Verde Valley area was, in many respects, a paradise. Plenty of water, a mild climate and abundant natural resources. So, the answer to the question of why the Sinagua left "paradise" seems to have been a combination of religious doctrine joined to a simultaneous decrease of natural resources and increase in population. Sound familiar? Destruction of natural resources combined with over-population is a potent combination for negatively impacting a society in yesterday's world as well as in today's.

—*Bryce Babcock*

Bibliography:

<u>Byrkit, James W.</u>, "The Palatkwapi Trail," Plateau, Magazine of the Museum of Northern Arizona, Vol. 59, No. 4, 1988.

<u>Fish, Paul R. and Fish, Suzanne K.</u>, "Verde Valley Archaeology: Review and Perspective," Museum of Northern Arizona Research Paper #8, 1977.

<u>Hartman, Dana</u>, "Tuzigoot: An Archeological Overview," Museum of Northern Arizona Research Paper #4, 1976.

<u>Pilles, Peter</u>, "The Southern Sinagua," in "People of the Verde Valley." Plateau, Magazine of the Museum of Northern Arizona, Vol. 53, No. 1, 1984.

Appendix D

The "Two Ronnies"

After thinking that I'd completed my book, I thought of something that I really intended to have included, but had slipped from my increasingly porous memory. Rather than try to rewrite and reprint half the book, I decided that I'd just include it here in the Appendix section. It really belongs in Chapter 31 where I'm recounting my association with best friend Charles Mossop and our time together as "The Reivers."

In addition to performing as Celtic singers, Charles and I also performed together doing comedy skits. We'd become familiar with the performances of the British com-edians, Ronnie Barker and Ronnie Corbett, whose acts as **The Two Ronnies** we watched weekly on PBS television. Their repertoire of various kinds of skits, included song and dance numbers as well as rapid-fire dialog. But always included was a comedy "news broadcast" in which they took turns relating imaginary "news" items that were always hilarious. Charles and I found that we could do the same sort of thing.

Cariboo College always had a yearly Christmas Party and Charles and I had partici-pated in the entertainment by singing a few Irish or Scottish songs which were well received. Why not add a comedy "news" report, *a la* The Two Ronnies, only inventing news stories involving members of our college family? So we proceeded in a joint effort to put a Two Ronnies type comedy "newscast" together. Our efforts both as singers and comedians were very well received, even by those we may have poked fun at, and we did our Two Ronnies bit for several years.

Later, when I worked for the National Park Service, Arizona State Park Service and for the Verde Canyon Railroad, I discovered that each of those organizations also had annual Christmas Parties. I drafted different persons to join me in the same kind of skits over a period of quite a few years. These I wrote alone, borrowing much of my material from the "broadcasts" that Charles and I had done at Cariboo College. Needless to say, they suffered from not having the original input of Charles, but these audiences were also extremely appreciative.

I had a great time doing these skits, both at Cariboo College and later adapting them to my U.S. employer's holiday parties. If you've never seen The Two Ronnies comedy acts, you're missing some **great** humor. Some of their performances are available on DVD's through Amazon.com, although most are not in the format that can be played and watched in North America, so if you buy, be careful. Perhaps a better alternative is just to go online to ***You Tube***. Many of their acts are available there. Go to *You Tube* and do a search for **The Two Ronnies.** I think you'll enjoy them—Bryce

~END~